W9-CUB-139

NEW DEVELOPMENTS IN

A0668000T00T

New Developments in Political Science

New Developments in Political Science

An International Review of Achievements and Prospects

Edited by Adrian Leftwich

Edward Elgar

Published by
Edward Elgar Publishing Limited
Gower House
Croft Road
Aldershot
Hants GU11 3HR
England

Gower Publishing Company
Old Post Road
Brookfield
Vermont 05036
USA

Printed in Great Britain by
Billing & Sons Ltd, Worcester

British Library Cataloguing in Publication Data
New developments in political science: an international
  review of achievements and prospects.
  1. Political science
  I. Leftwich, Adrian
  320

Library of Congress Cataloging-in-Publication Data
New developments in political science: an international review of
  achievements and prospects/ edited by Adrian Leftwich.
  p. cm.
  1. Political science. I. Leftwich, Adrian.
  JA71.N475 1990   89–23635
  320--dc20   CIP

  ISBN 1-85278-107-6

Contents

List of figures   vi
List of tables   vii
The Contributors   viii
Acknowledgements   x

1. Introduction: Politics and Political Science   1
    Adrian Leftwich
2. The Contemporary Polarization of Democratic Theory:
    The Case for a Third Way   8
    David Held
3. Feminism and Politics   24
    Diana Coole
4. Putting States in Their Place: State Systems and State Theory   43
    Bob Jessop
5. Comparative Politics: From Political Sociology to
    Comparative Public Policy   61
    Jan-Erik Lane and Svante Ersson
6. Politics and Development Studies   82
    Adrian Leftwich
7. Public Administration: Lost An Empire,
    Not Yet Found a Role?   107
    Christopher Hood
8. Weight Or Lightness? Political Philosophy and Its Prospects   126
    John Horton
9. International Relations   143
    Steve Smith
10. Marxism and Power   161
    Alex Callinicos
11. Elections and Voting Behaviour   176
    Pippa Norris
12. Rational Choice and Political Analysis   196
    Albert Weale

Index   212

Figures

5.1 Comparative approaches 63

12.1 The pattern of cyclical preferences 200

12.2 The open structure of an agenda under majority rule when preferences are cyclical 201

12.3 Conventional agenda rules as a structure-inducing equilbrium 204

12.4 The Prisoners' Dilemma 206

Tables

5.1   Countries classified as stable democracies   65

5.2   Correlations between different measures of democracy
(circa 1960)   67

5.3   Correlations between different measures of democracy
(circa 1980)   67

5.4   Correlation between measures of democracy
for different periods   68

5.5   The world of democracy   70

5.6   The affluence model: democracy and wealth   71

5.7   Democratic conditions: correlations between democracy
indices and social structure factors (1980s, 1970s, 1960s)   72

5.8   Democratic performance: correlations between
democracy indicators and output and outcome indicators
(1980s, 1970s, 1960s)   74

The Contributors

Alex Callinicos is a Lecturer in Politics at the University of York. His many previous books on politics in Southern Africa and Marxism include *Althusser's Marxism* (Pluto, 1976), *Is There a Future for Marxism* (Macmillan, 1982), *Marxism and Philosophy* (Oxford, 1983), *Making History* (Polity, 1987) and *South Africa between Reform and Revolution* (Bookmarks, 1988).

Diana Coole is a Lecturer in Politics (political theory) at the University of Leeds, and has published a number of articles on feminist thought and contemporary French political thought. She is also the author of *Women in Political Theory. From Ancient Misogyny to Contemporary Feminism* (Wheatsheaf, 1988).

Svante Ersson is a Lecturer in Political Science at the University of Umeå in Sweden and has published widely in the fields of political sociology and comparative public policy, including *Politics and Society in Western Europe* with Jan-Erik Lane (Sage, 1987).

David Held is Senior Lecturer in Social Science at the Open University. His previous publications include *Models of Democracy* (Polity, 1987), and he is co-editor of many collections including *Classes, Power and Conflict* (Macmillan, 1982), *States and Societies* (Martin Robertson, 1983), *The Idea of the Modern State* (1984) and *New Forms of Democracy* (Sage, 1986).

Christopher Hood is Professor of Public Administration and Public Policy at the London School of Economics. He has published widely in his field and his books include *The Limits of Administration* (Wiley, 1976), *Bureaumetrics*, with Andrew Dunsire (Gower, 1987), *The Tools of Government* (Macmillan, 1983) and *Administrative Analysis* (Wheatsheaf, 1986).

John Horton is a Lecturer in Politics at the University of York. He has published articles in the field of political philosophy and is co-editor, with Susan Mendus, of *Aspects of Toleration* (Methuen, 1985).

Bob Jessop is Senior Lecturer in Government at the University of Essex.

His previous books include *Social Order, Reform and Revolution* (Macmillan, 1972), *Traditionalism, Conservatism and British Political Culture* (Allen and Unwin, 1974), *Nicos Poulantzas* (Macmillan, 1985), *The Capitalist State* (Blackwell, 1982), and, as co-author, *Thatcherism* (Polity, 1988).

Jan-Erik Lane is Professor of Public Administration in the University of Umeå, Sweden and currently holds a research position in the Department of Economics at Lund University. He has published widely in the fields of political theory, public policy, political economy and comparative politics. He is the Chairman of the Committee on Conceptual and Terminological Analysis of IPSA, ISA and ISSC. He has published textbooks on bureaucracy and political theory in Swedish, is also the author of *Politics and Society in Western Europe* (Sage, 1987), and has edited *State and Market* (Sage, 1985) and *Bureaucracy and Public Choice* (Sage, 1987).

Adrian Leftwich is Senior Lecturer in Politics at the University of York. His work is in the field of the politics of development and different approaches to the analysis and teaching of politics. He has published in the area of teaching methods and is the author of *Redefining Politics. People, Resources and Power* (Methuen, 1983) and has also edited *South Africa. Economic Growth and Political Change* (Allison and Busby, 1974), and *What is Politics?* (Blackwell, 1984).

Pippa Norris is in the Department of Politics at the University of Edinburgh. She has published widely in the fields of electoral behaviour, public opinion and gender politics. She is the author of *The Politics of Sexual Equality* (Harvester, 1987) and *The Volatile Electorate: British By-Elections Since the War* (Oxford University Press, forthcoming).

Steve Smith is Senior Lecturer in International Relations in the University of East Anglia. He has edited and co-edited *International Relations: British and American Perspectives* (Basil Blackwell, 1985), *Foreign Policy Implementation* (Allen and Unwin, 1985), *The Cold War Past and Present* (Allen and Unwin, 1987), *British Foreign Policy* (Allen and Unwin, 1988) and *Belief Systems and International Relations* (Basil Blackwell, 1988).

Albert Weale is Professor of Politics in the University of East Anglia and has published widely in the fields of political theory and social policy. His books are *Equality and Social Policy* (Routledge, 1978), *Political Theory and Social Policy* (Macmillan, 1983) and he has co-authored *Lone Mothers, Paid Work and Social Security* (Bedford Square Press, 1984).

Acknowledgements

My main thanks must go to the authors for responding so positively to the idea of producing this book, for helping to make it happen in practice and for keeping so closely to the timetable for its production. Without that kind of cooperation, editing volumes of this kind would be very difficult indeed.

My thanks, also, to the publisher, Edward Elgar, for his careful attention to detail and for both the reliability and swiftness of his handling of queries and the general administration of this project.

Adrian Leftwich
Department of Politics
University of York
Heslington
York
United Kingdom.

1. Introduction: Politics and Political Science

Adrian Leftwich

> Political science should be the master science; it seems to have become marginalised.
>   – F F Ridley (1982)

INTRODUCTION AND SCOPE

The idea for this book grew out of the conviction that from time to time it is useful for scholars to stand back from the specifics of their own research in order to survey the broader fields of their specialist areas, to identify recent major achievements and problems in them and to point the way forward for further research.

Since the early 1960s there has been an enormous expansion in the number of people teaching and studying Politics, worldwide, as well as an explosion of publications and journals. While it is a full-time task to keep up-to-date with developments in our own fields, it has become almost impossible for us to know what has been happening beyond them. Given, thus, the proliferation of research in the main subfields of the discipline (and their shifting boundaries), as well as the emergence of new fields since the 1960s, it seemed an appropriate time for some kind of stocktaking. A volume such as this can provide an advanced survey of central issues and problems in key areas of the discipline for both practising political scientists and graduate students alike. It can also offer a useful contribution to the assessment of the state of the discipline, or at least aspects of it.

Moreover, the end of the twentieth century is only a decade away, and thus an assessment of achievements and limitations of the last 25 years, or so provides the opportunity, too, for identifying gaps which need filling or priorities that need attention in the study of politics into the twenty-first century.

The authors were thus asked to provide a thematic overview of what they regarded as the main characteristics and achievements in their fields, to identify the problems and anomalies that had arisen and to try to indicate some of the directions in which they thought future research would need to go.

1

Of course, this collection of essays is not a comprehensive survey of all the fields and subfields of the discipline, nor is it meant to be. There are volumes (or sets of volumes) which have sought more or less to do that, for the discipline as a whole or for subfields within it, and most of them have been prepared and published in the USA. These tend to be reference books (Greenstein and Polsby, 1975; Finifter, 1983; Wiarda, 1985).

But this is not such a book. There are thus many specialist subfields which are not systematically covered here – for example, individual country specialisms, the comparative study of constitutions and institutions, strategies of political enquiry and more quantitative methodological questions. However, to make this book both manageable and readable, I preferred to select broader fields, recognizing at the same time that gains in readability and interest would involve losses in detail and comprehensiveness.

The authors were specifically asked not to write as if they were contributing to an official 'handbook' or book of reference, nor to offer reviews of the literature. Rather, they were asked to identify central themes and problem areas which have characterized their fields and to organize their chapters around these. They have done this with great skill, for there is nothing more difficult than to assess the work of 20 years or more in a short chapter in a manner that is informative, authoritative and interesting.

That, at least, was the intention of the book and our hope is that, by reading it, colleagues will learn much about areas of Politics outside their own, and perhaps see connections with them. We also hope that these contributions will provide a spur to further thought and debate about the nature of the discipline of Politics and its future, as well as help to defend and promote its collective importance in both higher education and social research in all countries. A few final and more general comments about the relationship between Political Science and politics are in order here.

CONTEMPORARY PARADOXES AND PROBLEMS IN THE STUDY OF POLITICS

The domain of modern politics and its study has been characterized by paradox and tension. First, in popular discourse, politics and politicians are usually regarded with a mixture of derision and contempt. At least, in the liberal and social democracies, stand-up comics in bars and clubs get a lot of mileage out of them. People tend to regard politics as a field dominated by deceit and trickery, where you never get a straight answer and – especially in the developing societies, but not only there – where people are involved in politics largely for what they can get out of it. Chinua Achebe's justly famous West African novel, *A Man of the People*, car bumper-stickers in Britain ('Don't re-elect your MPs: make them work') and Banfield's study of the politics of 'amoral familism' in an Italian village in the 1950s all seem to illustrate the point precisely (Achebe, 1967; Banfield, 1958). Yet at the same time people know that everywhere in the modern world politics is crucial and that what politicians and governments do will influence their life chances, job prospects, incomes, health, welfare and much else.

There is a second paradox. The fact of the matter is that, unless one adopts a very narrow view of it, politics is a pervasive feature of collective human life. It is not only associated with government, but it occurs in all organizations, public and private, formal and informal, permanent and temporary. It is practised in churches, companies, colleges and families (Leftwich, 1983; 1984). Yet despite the obvious importance of politics in their lives, people seem reluctant to try to understand it analytically, preferring often to confine argument and discussion to debates about their differences in values, interests, preferences and ideologies. It is these differences and the patterns of conflict and cooperation which surround them – their provenance, forms and outcomes – which interest political scientists. Governments, moreover, appear unwilling to fund wide-scale public programmes which might promote the understanding of politics and political life through research and teaching, whether formal or informal. And thus, despite its centrality to our existence, the study of politics is probably one of the most poorly funded fields of research. Furthermore, governments often seem concerned to 'take politics out' of many questions – such as sport, road-building or the environment – preferring to present such issues as simply 'technical'. But they never can be, precisely because people have such diverse interests in all these and other social affairs.

From an analytical point of view, academic political scientists take politics more seriously, as the chapters which follow clearly bear out. Yet we, too, are caught – more or less uneasily – in a third paradox, identified for American Political Science by David Ricci as a 'tragedy'. He sees this as the tension between a commitment to 'democracy' on the one hand and 'scientific' enquiry on the other. In his view, political scientists in the USA have paid too much attention to 'science' while ignoring 'morals' and values (Ricci, 1984: 24 and 304). Some people might argue that the opposite was true in the United Kingdom: that Politics (and sociology) are characterized by a relatively low level of 'quantitative' rigour or 'scientific' enquiry. By this they usually mean an unwillingness or inability to use mathematical techniques, models or methodologies of measurement in the analysis of political phenomena (ESRC, 1987: 7, 9–10).

Such debates are, however, largely examples of a pervasive tension in all academic teaching and research in the social sciences, as Weber noted many years ago (Gerth and Mills, 1965). Should we seek to be (and is it possible to be) detached analysts of processes, or protagonists of policies and commitments, or both? And how far can 'scientific' analysis establish policies, or serve to strengthen or undermine them? It is an old dilemma about an old relationship in the academic world and it seems improbable that it will ever be finally resolved.

These considerations suggest that the relationship in practice between politics (the activity out there in the world) and Political Science or Politics (the discipline) constitutes a broad front of interactions that is both extensive and complicated. I suggest that these paradoxes and tensions are not only inevitable but are the lifeblood of Politics, precisely because they express within the discipline some of the enduring tensions in all human affairs: between interest and reason, heart and head, emotion and argument. Because of them, I would argue, political scientists need to assert more and more the complex primacy of politics in human affairs, to resist the further marginalization of the discipline and help to educate both students and wider publics about the different ways in which the state of our politics may be interpreted, about the diverse ways in which problems might be overcome and the relative costs and benefits of each.

Perhaps the central problem of all politics, and it may even be what defines politics and establishes the need for it, is how the interests and preferences of individuals (or groups of individuals) may be protected and promoted at the same time as protecting and promoting not only the interests and preferences of other individuals (or groups of individuals), but of the society as a whole, whether local or global. This is true for all societies, it always has been and always will be. Disputes about improper hunting behaviours or meat-sharing in a small-scale hunting-and-gathering society illustrate this just as clearly as do contemporary arguments about pollution damage caused by some large industrial companies, the international relations between states, or the relationship between democracy and development in formally 'socialist' countries. The central political problem in, and between, human societies is this: what political arrangements will promote the collective welfare of all and, simultaneously, the fulfilment and potential of each, or, in Marxian terms, will achieve a result where '. . . the free development of each is the condition for the free development of all' (Marx and Engels, 1872).

Most politics revolves around this central problem in a context where resources are scarce, and most prescriptive solutions seek to resolve it. But even if we assume that scarcity can be overcome or that current abundance in some areas can be more evenly distributed, the problem will not go away. We will still be faced with the problem that different people (or groups) may put, or want to put, these (now abundant) resources to different uses in ways that may have adverse implications for others.

It is the centrality and ubiquity of these and related issues in human affairs that makes politics an inevitable, necessary and enduring feature of all groups and societies, at least for the foreseeable future. The problems present themselves in countless ways, some old and some new, some at macro levels, some at micro, in the public and private arenas.

It seems clear that the extent and complexity of these issues has broadened and deepened since the end of the Second World War, as the scope, scale and intensity of human and social interactions have so dramatically increased, both within and between societies. The systematic internationalization of economic activity and the emergence of new states around the world are but two obvious indications of this. It is arguable that the politicization (as defined here) of human affairs is increasing worldwide, in the East and West and the North and the South. As competitive market forces are allowed, by policy changes, to play a greater role in the economic and social life of societies, so there is a proliferation of interest and pressure groups, some competing and some cooperating, but all acting politically to influence the outcome of events to their own advantage. This has clearly begun to happen even in the Soviet Union and China, following the reforms of the 1980s, where politics of this kind was formerly more limited.

Within societies, moreover, groups which were previously denied equal access to rights, opportunities and resources by existing political arrangements have mounted major campaigns to alter these, in both the private and the public spheres. There is perhaps no better example of this than the women's movement, associated with 'second-wave' feminism, and the impact it has had, and is having, everywhere, not only on social and economic relations but on the way people are coming to think about relations between the sexes.

THE PRIMACY OF POLITICS

This proliferation and intensification of politics serves to underline the main thesis here, that politics is central, not marginal, to the organization of affairs in all human societies, and is becoming increasingly so.

Precisely for this reason the discipline of Politics must seek to claim its 'master science' status – its place at the core of the social sciences. As I have suggested, the essential problem of politics at any level, or in any group, can be described as either an intrinsically normative one with far-reaching organizational implications, or as an intrinsically organizational one with far-reaching normative implications. More simply: how may we best live together and organize our affairs so as to provide simultaneously for the individual fulfilment of each and the collective well-being of all?

This problem will no doubt be treated in different ways around the world in diverse socioeconomic and cultural contexts, as will its solutions. But it is impossible to separate the normative and organizational. Hence all of the many competing normative solutions to the essential political problem (liberal–democratic, social–democratic, socialist, managerial, authoritarian–conservativism of a secular or religious kind, for instance) also need to be understood analytically – that is, with respect to their organizational characteristics and practical implications.

This being so, the world of politics presents Political Science with an inextricable mixture of normative and analytical challenges with which political scientists must grapple. Sometimes new approaches and new subfields emerge in response to the problems. The feminist contribution to the analysis of politics, power and the state is one such development, incorporating very clear normative and analytical components; another is development studies. From yet another point of view, the rational or public choice approaches represent attempts (often by economists) to explore the problem of collective choice in politics, and these too have strong implications for normative questions, and vice-versa.

Although they take different views, all the chapters which follow illustrate how intimate are the normative and analytical considerations in each of the fields, and how important it is that this be the case. To this extent they show, first, that politics is central as a means of social action and change; and, second, that Politics, as 'master science', is also central as a means of social understanding. The society-wide educational implications of enhancing this relationship between action and understanding are profound. In this regard, the discipline of Politics will continue to have a unique and expanding contribution to make, not a reduced one.

REFERENCES

Achebe, C. (1967), *A Man of the People* (Garden City, New York, Doubleday).

Banfield, E. C. (1958), *The Moral Basis of Backward Society* (New York, The Free Press).

ESRC (Economic and Social Research Council) (1987), *Horizons and Opportunities in the Social Sciences* (London, ESRC).

Finifter, A. (ed.) (1983), *Political Science. The State of the Discipline* (Washington, APSA).

Gerth, H. H. and Mills, C. W. (eds) (1958), *From Max Weber: Essays in Sociology* (New York, 1958).

Greenstein, F. and Polsby N. W. (eds) (1975), *Handbook of Political Science*, 8 vols. (Reading, Mass., Addison-Wesley).

Leftwich, A. (1983), *Redefining Politics: People, Resources and Power* (London: Methuen).

Leftwich, A. (ed.) (1984), *What is Politics? The Activity and Its Study* (Oxford, Basil Blackwell).

Marx, K. and Engels, F. (1958), 'Manifesto of the Communist Party' in *Selected Works* (Moscow, Foreign Languages Publishing House).

Ricci, D. (1984), *The Tragedy of Political Science* (New Haven, Yale University Press)

Ridley, F. F. (1982), 'If the devil rules, what can political science achieve?' in *Government and Opposition* 15 (3–4).

Wiarda, H. J. (ed.) (1985), *New Directions in Comparative Politics* (Boulder, Colorado, Westview).

2. The Contemporary Polarization of Democratic Theory: The Case for a Third Way

David Held

INTRODUCTION

On both the right and left of the political spectrum today a search is underway for new political policies, strategies and institutional arrangements. In the West the crisis of the welfare state, linked to protracted economic and political difficulties, has forced a rethinking of the relation between the economy and the state, and between the sphere of private initiative and public regulation, across the political spectrum. In the East there has been a growing recognition of deeply rooted problems affecting the entire structure of state-directed rule. With it has come a fundamental questioning of the connections between planning institutions, bureaucracy and market relations, among other things. And, in West and East, renewed concern about the direction of contemporary politics has given way, most notably, to fresh consideration of the very essence of democracy.[1]

This chapter focuses on the renaissance of reflection on possible democratic futures by, first, tracing current controversies; second, setting out a number of unresolved fundamental issues; third, exploring an alternative way of thinking about democracy; and, fourth, elaborating some oustanding questions which require further theoretical and practical inquiry. In tracing contemporary political disputes, the chapter concentrates on two of the most prominent 'voices' in current political discourse; those of the New Right and New Left. It is a particularly opportune moment to examine these voices because the twentieth anniversary of May '68 has taken place in the context of the political dominance of governments led by champions of the New Right, in the Anglo-American world at least. This circumstance is certainly not without its ironies and clearly offers food for thought, and the occasion for thinking ahead.

CURRENT CONTROVERSIES

The New Right (or neo-liberalism as it is sometimes called) is, in general, committed to the view that political life, like economic life, is (or ought to be) a matter of individual freedom and initiative (see Hayek, 1960, 1976 and 1982; and Nozick, 1974). Accordingly, a *laissez-faire* or free market society is the key objective along with a 'minimal state'. The political programme of the New Right includes: the extension of the market to more and more areas of life; the creation of a state stripped of 'excessive' involvement both in the economy and in the provision of opportunities; the curtailment of the power of certain groups (for instance, trade unions) to press their aims and goals; the construction of a government capable of enforcing law and order.[2]

In the late 1970s and 1980s, the governments of Margaret Thatcher and Ronald Reagan advocated 'rolling back the state' on grounds similar to those of the New Right and of some of the theorists of 'overloaded government' (see Held, 1984; McLennan, 1984). They insisted that both individual freedom and individual responsibility had been diminished because of the proliferation of bureaucratic state agencies attempting to meet the demands of those involved in 'pressure group' politics. In so arguing, they committed themselves to the classic liberal doctrine that the collective good (or the good of all individuals) can be properly realized in most cases only by private individuals acting in competitive isolation and pursuing their sectoral aims with minimal state interference.

At root, the New Right is concerned to advance the cause of 'liberalism' against 'democracy' by limiting the possible uses of state power. A government can only legitimately intervene in society to enforce general rules – rules which broadly protect 'life, liberty and estate'. Hayek, one of the leading advocates of these ideas, is unequivocal about this: a free, liberal order is incompatible with the enactment of rules which specify how people should use the means at their disposal (1960: 231–2). Governments become coercive if they interfere with people's own capacity to determine their objectives. The prime example Hayek gives of such coercion is legislation which attempts to alter 'the material position of particular people or enforce distributive or "social" justice' (*ibid.*: 231). Distributive justice always imposes on some another's conception of merit or desert. It requires the allocation of resources by a central authority acting as if it knew what people should receive for their efforts and how they should behave. The value of individuals' services can, however, only justly be determined by their fellows in and through a decision-making system which does not interfere with *their* knowledge, choices and decisions. And there is only one sufficiently sensitive mechanism for determining 'collective' choice on an individual basis – the free market. When protected by a constitutional state, no system provides a mechanism of collective choice as dynamic, innovative and responsive as the operations of the free market.

The free market does not always operate perfectly; but, Hayek insists, its benefits radically outweigh its disadvantages (1960 and 1976; and see Rutland, 1985). A free market system is the basis for a genuinely liberal order; for 'economic freedom is', as Friedman put it, 'an essential requisite for political freedom' (1980: 21). In particular, the market can ensure the coordination of decisions of producers and consumers without the direction of a central authority; the pursuit by everybody of their own ends with the resources at their disposal; the development of a complex economy without an élite who claim to know how it all works. Politics, as a governmental decision-making system, will always be a radically imperfect system of choice when compared to the market. Thus 'politics' or 'state action' should be kept to a minimum – to the sphere of operation of an 'ultra-liberal' state (Hayek, 1976: 172). An 'oppressive bureaucratic government' is the almost inevitable result of deviation from this prescription.

Thinkers like Hayek, along with the New Right movement more generally, have contributed significantly to a discussion about the appropriate form and limits of state action (Held and Keane, 1984). They have helped once again to make the relationship among state, civil society and subject populations a leading political issue. Conceptions about the proper character of this relationship are perhaps more unsettled now than at any point during the post-war years.

But the New Right, of course, is not the only tradition with a claim to inherit the vocabulary of freedom. The 'New Left' has developed profound claims of its own to this lexicon. It is worth stressing that the New Left did not develop principally as a 'counter-attack' on the New Right. (Indeed the contrary is true.) While the presence of the New Right has, in recent times, sharpened New Left views, the latter emerged primarily as a result of the political upheavals of the 1960s, internal debates on the left and dissatisfaction with the heritage of both liberal and Marxist political theory.[3] I shall focus the brief discussion below on the work of two people who have contributed, in particular, to the rethinking of left conceptions of democracy: Pateman (1970; 1985) and Poulantzas (1980).

The extent to which individuals are 'free' in contemporary liberal democracies is questioned by the New Left theorists. To enjoy liberty means not only to enjoy equality before the law, important though this unquestionably is, but also to have the capacities (the material and cultural resources) to be able to choose between different courses of action. As

Pateman put it, 'the "free and equal individual" is, in practice, a person found much more rarely than liberal theory suggests' (1985: 171). Liberal theory – in its classical and contemporary guises – generally assumes what has, in fact, to be carefully examined: namely, whether the existing relationships among men and women, working, middle and upper classes, blacks and whites, and various ethnic groups allows formally recognized rights to be actually realized. The formal existence of certain rights in democratic theory and ideology is, while not unimportant, of little value if they cannot be exercised in everyday practice. An assessment of freedom must be made on the basis of liberties that are tangible, and capable of being deployed within the realms of both state and civil society. The famous cynical comment on equality before the law – 'The doors of the Court of Justice stand open to all, like the doors of the Ritz Hotel' – applies equally to democratic participation and access to ordinary amenities. Without a concrete content – as particular freedoms – liberty can scarcely be said to have profound consequences for everyday life. If liberals or neo-liberals were to take these issues seriously, they would discover that, for want of a complex mix of resources and opportunities, massive numbers of individuals are restricted systematically from participating actively in political and civil life. Inequalities of class, sex and race substantially hinder the extent to which it can legitimately be claimed that individuals are 'free and equal'.

Furthermore, the very liberal claim that there can be a clear separation between 'civil society' and 'the state' is, Pateman argues, flawed, with fundamental consequences for key liberal tenets (1985: 172ff.). If the state is separate from the associations and practices of everyday life, then it is plausible to see it as a special kind of apparatus which the citizen ought to respect and obey. However, if the state is enmeshed in these associations and practices, then the claim that the state is an 'independent authority' or 'circumscribed impartial power' is radically compromised. In Pateman's judgement (and that of many contemporary Marxists and neo-pluralists), the state is inescapably locked into the maintenance and reproduction of the inequalities of everyday life. Accordingly, the whole basis of its claim to distinct allegiance is in doubt (1985: 173ff.; Lindblom, 1977; Offe, 1985). This is unsettling for the whole spectrum of questions concerning the nature of public power, the relation between the 'public' and the 'private', the proper scope of politics and the appropriate reach of democratic governments.

If the state, as a matter of routine, is neither 'separate' nor 'impartial' with respect to society, then it is clear that citizens will not be treated as 'free and equal'. If the 'public' and 'private' are interlocked in complex ways, then elections will always be insufficient as mechanisms to ensure the accountability of the forces actually involved in the 'governing' process. Moreover, since the 'meshing' of state and civil society leaves few, if any, realms of 'private life' untouched by 'politics', the question of the proper form of democratic regulation is acute. What form democratic control should take, and what the scope of democratic decision-making should be, becomes an urgent matter. However, the 'traditional' left response to these issues needs to be treated with caution, since 'New Left' thinkers generally accept that there are fundamental difficulties with orthodox Marxist theory (see Macpherson, 1977).

In common with other New Left thinkers, Poulantzas has tried to develop a position which moves beyond a rigid juxtaposition of Marxism with liberalism. For Poulantzas, the development of Stalinism and a repressive state in Russia is not merely due to the peculiarities of a 'backward' economy – as many Marxists today still argue – but can be traced to problems in Marx's and Lenin's thought and practice. Marx's and Lenin's belief that the institutions of representative democracy can be simply swept away by organizations of rank and file democracy is erroneous. Lenin, above all, mistook the nature of representative democracy when he labelled it simply as bourgeois (Polan, 1984). Underlying this typical Leninist view is a mistaken distrust of the idea of competing power centres in society. Moreover, it was because of distrust of this kind that Lenin ultimately undermined the autonomy of the Soviets after the 1917 Revolution, and set the Revolution on an 'anti-democratic' road. Poulantzas affirms the view that 'without general elections, without unrestricted freedom of press and assembly, without a free struggle of opinion, life dies out in every public institution' (Rosa Luxembourg, quoted by Poulantzas, 1980: 283).

Poulantzas argues that the whole relation between socialist thought and democratic institutions needs to be rethought in the light not only of the reality of Eastern European socialism but also of the moral bankruptcy of the social democratic vision of reform. Social democratic politics has led to the adulation of 'social engineering', proliferating policies to make relatively minor adjustments in social and economic arrangements. The state has, accordingly, grown in size and power undermining the vision that social democratic politics might once have had.

What, then, is the way forward? Institutions of direct democracy or self-management cannot simply replace the state for, as Max Weber predicted, they leave a coordination vacuum readily filled by bureaucracy. Poulantzas emphasizes two sets of changes which he believes are vital for the transformation of the state in West and East into forms of what he calls 'socialist pluralism'. The state must be democratized by making parliament, state bureaucracies and political parties more open and accountable while new forms of struggle at the local level (through factory-based politics, the women's movement, and ecological groups) must ensure that society, as well as the state, are democratized – that is, subject to procedures which ensure accountability. But how these processes interrelate Poulantzas does not say, stressing instead that there are 'no easy recipes'.

While the New Left theorists have highlighted a number of fundamental difficulties with liberal accounts of democracy and, in particular, with the New Right position, the New Left conception of democracy, both as it is and as it could be, cannot simply be accepted. Too many fundamental issues are left unaddressed. Little is said, for instance, about how the economy is actually to be organized and related to the state apparatus, how institutions of representative democracy are to be combined with those of direct democracy, how the scope and power of administrative organizations are to be checked, how those who wish to 'opt out' of the political system might do so, how the problems posed by the ever-changing international system could be dealt with. Moreover, the arguments pass over the question of how the 'model' could be realized, over the whole issue of transitional stages and over how those who might be worse off in some respects as a result of its application (those whose current circumstances allow them to determine the opportunities of others) might react and should be treated.

Furthermore, New Left theorists tend to assume that people in general want to extend the sphere of control over their lives. What if they do not want to do so? What if they do not really want to participate in the management of social and economic affairs? What if they do not wish to become creatures of democratic reason? Or, what if they wield democratic power 'undemocratically' – to limit or end democracy?

These are complex and difficult questions, not all of which, of course, one could reasonably expect each theorist to address fully. None the less, they are important questions to ask of 'participatory democracy', precisely because it is a version of democratic theory which champions not only a set of procedures, but a form of life as well.

FUNDAMENTAL ISSUES

The New Left theorists are correct, I believe, to pursue the implications of democratic principles for the organizational structure of society as well as of the state. However, this leaves them vulnerable to criticism – in particular to the charge that they have attempted to resolve prematurely the highly complex relations between individual liberty, distributional matters (questions of social justice) and democratic processes. By focusing squarely on the desirability of collective decision-making, and by allowing democracy to prevail over all other considerations, they tend to leave these relations to be specified in the ebb and flow of democratic negotiation.

However, it is precisely in criticizing such a standpoint that the New Right thinkers are at their most compelling. Should there be limits on the power of the *demos* to change and alter political circumstance? Should the nature and scope of the liberty of individuals and minorities be left to democratic decision? Should there be clear constitutional guidelines which both enable and limit democratic operations? By answering questions such as these in the affirmative, the New Right recognizes the possibility of severe tensions between individual liberty, collective decision-making and the institutions and processes of democracy. By not systematically addressing these issues, the New Left, in contrast, has too hastily put aside the problems.[4] In making democracy at all levels the primary social objective to be achieved, the New Left thinkers have relied upon 'demo-cratic reason' – a wise and good democratic will – for the determination of just and positive political outcomes. Can an essentially democratic *demos* be relied upon? Can one assume that the 'democratic will' will be wise and good? Can one assume that 'democratic reason' will prevail? Hayek and other New Right thinkers have suggested good grounds for at least pausing on this matter.

It was precisely around these issues that the New Right generated so much political capital by directly acknowledging the uncertain outcomes of democratic politics – the ambiguous results, for instance, of the 'well-intentioned' democratic welfare state. By highlighting that democracy can lead to bureaucracy, red tape, surveillance and excessive infringement of individual options (and not just in East European societies), they have struck a chord with the actual experience of those in routine contact with certain branches of the modern state, experience which by no means necessarily makes people more optimistic about collective decision-making. The New Right has, then, contributed to a discussion about the desirable limits of democratic collective regulation with which others must engage if the model of a more participatory democracy is to be adequately defended. Such an engagement might well have to concede more to the liberal tradition than has hitherto been allowed by left-wing thinkers. The central question then is: how can individuals be 'free and equal' and enjoy equal opportunities to participate in the determination of the framework which governs their lives without surrendering important issues of indivi-dual liberty and distributional questions to the uncertain outcomes of the democratic process?

I believe that the surrender need not take place if enhanced political participation is embedded in a legal framework that protects and nurtures individuals as 'free and equal' citizens. Accordingly, one cannot escape the necessity of recognizing the importance of a number of fundamental liberal tenets concerning the centrality, in principle, of an 'impersonal' structure of public power, of a constitution to help guarantee and protect rights, of a diversity of power centres within and outside the state, and of mechanisms to promote competition and debate between alternative political platforms. What this amounts to, among other things, is confirmation of the fundamental liberal notion that the 'separation' of the state from civil society must be a central feature of any democratic political order. Models of democracy that depend on the assumption that 'state' could ever replace 'civil society' or vice versa must be treated with the utmost caution.

Within the history of liberalism alone the concept of 'civil society' has been interpreted in a variety of different ways (Bobbio, 1985; Pelczynski, 1985; Keane, 1988). There is a profound sense, moreover, in which civil society can never be 'separate' from the state; the latter, by providing the overall legal framework of society, to a significant degree constitutes the former. None the less, it is not unreasonable to claim that civil society retains a distinctive character to the extent that it is made up of areas of social life – the domestic world, the economic sphere, cultural activities and political interaction – which are organized by private or voluntary arrangements between individuals and groups outside the direct control of the state (Hall, 1983). It is in this sense that the notion is used here. Thus understood, the terms of the argument I wish to make in the remainder of the chapter can be stated as follows: centralized state institutions – *pace* the advocates of highly radical models of the market or democratic life – must be viewed as necessary devices for enacting legislation, enforcing rights, promulgating new policies and containing inevitable conflicts between particular interests. And representative electoral institutions, including parliament and the competitive party system, must be seen as an inescapable element for authorizing and co-ordinating these activities.

However, to make these points is not to affirm any one liberal democratic model as it stands. There are profound difficulties with each major model of liberal democracy (Held, 1987). For example, advocates of liberal democracy representing positions as diverse as those of Bentham, J. S. Mill and Schumpeter have tended to be concerned, above all else, with the proper principles and procedures of democratic government. By focusing on 'government', they have detracted attention from a thorough examination of the relation between: formal rights and actual rights; commitments to treat citizens as free and equal and practices which do neither sufficiently; conceptions of the state as, in principle, an independent authority and involvements of the state in the reproduction of the inequalities of everyday life; notions of political parties as appropriate structures for bridging the gap between state and society and the array of power centres which such parties and their leaders cannot reach; and conceptions of politics as governmental affairs and systems of power which negate this concept. As the New Left thinkers have correctly pointed out, no current conception of liberal democracy is able adequately to specify the conditions for the possibility of political participation by all citizens, on the one hand, and the set of governing institutions capable of regulating the forces which actually shape everyday life, on the other. The problems, in sum, are twofold. First, the structure of civil society (including private ownership of productive property, vast sexual and racial inequalities), which is misunderstood or endorsed by liberal democratic models, does not create conditions for effective participation, proper political understanding and equal control of the political agenda (Dahl, 1985). Second, the structure of the liberal democratic state (including large, frequently unaccountable bureaucratic apparatuses, institutional dependence on the process of capital accumulation, and political representatives preoccupied with their own re-election) does not create an organizational force which can adequately regulate 'civil' power centres.

DEMOCRACY: A DOUBLE-SIDED PROCESS

The implications of these points are profound: for democracy to flourish today it has to be reconceived as a double-sided phenomenon concerned, on the one hand, with the reform of state power and, on the other, with the restructuring of civil society (Held and Keane, 1984). This entails recognizing the indispensability of a process of 'double democratization' – the interdependent transformation of both state and civil society. Such a process must be premised by the acceptance of the principle that the division between state and civil society must be a central feature of democratic life, and the notion that the power to make decisions must be free of the inequalities and constraints imposed by the private appropriation of capital. But, of course, to recognize the importance of both these positions is to recognize the necessity of substantially recasting their traditional connotations. This requires us to rethink the forms and limits of both state action and civil society.

The questions arise: how, and in what ways, might state policy be made more accountable? How, and in what ways, might 'non-state' activities be democratically re-ordered? To address these problems with any thoroughness is beyond the scope of this chapter (although it is a task begun in Held and Pollitt, 1986, and a central concern of Held, 1987 and forthcoming).

However, it is clearly important to add some institutional detail to the argument presented so far, if the conditions of enactment of a 'double-sided' conception of democracy are to be envisaged at all. What follows, however, is nothing other than the briefest of sketches – some elements of an agenda for further thought and research.

In many countries, both Western and Eastern, the limits of 'government' are explicitly defined in constitutions and bills of rights which are subject to public scrutiny, parliamentary review and judicial process. This idea is fundamental, and fundamental to democracy conceived as double-sided process. However, such a conception of democracy requires these limits on 'public power' to be reassessed in relation to a far broader range of issues than has been hitherto commonly presupposed. If people are to be free and equal in the determination of the conditions of their own lives, and enjoy equal rights in the specification of the framework which generates and limits the opportunities available to them, they must be in a position to enjoy a range of rights not only in principle, but also in practice. The rights of citizens must be both formal and concrete. This entails the specification of a far broader range of rights, with a far more profound 'cutting edge', than is typically allowed.

A democracy would be fully worth its name if citizens had the actual power to be active as citizens; that is to say, if citizens were able to enjoy a bundle of rights which allowed them to *command* democratic participation and to treat it as an entitlement (see Sen, 1983: ch. 1). Such a 'bundle of rights', it is important to stress, should not be thought of as merely an extension of the sphere of accumulated private demands for rights and privileges over and against the state, as many liberal thinkers have conceived rights (see Held, 1987: ch. 2). Nor should it be thought of as simply redistributive welfare measures to alleviate inequalities of opportunity, as many of the theorists of the welfare state have interpreted rights (see Marshall, 1973). Rather, it should be seen as entailed by, and integral to, the very notion of democratic rule itself. It is a way of specifying certain socioeconomic conditions for the possibility of effective democratic participation. *If one chooses democracy, one must choose to operationalize a radical system of rights.*

What would be included in such a system of rights? A constitution and bill of rights which enshrined the idea of democracy as a 'double-sided' process would specify equal rights with respect to the processes that determine state outcomes. This would involve not only equal rights to cast a vote, but also equal rights to enjoy the conditions for enlightened understanding, involvement in all stages of collective decision-making and the setting of the political agenda. Such broad 'state' rights would, in turn, entail a broad bundle of social rights linked to reproduction, childcare, health and education, as well as economic rights to ensure adequate economic and financial resources for democratic autonomy. Without tough social and economic rights, rights with respect to the state could not be fully enjoyed; and, without state rights, new forms of inequality of power, wealth and status could systematically disrupt the implementation of social and economic liberties.

A system of rights of this type would specify certain responsibilities of the state to groups of citizens, which particular governments could not override, unless permitted by an explicit process of constitutional amendment. In principle, the authority of the state would thus be clearly circumscribed; its capacity for freedom of action would be bounded. For example, a right to reproductive freedom for women would entail making the state responsible not only for the medical and social facilities necessary to prevent or assist pregnancy, but also for providing the material conditions which would help make the choice to have a child a genuinely free one, and, thereby, ensure a crucial condition for women if they are to be 'free and equal'. A right to economic resources for women and men, in order that they may be in a position to choose among possible courses of action, would oblige the state to be preoccupied with the ways in which wealth and income can be far more equitably distributed. Such resources might be made available through, among other things, a guaranteed income for all adults irrespective of whether they are engaged in wage-labour or household-labour (Jordan, 1985). Although strategies of the latter type should be treated with some caution since their implications for collective or societal wealth creation and distribution are complex and by no means fully clear, without a minimum resource base of some kind, many people will remain highly vulnerable and dependent on others, unable to exercise fully an independent choice or to pursue different opportunities that are formally before them. Thus, the 'rule of law' must involve a central concern with distributional questions and matters of social justice: anything less would hinder the realization of democratic rule.

Accordingly, in this scheme of things, a right to equal justice would entail not only the responsibility of the state to ensure formal equality before the law, but also that citizens would have the actual capacity (the health, skills and resources) to take advantage of opportunities before them. Such a constitution and bill of rights would radically enhance the ability of citizens to take action against the state to redress unreasonable encroachment on liberties. It would help tip the balance from state to parliament and from parliament to citizens and would thus be an 'empowering' legal system. As such, it would break with any assumption that the state can successfully define citizens' wants and needs and become the 'caretaker of existence' (Held, 1986). Of course, 'empowerment' would not thereby be guaranteed, since no legal system alone is able to offer such guarantees, but it would specify rights which could be fought for by individuals, groups and movements (wherever pressure could most effectively be mounted), and which could be tested in open court, among other places.[5]

In part, the implications for civil society are clear. To the extent that its structures comprise elements that undermine the possibility of effective collective decision-making, they would have to be progressively transformed. A democratic state and civil society is incompatible with the existence of powerful sets of social relations and organizations which, by virtue of the very basis of their operations, can distort democratic processes, and hence outcomes. At issue here is, among other things, the curtailment of the power of corporations to constrain and influence the political agenda, the restriction of the activities of powerful interest groups (whether they be representatives of particular industries or some trade unions with workers in key industrial sectors) to pursue unchecked their own interests, and the erosion of the systematic privileges enjoyed by some social groups (for instance, certain racial groups) at the expense of others. The state and civil society must, then, become the condition for each other's democratic development.

Under such conditions, strategies would have to be adopted to break up old patterns of power in civil society and to create new circumstances permitting citizens to enjoy greater control of their own projects (Keane, 1988). If individuals are to be free and equal in the determination of the conditions of their own existence, there must be a multiplicity of social spheres – for example, socially-owned enterprises, independent communications media and health centres – which allow their members control of the resources at their disposal without direct interference from the state, political agencies or other third parties. The models for the organization of such spheres would have much to learn from the conceptions of direct participation mentioned earlier. But an experimental view of such organizational structures would have to be taken. The state of democratic theory and the knowledge we have of radical democratic experiments does not allow wholly confident predictions about the most suitable strategies for organizational change (see Held and Pollitt, 1986). In this particular sense, the 'music of the future' (Marx) can only be composed in practice through innovation and research.

OUSTANDING QUESTIONS

The model of democracy sketched above – which I call 'democratic autonomy' or 'liberal socialism' – seeks to place at its centre the right of all citizens to participate in public affairs. What is at issue is the provision of a *rightful share* in the process of 'government'. However, it is one thing to recognize a right, quite another to say that everyone must, irrespective of choice, actually participate in public life. Participation is not a necessity.

It has been argued that one of the most important negative liberties established since the end of the ancient world is 'freedom from politics', and that such a liberty is an essential part of the contemporary democratic heritage (Arendt, 1963: 284). The model of democratic autonomy strives to be compatible with this element of our heritage. Citizens may decide that extensive participation is unnecessary in certain circumstances, and they may decide this for very rational reasons including a conviction that their interests are already well protected (see Mansbridge, 1983). Clearly, all systems of law – and the legal system of democratic autonomy would be no exception – specify a variety of obligations. Within the model of democratic autonomy, obligations would clearly exist. Citizens would be obliged to accept democratic decisions in a variety of circumstances – at sites of politics, work and community life – unless it could be proved that their rights were violated by such decisions. But the obligation to become involved in all aspects of public life would not be a legal obligation. The right to a life of one's own, within a framework of democratic autonomy, is indisputably important.

This position, of course, raises difficult issues. What exact bundle of rights and obligations does the model of democratic autonomy create? Precisely which obligations would citizens have to accept? Under what circumstances could they legitimately refuse such obligations? If citizens were to be entitled to refuse a decision on the grounds that it violated their rights, what means of resistance would they be justified in deploying in these circumstances? These are just a few of the problems which a fully explicated model of democratic autonomy would have to address, and which require further theoretical inquiry.

In any given political system there are clearly constraints on the extent of liberty which citizens can enjoy: liberty is limited. What distinguishes the model of democratic autonomy from other models, especially those in the liberal tradition like that of the New Right, is a fundamental commitment to the principle that the liberty of some individuals must not be allowed at the expense of others, where others are often a majority of citizens. In this sense, the concept of liberty presupposed by the model of democratic autonomy allows, in some respects, a smaller range of actions for certain groups of individuals. If the aims of the model are to be realized, then some people will no longer have the scope to, for instance, accumulate a vast amount of resources, or pursue their own careers at the expense of the careers of their lovers, wives or children. The liberty of persons within the framework of democratic autonomy will have to be one of progressive accommodation to the liberty of others. While, therefore, the scope of action may be more limited for some in certain respects, it will be radically enhanced for others.

It does not follow from this, as is sometimes remarked about related theoretical positions, that such a fundamental transformation of life opportunities entails the end of the division of labour or the end of a role for specialized competencies. As one critic rightly commented: 'a political future which promised to dispense with expertise will be necessarily an idiot's promise or a promise made in the deepest bad faith' (Dunn, 1979: 19). The model of democratic autonomy is, and must be, fully compatible with people choosing to develop particular talents and skills. The conditions of such choices will be different, but this does not mean that there will be no choices (see Burnheim, 1985). Moreover, the model of democratic autonomy explicitly presupposes the existence of centralized decision-making in government. Democratic autonomy does not promote the levelling of all authority and of those clusters of institutions which can provide skilled, predictable administration. Weber's argument about the importance of the latter in preventing public affairs becoming a quagmire of in-fighting among factions, wholly inefficient in settling pressing collective issues, is particularly significant (see Weber, 1978, II: 949, 951–2), but the form and structure of such institutions would have to be changed. It would, again, be quite fallacious to claim that one can know exactly how, and in what precise ways, this should happen. Much further reflection and research is unquestionably necessary on the types and forms of possible political organization and their connecting relations with markets when the latter function within a framework of broad equality of conditions.

CONCLUSION

If democratic life involves no more than a periodic vote, the locus of people's activities will be the 'private' realm of civil society and the scope of their actions will depend largely on the resources they can command. Few opportunities will exist for citizens to act as citizens, as participants in public life. But if democracy is understood as a 'double-sided' process, this state of affairs might be redressed by creating opportunities for people to establish themselves 'in their capacity of being citizens' (Arendt, 1963: 256). Of course, this model of democracy faces an array of possible objections which cannot be pursued here. Hopefully, however, the necessity to think beyond the positions of the New Right and New Left has, at the very least, been established.

NOTES

1. I have discussed these issues at greater length in *Models of Democracy* (1987) and in *New Forms of Democracy* (Held and Pollitt, 1986). Some of the material in this chapter is adapted from *Models* as well as from Chapter 1 of *New Forms*, although I have sought to tighten up some of my earlier formulations here. I am indebted to Adrian Leftwich for many helpful comments on a draft of this essay.
2. It might be noted that item four of this programme is arguably inconsistent with items one and two. In fact, a tension exists in conservatism generally and in the New Right in particular between those who assert individual freedom and the market as the ultimate concern, and those who believe in the primacy of tradition, order and authority, because they fear the social consequences of rampant *laissez-faire* policies. My account of the New Right concentrates on the former group, who have been most influential in current politics. See Levitas (1986) for an analysis of different elements in New Right thinking.
3. The New Left, like the New Right, consists of more than one strand of political thought: at the very least, it consists of ideas inspired by Rousseau, anarchists and a variety of Marxist positions. A number of figures have contributed to the reformulation of left conceptions of democracy and freedom. See Pierson (1986) and Held (1987: ch. 8).
4. This is not to say that the problems are unrecognized (see, for instance, Macpherson, 1977: ch. 5).
5. The existing judicial system in most countries is unlikely to provide sufficiently representative personnel to oversee such a judicial process. An alternative would have to be found, comprising perhaps judicial bodies composed of people who were chosen from a 'statistically representative' sample of the population – that is, who were statistically representative of key social categories (gender, race, age) (see Burnheim, 1985). There is no reason to suppose that such bodies would be less capable of independent judgement than the existing judiciary and many reasons for believing that their judgements over the specific matter of how to interpret human rights would be more representative of collective opinion.

REFERENCES

Arendt, H. (1963), *On Revolution* (New York, Viking Penguin).

Bobbio, N. (1985), *Stato, Govern, Societa: Per Una Teoria Generale della Politica* (Turin, Einaudi).

Burnheim, J. (1985), *Is Democracy Possible?* (Cambridge, Polity Press).

Cohen, J. L. (1982), *Class and Civil Society: the limits of Marxian critical theory* (Oxford, Martin Robertson).

Dahl, R. A. (1985), *A Preface to Economic Democracy* (Cambridge, Polity Press).

Dunn, J. (1979), *Western Political Theory in the Face of the Future* (Cambridge, Cambridge University Press).

Friedman, M. R. (1980), *Free to Choose: a personal statement* (Harmondsworth, Penguin).

Hall, S. (1983), 'Themes and questions' in *The State and Society*, **3(7)** (Milton Keynes, Open University Press).

Hayek, F. A. (1960), *The Constitution of Liberty* (London, Routledge and Kegan Paul).

Hayek, F. A. (1976), *The Road to Serfdom* (London, Routledge and Kegan Paul).

Hayek, F. A. (1982), *Law, Legislation and Liberty*, vol. 3 (London, Routledge and Kegan Paul).

Held, D. (1984), 'Power and legitimacy in contemporary Britain' in G. McLennan, D. Held and S. Hall (eds), *State and Society in Contemporary Britain* (Cambridge, Polity Press).

Held, D. (1986), 'Liberalism, Marxism and the future direction of public policy' in P. Nolan and S. Paine (eds), *Re-thinking Socialist Economics* (Cambridge, Polity Press).

Held, D. (1987), *Models of Democracy* (Cambridge, Polity Press).

Held, D. (1988), 'Citizenship and autonomy' in D. Held and J. B. Thompson (eds) *Social Theory of Modern Societies* (Cambridge, Cambridge University Press).

Held, D. (forthcoming), *The Foundations of Democracy* (Cambridge, Polity Press).

Held, D. and Keane, J. (1984), 'Socialism and the limits of state action' in J. Curran (ed), *The Future of the Left* (Cambridge, Polity Press).

Held, D. and Pollitt, C. (eds) (1986), *New Forms of Democracy* (London, Sage).

Jordan, B. (1985), *The State: authority and autonomy* (Oxford, Basil Blackwell).

Keane, J. (1988), *Democracy and Civil Society* (London, Verso).

Levitas, R. (ed.) (1986), *The Ideology of the New Right* (Cambridge, Polity Press).

Lindblom, C. E. (1977), *Politics and Markets* (New York, Basic Books).

Macpherson, C. B. (1977), *The Life and Times of Liberal Democracy* (Oxford, Oxford University Press).

Mansbridge, J. J. (1983), *Beyond Adversary Democracy* (Chicago, Chicago University Press).

Marshall, T. H. (1973), 'Citizenship and social class' in T. H. Marshall, *Class, Citizenship and Social Development* (Westport, Conn., Greenwood Press).

McLennan, G. (1984), 'Capitalist state or democratic polity? Recent developments in Marxist and pluralist theory' in G. McLennan *et al.* (eds), *The Idea of the Modern State* (Milton Keynes, The Open University Press).

Nozick, R. (1974), *Anarchy, State and Utopia* (Oxford, Basil Blackwell).

Offe, C. (1984), *Contradictions of the Welfare State* (London, Hutchinson).

Offe, C. (1985), *Disorganized Capitalism* (Cambridge, Polity Press).

Pateman, C. (1970), *Participation and Democratic Theory* (Cambridge, Cambridge University Press).

Pateman, C. (1985), *The Problem of Political Obligation: a critique of liberal theory* (Cambridge, Polity Press).

Pelczynski, Z. A. (ed.) (1985), *The State and Civil Society* (Cambridge, Cambridge University Press).

Pierson, C. (1986), *Marxism or Politics?* (Cambridge, Polity Press).

Polan, A. J. (1984), *Lenin and the End of Politics* (London, Methuen).

Poulantzas, N. (1980), *State, Power, Socialism* (London, Verso/NLB).

Rutland, P. (1985), *The Myth of the Plan* (London, Hutchinson).

Sen, A. (1983), *Poverty and Famine* (Oxford, Oxford University Press).

Weber, M. (1978), *Economy and Society*, 2 vols. (Berkeley, University of California Press).

3. Feminism and Politics

Diana Coole

INTRODUCTION

Feminism has provided a new perspective for Politics by focusing on women as its subject matter and by looking at gender relations as a significant example of a power relationship. It has not, however, been content merely to constitute another subfield within the discipline. Besides insisting that women be included in all branches of political research, it has criticized the conventional values, models and methodologies of political studies and seeks to replace them with a feminist alternative.

Its intellectual contribution to the discipline must be seen in the light of feminism's broader political goals within the women's movement. In challenging traditional ways of conceiving and studying the political, it perceives itself as participating in a wider struggle whose target is patriarchy – the domination of women by men – in all its manifestations. For feminists, the sexual inequality that is evident in academic institutions, as well as the representations of the feminine that are promulgated in their disciplines, are but particular expressions of the patriarchal relations which criss-cross society as a whole. Feminism therefore challenges both the overwhelmingly male constitution of university and college Politics departments and the masculine values and assumptions with which politics and its study have always been associated. In other words, feminism sees its engagement with the academic discipline of Politics as a political act within a broader political strategy.

Feminism is, then, both an intellectual perspective and a social movement; its theories and its practice are interwoven. This lends to its engagement with the discipline of Politics a peculiar sort of self-reflexiveness. When feminists discuss such issues as equal opportunities, for example, they speak as members of a group (a 'sex-class') which suffers from discrimination and looks to equal opportunity as a contribution to its own advancement. They also recognize that the way politics is delineated and studied is part of a broader cultural milieu in which gendered identities and relations are defined. And, by a further twist, feminism finds itself the object of research to the extent that its exponents become

24

recognizable political actors, to be discussed according to the perspectives and methods of mainstream Political Science.

THE HISTORY OF FEMINIST THOUGHT

It will be useful to begin with a brief overview of the development of feminism in relation to the study of politics. Feminism is not a recent development: it emerged in the late seventeenth century as a corollary of liberalism, when women began to recognize their unequal status as a sex. For two centuries, its exponents struggled to gain access for women to educational establishments and the professions, as well as to the civil and political rights enjoyed by men. The movement went into eclipse during the middle decades of this century and a 'second wave' appeared only in the late 1960s. The latter's aims have been far more radical than those of its predecessor: among them is nothing less than a transformation of Western culture, including its intellectual frameworks and its epistemology. This process has been more self-consciously pursued as women have become increasingly aware of the ideological dimensions of their oppression, in which the social sciences, *inter alia*, have played a significant role (Millett, 1977: 220–33).

Early feminists of the 'second wave' were less interested in contributing to the discipline of Politics *per se*, than in composing political writings which would disclose the dimensions of women's oppression. It was an irony of their position that not only were women largely invisible as public agents, but a sceptical establishment – and even many women themselves – had to be convinced that they were oppressed at all. Some of these early writings have become classic texts to be studied in their own right: Simone de Beauvoir's *The Second Sex* (1949), Betty Friedan's *The Feminine Mystique* (1963), Shulamith Firestone's *The Dialectic of Sex* (1970) and Juliet Mitchell's *Woman's Estate* (1971) were all early attempts at identifying and explaining women's subjection. They were theoretical works which tried to shift our focus on the social world, but they did so with the aid of conceptual frameworks already in existence (existentialist, liberal, Marxist), twisting and adapting them in an effort to apply them to previously invisible dimensions of power. Subsequently, however, a suspicion grew that these theoretical frameworks, like the social sciences, might be less gender-neutral than they seemed: in using them, feminists unwittingly reproduced patriarchal images of gender and a masculine construction of the world. During the 1970s a radical feminist position thus emerged, seeking a new approach to women that would apply feminist concepts and points of reference to them (Eisenstein, 1984: ch. 5).

This marks one of two central developments (and divisions) in feminism's contribution to the study of politics. On the one hand, there are those who have fought to expand the subject areas which are studied to include women's issues and activities, but who continue to use the intellectual tools and concepts of the discipline. On the other, there are those who see in these tools and concepts an expression of masculine hegemony and who therefore seek new ways of looking at the social world as well as an expanded area of research.

A second development has nevertheless been important, and this is the recent growth in empirical political research in relation to women. Writing as recently as 1986, Joni Lovenduski was still able to lament the scant attention paid to women's political position outside of the United States as well as the lack of a database on which such attention might build (Lovenduski, 1986: 1). Although the collection and processing of data is more in conformity with the traditional methods of Political Science which have been criticized by some feminists, there is surely an urgent need for such research by women (and men!) who work within the discipline. That this should finally be happening is perhaps unsurprising, since the very success of the women's movement in involving women in mainstream politics has made them an important research topic. During the 1980s, more empirical research has accordingly been undertaken in relation to women's voting behaviour and preferences; their activities in pressure groups and parties; their fortunes in getting elected, and so on. Pippa Norris's *Politics and Sexual Equality* (1987) and Lovenduski's *Women and European Politics* (1986) are both good examples of this type of work, which also have the advantage of a comparative approach. Yet despite the use of more conventional analytic tools in such research, these scholars emphasize the political context within, and purpose for which, such data is collected. Lovenduski illustrates this point well when she associates her choice of subject matter with a commitment to political feminism and to a crusade against sexual discrimination (Lovenduski, 1986: 1). The approach is explicitly feminist, then, but there is no suggestion that its methods are in any way feminine. To put it another way: the methodology aims for objectivity, but within a value-context.

In a rather different sense, this more empirical approach has recently found favour in the theoretical camp. During the 1970s, the major theoretical debate was between Marxist feminists, who sought (ultimately unsuccessfully) an integrated theory of sexual and class oppression (Hartmann, 1979; Barrett, 1980; Phillips, 1987), and radical feminists who pursued (equally unsuccessfully, many would argue) a grand general theory of patriarchy (Beechey, 1979). Accusations of racism and ethnocentric bias against both positions (for example, Amos and Parmar,

1984), as well as an inclination towards a post-modernism which recognizes a plurality of fractured identities, have led in the 1980s to some retreat from this theoretical high ground. There has been some shift towards detailed case studies of the way sex, class and race articulate with one another in different times and places to produce shifting patterns of oppression.

THE QUEST FOR VALUE: FEMINISM AND FEMININITY

In the rest of this chapter I intend to focus on the more radical aspirations of feminism regarding a reconceptualization of the political. However, four caveats are in order before I begin. First, feminists do not always distinguish in this task between the theory and practice of politics, and so challenges to Politics as a discipline cannot always be isolated from challenges to the experience it interprets and/or constructs. Second, feminism is no monolithic body of ideas and there are few which can be generalized across the spectrum without distorting some positions. I have tried to avoid the rather tedious practice of dividing discussions into liberal, socialist/Marxist and radical perspectives, but it has on occasion been necessary to distinguish between different political or philosophical allegiances. Third, in order to examine feminism's contribution to Politics, it will often be necessary to dwell on theoretical developments within feminism itself and only then will their implications for the political be surmised. And finally, it must be admitted that the developments I want to explore have neither been worked out in a systematic way, nor have they usually been directly related to the study of politics. The notion of a feminist political discourse in particular remains an adventure for the future and it is only possible here to explore a few ideas as to what it might look like.

It is radical feminism which can lay claim to the most profound criticism of conventional Politics and Political studies, although some of its arguments would also be accepted by women on the left. A radical position may be broadly classified as one which sees patriarchy as the most pervasive feature of social life. Although some of its exponents have found a material base beneath this male omnipotence (Delphy, 1977), priority has been more typically given to cultural and psychosexual factors. During the 1980s this has tended to lead radical feminists away from a 'sex-war' focus, where men and women engage in a recognizable conflict of interests, towards greater appreciation of how gendered identities are constructed. Language, epistemology and the unconscious –

the realms of meaning, knowledge and subjectivity – have come to the fore and, with them, approaches which have remained largely alien to other branches of political analysis, most notably structural linguistics, post-structuralism and psychoanalysis. These have allowed feminists to speak rather more confidently about notions of femininity or masculinity, while facilitating an attack on the methodology of the social sciences.

In the context of this chapter, such developments raise a central question: is there something about conventional politics, and the way it has been studied, that might identify it as patriarchal and/or as an expression of masculine hegemony? And, conversely, is it plausible to anticipate an alternative that would be recognizably feminist and/or feminine? If so, what might this look like? Such phrasing reveals an ambiguity: a conflation often occurs between the idea of a *feminist* and that of a *feminine* politics. These are not necessarily the same thing and so we need to ask first of all what it might mean to designate a politics, or a method, feminine (or masculine).

Historically, much of the thrust of feminist argument has lain in its rejection of a naturally gendered psychology or social function: the biological distinction between the sexes specifies only that it is females who have a capacity to bear offspring; it signifies nothing about whether and how they might do so, what roles they might play or what attitudes and capacities they might exhibit. All these are socially overdetermined. This position is not, however, incompatible with a recognition that women and men do in fact reveal differences in their personalities and preferences which might be conveniently labelled feminine and masculine. It merely insists that such distinctions are a result of social forces and are therefore contingent and changeable. The implication is, then, that sex and gender do not correlate in any essential way: under different historical and cultural conditions, men might demonstrate more feminine qualities (and vice versa), while the signficance of the terms will itself shift.

Such a position can accommodate a variety of political conclusions. One might reason, as have most liberals and some socialists, that a progressive politics (or Political Studies) would be one which refused to grant any relevance to sex or gender distinctions (Richards, 1982). A model of impartial procedures or methods applied by and to ostensibly asexual individuals would be the ideal. Its pursuit would involve a *feminist* politics since its success would depend upon gaining equal opportunities for women, but there is no sense in which this might be described as a *feminine* process. Many feminists would nevertheless judge such a politics inadequate to rectify gender inequality. It takes the public realm as already constituted, asking for women's inclusion there but granting them no role in creating it: it lacks vision. Nor does it ask whether there might not be something about the way in which the political process works, or is conceived, that reproduces the deprecation of women and perhaps of individuals in general. Thus, while such a politics might have feminist goals, it cannot suggest any specifically feminist means or values for it.

In order to avoid these limitations, a stronger association between a feminist politics and femininity has been suggested. It is this which allows an escalation from demands for equal rights, to a vision of a transformed political realm. Although there has been a substantial consensus as to the qualities and values that might be associated with such femininity, however, this masks a considerable variety of theories regarding its acquisition and status.

For liberals, gendered characteristics are primarily a result of cultural pressures and of socialization. Girls are taught the values and attitudes which society deems conducive to the roles it will assign them. For socialists, feminine consciousness results from experience: women's historical role as reproducers, carers, servicers (and the oppressed) of society has encouraged appropriate orientations in them and these are generationally reproduced in the family. In both cases, femininity is therefore seen as socially, not biologically, acquired; it does not predestine women for a particular place in the division of labour, yet it does yield a recognizable image of gendered behaviour. There is some ambivalence as to the political significance of this occurrence. While some have focused on the passivity, subservience and masochism of women – qualities which disadvantage them in competing with men and for whose elimination they should aim – others have found a more positive message in women's cooperative, sensitive, nurturing tendencies, which might offer hope for a superior mode of life-enhancing politics and of human relations generally.

The latter position opens the door to a politics which might be called both feminist and feminine. While it remains an open question whether women will continue to evince such qualities under different conditions or, indeed, whether such qualities will continue to attract the conventional label of feminine at all, it would be no accident that the women's movement should have adopted the values and priorities that it has. They reflect something about their exponents' gendered experience, exemplified in the ideals of sisterhood, as well as something which they believe to be inherently desirable for all human conduct. Conversely, the style of a conventional politics traditionally dominated by men might be identified as masculine in so far as it expresses men's historically acquired ambitions and behaviour.

More detailed studies of the connection between sex and gender have made use of psychoanalysis (for example, Mitchell, 1974; Dinnerstein, 1976; Chodorow, 1978; Marks and Courtivron, 1981). Nancy Chodorow

provides a good example of this in her use of post-Freudian Object
Relations theory. Central to her work is the fact that asymmetrical child-
rearing practices are virtually universal. It is women who are primary
carers and this, she argues, is the key to the appearance of gendered
personalities, where separation from the primary love-object is the central
factor in psychic development. The girl who is like her mother and
strongly identified with her, gains a secure sense of her sexual identity but
a weak sense of her own autonomy and ego-boundaries, owing to the
difficulty of separation. The boy, on the other hand, is always treated as
different and must gain a sense of his sexual identity from the absent
father; his masculinity is predicated on his being not-female. The result is a
weak and abstract sense of masculinity but a stronger notion of self-
identity.

From these early differences we see subsequent gendered proclivities for
different types of knowledge and being. Females evince a capacity for
empathetic relationships, for cooperation and caring; they feel at home in
the world and relate strongly to their environment. Men, on the other
hand, are more attracted to modes of abstract thought which reflect their
own sense of separation from the world. They distrust subjectivity and
favour rational, objective, impersonal forms of knowledge and association. They fear that which is associated with femininity and pursue
projects of domination over it.

This association between masculinity and a fear of the feminine, which
leads to the desire for control and manipulation, is explored by other
feminists in terms of a cultural symbolism (Griffin, 1972; Keller, 1978,
1982; Daly, 1979; Lloyd, 1984). They argue that Western culture has
always identified femininity with nature, chaos, and that which must be
suppressed if culture and knowledge are to bloom. Although these cultural
equations, like the child-rearing practices described by Chodorow, might
in principle be different (and feminists must demand that they become so),
they have so far given to femininity and masculinity fairly universal
connotations.

A more essentialist, biological, identity between women and femininity
(and men and masculinity) appears in the work of some radical feminists.
Mary Daly (Daly, 1979), Adrienne Rich (Rich, 1977) and some French
feminists, for example, have argued that women's corporeal experiences –
their ability to give birth, their experience of sexual penetration, their
multi-centred sexuality – grant them a more intimate relation to the world
and more fluid ego-boundaries and ways of relating to that which is not-I;
hence a capacity for a feminine way of knowing which rejects imperious
classification and dualistic thought in favour of a mobile, creative, holistic
approach. Nevertheless, such essentialist accounts are problematic for

feminists because they rely upon biological accounts of women's nature and merely revalorize it within a patriarchal world. Rather than suggesting ways in which politics might be reconceived and transformed in some way which might provisionally be labelled 'feminine', they equate femininity with a disavowal of all such activity. Critical, rational thought itself becomes identified with a masculine approach that is to be rejected, leaving no opportunity for practical or intellectual engagement. One is politically efficacious merely by expressing one's suppressed femininity.

I suggested that a purely feminist politics was inadequate because it could offer no critique of the conventional theory and practice of politics beyond their discrimination against women. At the other end of the spectrum, an essentialist link between women and femininity appears to render political engagement or critique impossible. Despite the undoubted dangers of using such notions as feminine and masculine, I would therefore suggest that some notion of *contingent* femininity is valuable in yielding women a conception of a different *style* of politics. This allows something to be said about the way women might engage in the political realm, which would be different from its current configuration. It also permits a radical critique of mainstream politics from a feminist perspective as well as offering grounds for a vision of social regeneration. Also, it can condemn the masculine ethos of conventional politics while allowing that reconstructed men might share in a feminist alternative.

While this link between sex and gender might rest on cultural, experiential, psychological or symbolic foundations, it is its historical contingency which must be kept in mind. It is also important to remember that femininity is a fluid and open referent whose meaning is a patriarchal construction as well as a response to experience. Nor are its qualities at any time unproblematically adopted by women, whose struggles to conform to prevailing notions of femininity contribute to their oppression. It is only in so far as feminists have identified certain historical orientations by women and have then *chosen* to develop these as models of a progressive politics that a feminist politics can usefully be designated feminine. The relationship between women and the values and attitudes femininity signifies, remains contingent but not gratuitous.

THE UBIQUITY OF POWER AND POLITICS

It is now possible to return to my earlier question: is there something about conventional politics and its study, which might designate it an expression of patriarchy and/or masculinity? Feminists have pointed to an explicit patriarchal domination in practice. The state and its apparatuses are 'manned' predominantly by men and they are used to sustain male power in the private realm. Legislation and social policy are used to define women's roles and rights in such areas as reproduction, economic status and the family (McIntosh, 1987; Barrett, 1980). Moreover, many feminists have found the impersonal and bureaucratic nature of the modern state problematic in relation to the personalized and participatory style of politics which they favour.

A Political Science which focuses on the state stands accused of colluding in women's invisibility and status as non-political actors, since it has ignored their public activity as well as their private subjugation. At the same time, feminists have been critical of the discipline's focus on the state as the most important and interesting aspect of political life because, like Marxists, they see it not as an autonomous institution which floats above the conflicts of civil society, but as a participant in those conflicts (in this case, in the struggle between the sexes). It is one expression of some more fundamental political relationship and it is this which the discipline needs to study.

This brings me to a central claim by feminists, that the personal is political. It is a claim that is both immensely fertile and profoundly problematic for the study of politics. Its basic point is precisely that politics cannot be confined to the macro-levels of state processes; that politics is defined not by proximity to a particular *institution* but by a kind of *relationship*, namely one in which power and domination/subordination are present (Millett, 1977: 23f). Since women suffer from domination in their everyday lives and in their most intimate relationships, it follows that power relations run throughout the social fabric and it is these which need to be elicited, described, explained and eliminated. In other words, it is not enough for political analysis merely to include women's contribution to, and interest in, the formal political process. An entirely new range of issues – such as rape, pornography, abortion, housework – and institutions – the family, the classroom, the workplace, language – become relevant, since they are all channels through which power is systematically exercised. In recognizing the density, pervasiveness and frequent invisibility of power relations, feminists have come increasingly to reject models of individuals or classes locked in an overt conflict in order to impose their will and pursue explicit interests, as too simplistic. In other words, if a feminist politics emphasizes the multiplicity and intimacy of personal contact, a feminist analysis of politics equally stresses the myriad channels through which power is exercised on a personal level. Political analysis for it entails far more complex models than who gets what, when and how, as well as a more subtle account of power than one person's ability to coerce or influence another. It requires a shift in focus away from institutions and mass–class behaviour, towards a greater concern with subjectivity. The latter is perhaps one of feminism's main contributions to the discipline.

If the idea of personal politics might enrich the discipline by inviting a deeper look at the threads of power and knots of consciousness, however, it has simultaneously rendered the notion of what counts as political highly problematic because it has erased the boundary traditionally drawn between the public (political) and private realms. If it has associated politics with power relationships, it has discovered that power is ubiquitous; that even discourse and the unconscious are sites of domination. In fields like cultural studies and literary criticism, this has been an immensely fertile development (and its exponents have had no difficulty in admitting to the political dimensions of their work! – see Greene and Kahn, 1985). However, it remains problematic for the study of politics as such, in so far as it raises the spectre of a definition that is sufficiently broad to include virtually all human relationships and expressions. For those who favour a truly interdisciplinary approach, this may be only a problem of semantics. For practitioners of the discipline it raises the question of whether politics is to be reclassified as coextensive with sociocultural life *per se*, or simply limited to the analysis of only certain types of power relation where power is public and overt.

David Miller has suggested that personal matters can become objects of political concern only where state activity is involved, and that in this sense women's personal relations are no different from, say, the protection of animals (thus presumably public provision of nurseries would be a political question, but not who performs domestic labour or how it conventionally becomes designated women's work). To describe personal relations as political is misleading, he insists: not all power relations are political and to claim that they are is to widen 'the idea of politics to the point of vacuity' (Miller, 1987: 391). While this solution neatly maintains the discipline's traditional boundaries, however, it does nothing to answer feminist contentions that the public–private distinction is itself a patriarchal one, nor can it allow political studies to come to terms with the issues raised by feminism regarding the micro-levels of domination. At stake is its willingness to acknowledge its own political nature. Feminist concerns thus raise fundamental questions regarding the compartmentalization and departmentalization of knowledge in both intellectual and institutional terms, where these are antithetical to its own holistic and interdisciplinary inclinations.

FEMINISM, SCIENCE AND THE SOCIAL SCIENCES

If feminists have been critical of the values and models of politics, it is perhaps on methodological and epistemological questions that their most contentious yet intriguing suggestions have been made. Is there something here, too, which might be characterized as masculine and invite a feminist alternative?

Feminist interest in methodology has been most relevant to the study of politics where the latter claims to be a science. Some of the feminist suspicion of science is reminiscent of that demonstrated by critical theory, while criticism of its positivist inclinations echoes some of the attacks on behaviouralism which were becoming fashionable during the formative years of contemporary feminism itself. What feminists have added to these critiques is a gender perspective: a scientific approach has been associated with a masculine orientation to control and the scientific approach of the social sciences has been more specifically identified as a means of sustaining and legitimizing a patriarchal *status quo*.

At the most general level, feminists have been critical of the epistemology of the sciences. Objective knowledge is said to cut the knower off from the world being described, thus robbing him of access to the sources of living meaning. It imprisons him in preconceived categories and repetition, and it is not open to new, eccentric phenomena nor to individual idiosyncracies. In the social world especially, it therefore produces a sterile and rigid sort of knowledge whose classifications distort and freeze living relationships. Its dualist epistemology produces an impoverished way of knowing, for it fails to see the interconnectedness of things; it releases only corpuscles of data, which it then assembles in an artificial way (for example, Daly, 1979).

This is contrasted with a more empathetic, engaged and open mode of feminine knowing of the (social) world of which the knower is a part and able to discern its underlying rhythms and complexity. Although this theme has dangers of reducing a feminist approach to one which renounces rational thought altogether, it does suggest that neither empiricism nor rationalism are epistemologies that feminism would favour. Certainly it would be critical of a science which overemphasized behaviouralism, quantification or an inductive theory of human behaviour. A more dialectical, descriptive approach might be favoured (perhaps a phenomenology); in the social sciences, perhaps participant observation or symbolic interactionism might be perceived as sympathetic methods. Hilary Rose suggests that something like this feminine (non-Cartesian) way of knowing emerges from the characteristics typical of women's work, where the manual, mental and emotional have not yet been severed (Rose, 1983).

The propensity for scientific theories to dominate and manipulate their subject matter is seen by feminists as a particularly masculine way of proceeding. As we have seen, they point to an association which runs through Western culture between knowledge and masculinity, where the wild and chaotic feminine realm must be controlled and tamed if culture and civilization are to advance. This domination of a nature long associated with femininity now threatens global destruction. The equation is, however, more than symbolic because, as we saw, psychoanalytic feminism suggests that men are particularly attracted to those scientific ways of knowing which harmonize with their own psychological predispositions. They favour its rigid self–other distinctions, its rational abstractions and absolutism, its quest for a disengaged, authoritative, value-free knowledge. All are contrary to a feminist–feminine way of proceeding. The metaphors of control that have characterized the natural sciences since Bacon become literal in the social sciences when women, in particular, are controlled by the social policies and legislation they inform.

Political Science lays claim to a scientific status in so far as its practitioners systematically collect and collate data in an objective way, in order to discern regularities in behaviour such that individual acts can be aggregated and explained in terms of recurrent patterns. Feminists question the alleged neutrality of this approach and a further strand of their attack on scientific method rests on its claims to a fact–value distinction which they find neither possible nor desirable. In part, this stems from their general epistemological point about the sterility and dishonesty of social knowledge gained by a disengaged observer. But they are also well aware that it is values which dictate the facts and problematics that will be selected for study. It is evident that Political Scientists have not found women an interesting topic: their invisibility within the discipline stems at least partially from its failure to collect data about them, and this in turn has political consequences. Women's interests, issues, activities, have received little attention and therefore appear non-existent, thus reinforcing the idea that the political realm is a male one. The description and classification of the world as it is also has a conservative force, since it precludes alternatives and occludes those relationships which might evince a different logic or which might (like many dimensions of patriarchal power) remain invisible.

Unlike the earlier condemnation of science as such, this latter argument does not necessarily imply that feminists should avoid scientific method. It finds nothing intrinsically wrong or masculine about it, provided that it is explicit about its values and performs its research within an acknowledged (feminist) value-context. A feminist science of politics is then quite acceptable – even necessary – from this point of view, provided that it does not confuse scientific method with the more extravagant epistemological claims of positivism and that it discredits the fiction that 'normal' Political Science is neutral about humanity as such. Given feminist sensitivity to the multitude of non-empirical, invisible forms of power, however, it would be inconsistent to argue that the social sciences should strive to become wholly scientific: the collection of data is but one tool among other forms of analysis, and science is but one way of approaching the world. Normative inquiries remain vital.

This kind of question nevertheless opens up an interesting debate regarding the status of a feminist Politics. Is the aim of feminism to achieve a genuinely universal account of political behaviour, which incorporates data about women in order to rectify its traditional partiality? Or does the very quest for universalism have more to do with power than with truth? That is, is the idea of a single reality, wherein some universal human type is active, merely a fiction propagated by the dominant (white, male) group? Should feminists thus anticipate a plurality of Political disciplines, taking into account a variety of realities and identities and accepting the resulting relativism this implies?

Further methodological difficulties are raised by feminism's commitment to a knowledge which does justice to personal relations and experience, as opposed to the scientific predilection for aggregating behaviour in order to discern typical patterns. Can a politics which looks to collectivities and classes of people, accommodate the personal dimension? Yet, obversely, is it possible to base a theory of politics on personal experience without becoming simplistic, myopic and limited to a mosaic of individual utterances which would lack any explanatory power?

One response to this latter dilemma has been to focus not on personal experience as such, but on the subjectivity which emerges out of patriarchal (phallocentric) structures. Poststructuralism's focus on language, for example, allows it to bring together questions of subjectivity, political power and social organization (see Weedon, 1987). On a more ideological level, the way in which a conception of patriarchy emerged out of radical feminist consciousness-raising groups, is perhaps indicative of a feminist approach to formulating general theory which did try to accommodate individual experience.

The challenge to an abstract and impersonal methodology in Political Science in many ways parallels the kind of criticisms which we earlier found feminists levelling against the state, where an aggregating approach was similarly accused of ignoring individual experience, although this time in a practical way. The methodological and institutional questions raised here require more careful study than they have received so far, perhaps due to feminists' tendency to assume either that change will occur within the context of present structures, or that it must sweep those structures away in their entirety, along with the reasons for their existence.

CONCLUSIONS AND ANTICIPATIONS

What, in conclusion, might feminism offer to Political Studies in the future? My suggestions here are necessarily personal and speculative. Least controversially, however, it seems obvious that there is much work to be done by those women who work within the conventional paradigms of the discipline, where the primary task is surely to render women more visible. Empirical and statistical data on women's activities must be collected in order to build up a database for further research. Critical readings of classic political texts must extrapolate and scrutinize what they say about women and discover what women have said about themselves. Female scholars must strive to produce more so that reading lists are no longer dominated by male authors. All these activities require a rigorous and critical approach to political questions. Feminists will continue to demand that women who have developed such skills have equal access to academic posts. Here they can fight against the marginalization of women's issues, while providing role models for students, which challenge traditional views that both politics and intellectual life are male preserves. It is also important that they question the social production of knowledge, asking who produces it, who has access to it, and under what conditions.

As well as extending the subject matter of Politics feminists try, as we have seen, to expand the scope of the political. The location of gender relations and of personal relations generally, as sites of power, poses a fundamental challenge to the narrowness with which the discipline has conceived itself. At the very least, it demands a more interdisciplinary approach which would take into account the sort of information furnished by sociologists or social psychologists, and the type of methodology used in linguistics or psychoanalysis. Without these it cannot really begin to make sense of subjectivity or the micro-levels of political relationships.

I have argued, however, that feminism aspires to do more than expand the concerns and definition of Politics in order to address the woman question. It challenges the values and assumptions that underlie mainstream politics in theory and practice and looks to a feminist alternative at this level. This can be simply illustrated by the way in which Politics might be taught. Feminist values imply a less hierarchical relationship between teacher and student, less formal teaching arrangements and methods of assessment, and less competitiveness between academics and between students. Group work, joint projects, empirical studies arising out of students' own experience, would all seem conducive to the reciprocity and egalitarianism which feminism favours. Its values and its political demands would also come together in pursuing less élitist recruitment to higher education, more part-time and flexible degree programmes, more open access and more mature students. These would especially benefit women who must often combine study with other commitments. While being aware of the importance of vocational training to women who are generally disadvantaged in the workforce, I think that many feminists would also support a less utilitarian attitude towards the pursuit of knowledge.

Feminist values offer some suggestions regarding a feminist methodology. This would emphasize the importance of evaluating as well as describing behaviour – for example, it would not just ask for a realistic account of what states do, but would question their values and goals in doing it, while using its own values to determine the *way* in which research is undertaken. Its style of collecting data and generating theory might embrace the following: an open, questioning, pluralist, anti-reductionist, holistic approach, in which the connections between things are sought; a renunciation of conceptual domination of its subject matter, refusing to force experience and change into rigid categories; and a greater commitment to sharing information and to cooperating in its generation. If it found scientific methods useful, it would undertake them in a value-context; it would not confound them with definitive or value-free truths. A feminist approach must ask why a particular piece of research is being undertaken and what its contribution might be to women's lives and to social well-being more generally. In particular, it is critical of the (social) scientist's failure to take responsibility for the uses to which a piece of research might be put.

A continuing feminist task must be to disclose the hidden (patriarchal) assumptions which underlie much of what passes for Political Science, and so much of its flavour will remain critical. In this context, feminists have set themselves two rather different sorts of agenda. From a radical or socialist point of view, Political Science fairly accurately describes what it defines as conventional political behaviour. Feminists' task is to reveal that this is not equivalent to some universal model of human activity. Its dangerous, destructive and downright unpleasant qualities should be exposed, as well as its gendered nature. Poststructuralist feminists, on the other hand, would argue that these conventional descriptions play an even more insidious role because they create, or construct, a particular type of subjectivity. From this perspective, language is a crucial site of political struggle and the most challenging task for women is to develop a feminist

political discourse in which alternative ways of being a political participant would come to the fore.

This latter approach has particular relevance for political theory. In
many ways, the feminist argument that Politics has played an ideological
role is more obvious here: the history of political thought is full of
descriptions of women as ill-equipped for political participation and
therefore legitimately excluded from it. As in other parts of the discipline,
feminists' first demands were that women be made more visible here: the
work of female thinkers like Mary Wollstonecraft was resurrected and the
pronouncements of the tradition on women were extrapolated and held up
for critical scrutiny (Okin, 1980; Elshtain, 1981; Coole, 1986, 1988;
Kennedy and Mendus, 1987. However, poststructuralism suggests
another way of reading these texts that is perhaps more radical.

The starting-point for poststructuralist criticism is a denial that language is a transparent medium for communicating an independently
existing truth: instead it claims that language constructs meaning. Discourses are sites of struggle over dominant meanings and can therefore be
analysed in terms of the power–knowledge relations found there. Political
theory would be one example of such discursive practice and the purpose
of a feminist poststructural reading would be to analyse how gender is
constructed; how power relations between the sexes are produced and
reproduced and where there might be disturbances or gaps allowing
change.

Political thought has, among other things, offered apparently natural
ways of being a man or woman and has spoken of the kinds of interest or
pleasure that 'naturally' arise from these. Conclusions regarding the
correct political role for the sexes have followed. But when an Aristotle or
a Rousseau, for example, spoke of women as irrational, passive or
sentimental, they were not describing real women. They were constructing
one possible way of being feminine, and one which served patriarchal
interests. Equally, when a Hobbes or Bentham spoke of human nature,
they not only constructed different possible types of subjectivity, they also
disguised the fact that their human subject was normatively male. Their
construction of the rational, self-interested agent became the central
representation of subjectivity in modern political discourse, precluding
alternative (that is, feminine) meanings or values. Political thought from a
poststructuralist perspective is thus itself part of a power struggle to
structure meaning and hence people's sense of themselves and of what is
appropriate behaviour. It is not a quest for (moral or scientific) truth and
should not be read as such. Terms like femininity and masculinity have no
fixed significance or natural base; they are fluid meanings which change
over time according to the balance of power. One goal of feminism would

therefore be to reconstruct the presentation of gender and of political subjects generally.

This kind of reading would seem to hold out some exciting prospects for reading the classic texts and might perhaps be usefully extended to a study of the ways in which law or social policy construct images of gender (or class or race). The way in which this reading is undertaken also has affinity with feminism, for traditional approaches may be said to privilege the author and critic as authoritative expositor and interpreter, respectively, of truth. The poststructuralist acceptance of meaning as always deferred and plural is more attuned to the openness and multiplicity of feminism.

Not all the developments which feminism implies are unproblematic or without difficulties. Perhaps the movement's greatest failure so far is that, despite the vast amount of literature it has generated, it still remains marginalized within mainstream Political Science. For most of the latter's practitioners there is still feminism and the question of women (an esoteric, dangerous area that is perhaps too political to be taken seriously) and then there is the discipline in its ungendered innocence. At best, the mainstream might include data on women in British government or policy-making, or a session on feminism in a modern ideologies course. This is largely, of course, a failure of the discipline itself, but feminists have not been entirely blameless. Much of their more radical work has been hived off into women's studies programmes, which have themselves been seen as a sanctuary for female students tired of male-dominated faculties and the lack of relevance to women of their courses. Unfortunately, this allows the more traditional fields within Political Studies to remain unreconstructed. This tendency to intellectual separatism parallels the preference for separatist politics and lifestyles among some radical feminists, offering similar attractions and hazards.

To some extent, this position has also undermined women who do work within the discipline and who have been accused of selling out and of being coopted. Feminists have rightly been wary of defusing the radical and practical implications of their perspective by translating it into a sterile academic discipline with its classic texts and statistical verities. But this is why the development of a feminist approach to studying *all* aspects of political life, is so crucial.

On the question of a feminist approach, or rationality, or epistemology, there has been a tendency among some radicals to reject intellectualism, logic and rigour as antithetical to a feminine way of knowing. The latter is associated with intuitiveness and a poetic, anecdotal, impressionistic mode of expression. While these might indeed have their place in artistic creation (and the idea of a feminist aesthetics is no less fascinating than that of a feminist epistemology or ethics), it is difficult to see how they could allow feminists seriously to engage the patriarchal structures of politics or criticize the masculine hegemony of its discourses. A commitment to historically mediated feminine values in research is very different from the pursuit of essentialist female qualities and must remain so. As long as this distinction is kept in mind, the way is open for feminism greatly to enrich the discipline of Politics in the future, provided that it is itself open to such advances.

REFERENCES

Amos, V. and Parmar, P. (1984), 'Challenging imperial feminism', *Feminist Review,* **17**.

Barrett, M. (1980), *Women's Oppression Today* (London, Verso).

Beechey, V. (1979), 'On Patriarchy', *Feminist Review,* **3**.

Chodorow, N. (1978), *The Reproduction of Mothering* (Berkeley, University of California Press).

Coole, D. (1986), 'Re-reading political theory from a woman's perspective', *Political Studies,* **34(1)**.

Coole, D. (1988), *Women in Political Theory. From Ancient Misogyny to Contemporary Feminism* (Brighton, Wheatsheaf).

Daly, M. (1979), *Gyn/Ecology. The Meta-Ethics of Radical Feminism* (London, The Women's Press).

Delphy, C. (1977), *The Main Enemy* (London, Women's Research and Resources Centre).

Dinnerstein, D. (1976), *The Mermaid and the Minotaur* (New York, Harper and Row).

Eisenstein, H. (1984), *Contemporary Feminist Thought* (London, Unwin).

Elshtain, J. B. (1981), *Public Man, Private Woman* (Oxford, Martin Robertson).

Greene, G. and Kahn, C. (1985), *Making a Difference: French literary criticism* (London, Methuen).

Griffin, S. (1972), *Woman and Nature: The Roaring Inside Her* (New York, Harper and Row).

Hartmann, H. (1979), 'The unhappy marriage of Marxism and feminism: towards a more progressive union', *Capital and Class,* **8**.

Keller, E. F. (1978), 'Gender and science', *Psychoanalysis and Contemporary Thought,* **1**.

Keller, E. F. (1982), 'Feminism and science', *Signs,* **7(3)**.

Kennedy, E. and Mendus, S. (eds) (1987), *Women in Western Political Philosophy* (Brighton, Wheatsheaf).

Lloyd, G. (1984), *The Man of Reason. 'Male' and 'Female' in Western Philosophy* (London, Methuen).

Lovenduski, J. (1986), *Women and European Politics: contemporary feminism and public policy* (Brighton, Wheatsheaf).

Marks, E. and Courtivron, I. (1981), *New French Feminisms* (Brighton, Harvester).

McIntosh, M. (1987), 'The state and the oppression of women' in A. Kuhn and A. Wolpe (eds), *Feminism and Materialism* (London, Routledge and Kegan Paul).

Miller, D. (1987), 'Politics' entry in D. Miller *et al.* eds, *The Blackwell Encyclopedia of Political Thought* (Oxford, Basil Blackwell).

Millett, K. (1977), *Sexual Politics* (London, Virago).

Mitchell, J. (1971), *Woman's Estate* (Harmondsworth, Penguin).

Mitchell, J. (1974), *Psychoanalysis and Feminism* (Harmondsworth, Penguin).

Norris, P. (1987), *Politics and Sexual Equality: the comparative position of women in Western democracies* (Brighton, Wheatsheaf).

Okin, S. (1980), *Women in Western Political Thought* (London, Virago).

Phillips, A. (1987), *Divided Loyalties. Dilemmas of Sex and Class* (London, Virago).

Randall, V. (1982), *Women and Politics* (London, Macmillan).

Rich, A. (1977), *Of Woman Born* (London, Virago).

Richards, J. R. (1982), *The Sceptical Feminist* (Harmondsworth, Penguin).

Rose, H. (1983), 'Hand, brain and heart: a feminist epistemology for the natural sciences' *Signs,* **9(1)**.

Rowbotham, S. *et al.* (1979), *Beyond the Fragments. Feminism and the Making of Socialism* (London, Merlin Press).

Segal, L. (1987), *Is the Future Female? Troubled Thoughts on Contemporary Feminism* (London, Virago).

Spender, D. (1985), *For the Record. The Making and Meaning of Feminist Knowledge* (London, The Women's Press).

Weedon, C. (1987), *Feminist Practice and Poststructuralist Theory* (Oxford, Basil Blackwell).

4.   Putting States in Their Place: State Systems and State Theory

Bob Jessop

After its initial post-war neglect under American intellectual hegemony, the state re-entered the social scientific mainstream some 20 years ago.[1] Efforts to theorize the state soon proliferated and empirical research multiplied on specific aspects of the state apparatus and state power. The Miliband–Poulantzas debate played a key role in stimulating this interest in the Anglophone world but many other currents, American as well as European, fed into the same theoretical stream. Moreover, if attempts to 'bring the state back in' during the 1970s were largely associated with Marxists, it is mainly macro-sociologists and orthodox political scientists who are now in the vanguard. The reasons for this shift are too complex to be examined here and the available space is even too limited for a general critique of the main approaches to the state currently on offer (useful surveys of recent state theory include: Jessop, 1982; Carnoy, 1984; Thomas and Meyer, 1984; Alford and Friedland, 1985; Benjamin and Elkins, 1985; Evans *et al.*, 1985; Dunleavy and O'Leary, 1987). Instead I will focus on five key issues in recent theorizing about the state. The first is the nature of the state as a theoretical object; the second is the theoretical validity of the recent fashion for 'state-centred' theorizing; the third concerns the paradoxical relation between the state and society; the fourth their mediations; and the fifth is the agenda for future research in state theory. These issues are closely interrelated and I will adopt the same general theoretical approach in dealing with each of them.

WHAT IS THE STATE?

This innocuous-looking question is the first and the most fundamental problem facing all theories of the state. Some system theorists still argue that the state should be abandoned as a topic of research since it produces vapid debates and a conceptual morass (e.g., Easton, 1981: 321–2; and, for a counter-critique, Hoffman, 1988: 26–8). The balance of opinion still favours the state as a focus of research but, beyond this agreement, the conceptual swamp that Easton predicted continues.

Among the many questions which provoke debate (vapid or not) are the following sets. Is the state itself best defined by its legal form, its coercive capacities, its institutional composition and boundaries, its internal operations and modes of calculation, its declared aims, its functions for the broader society, or its sovereign place in the international system? Is it a thing, a subject, a social relation, or simply a construct which helps to orient political action? Is stateness a variable and, if so, what are its central dimensions? What is the relationship between the state and law, the state and politics, the state and civil society, the public and the private, state power and micro-power relations? Can the state be studied on its own; should it be studied as part of the political system; or, indeed, can it only be understood in terms of a more general social theory? Does the state have any autonomy and, if so, what are its sources and limits? Answers to such questions can clearly vary from one set to another but viewing the state as a social relation provides a relatively coherent solution to most of them.

The Complexities of the State and State Theory

As already indicated there is little agreement on how to define the state. Among the many reasons for this, two merit discussion here. First, any actually existing state comprises a more or less distinct ensemble of multifunctional institutions and organizations which have at best a partial, provisional, and unstable political identity and operational unity and which involve a complex, overdetermined dynamic. Thus differences can legitimately arise as to which particular features are treated as primary or definitive and which as secondary or contingent. Second, discounting the complexities of states themselves, differences also arise because the concept of the state has a central role in political life itself. This holds not only for disputes about the boundaries, purposes, and limits of any given state but also for processes of state-building and reorganization intended to transform that state. This suggests that the concept is not just essentially contested[2] but also that dominant conceptions can influence the nature of the state itself. This is why some commentators even doubt whether, in the absence of a developed concept of the state, states can really be said to exist in the UK or the USA (for example, Nettl, 1968; Dyson, 1982; Badie and Birnbaum, 1983).

If I had to offer a general definition of the state, I would phrase it in terms of political discourse as well as institutions. Specifically, the core of the state apparatus comprises a distinct ensemble of institutions and organizations whose socially accepted function is to define and enforce collectively binding decisions on the members of a society in the name of their common interest or general will. This abstract, formal, 'cluster' definition[3] identifies the state in terms of its generic features as a specific form of macro-political organization with a specific type of political orientation; it also establishes clear links between the state and the political sphere and, indeed, the wider society. Thus, not all forms of macro-political organization can be classed as state-like nor can the state simply be equated with government, law, bureaucracy, a coercive apparatus, or another political institution. Indeed, this definition puts the contradictions and dilemmas necessarily involved in political discourse at the heart of work on the state (cf. Hoffman, 1988). For claims about the general will or common interest are a key feature of the state system and distinguish it from straightforward political domination or violent oppression. At the same time, adopting this approach serves as a basis for describing specific states and political regimes as well as for exploring the conditions in which states emerge, evolve, enter into crisis, and are transformed.

This said, certain qualifications are required. First, above, around, and below its core are found institutions and organizations whose relation to the core ensemble is uncertain. States never achieve full closure or complete separation from society and their precise boundaries are normally in doubt. Their operations also depend on a wide range of micro-political practices dispersed throughout society but concentrated and condensed in the core of the state. And they also enter into links with emergent state-like institutions at an interstate level. Second, the nature of these institutions and organizations, their articulation to form the ensemble, and their links with the wider society will depend on the nature of the social formation and its past history. The capitalist type of state will differ from the feudal, and specific forms of regime will differ from one capitalist society to another.[4] Third, although the socially acknowledged character of its political functions for society is a defining feature of the normal state, the forms in which this legitimacy is institutionalized and expressed will also vary and, even in single states, they can often prove multiple and even mutually contradictory.[5] Fourth, although coercion is the state's ultimate sanction, it has other methods of enforcement and violence is rarely the first resort. Fifth, the society whose common interest and general will are administered by the state should no more be interpreted as an empirical given than the state. The boundaries and identity of the society are often constituted in and through the same processes by which states are built, reproduced, and transformed. Indeed, it is one of the more obvious conclusions of the state-centred approach that state- and nation-building are strongly influenced by the emergent dynamic of the emergent international system formed through the interaction of sovereign states. Finally, whatever the political rhetoric of the common interest or general will might suggest, these are always 'illusory' in so far as any attempt to define them occurs on a strategically selective terrain and involves the differential articulation and aggregation of interests, opinions, and values (cf. Jessop, 1983).

In this context the state can be analysed on three levels: the forms of its basic institutional separation from the rest of the society whose general interests it is supposed to represent; the nature of its internal organization, modes of political calculation and operating procedures; and the political practices and discourses in and through which the common interests are articulated and promoted. These three levels correspond to the basic organizing principles of a given social formation, the organizing principles of the state as an institutional ensemble, and the actual political struggles which occur within, around, and at a distance from the state (cf. the threefold structure of Poulantzas's theorization of the state as discussed in Jessop, 1985).

To make this analysis more specific, a hierarchy of concepts is needed which moves from the abstract formal concept of statehood down to more specific regime types. Operating on the three levels identified above, this hierarchy would provide the means to generate a typology of state forms and/or to specify any given state. Below the concept of statehood would come different types of state associated with different types of social formation. For example, if social formations are identified in terms of their dominant mode of production, these could include the feudal, absolutist, capitalist, and state socialist types of state. Moreover, if it seems appropriate to periodize social formations, then typical variant historical forms could also be specified. Thus, for capitalist social formations, one might define liberal, monopoly, and state monopoly forms. Next would come concepts relating to normal and exceptional regimes[6] (and their variant forms, such as presidential or parliamentary democracies, fascist or military dictatorships); these could be further specified in terms of regime types (in terms of party systems, modes of policy-making, and so on). Such a hierarchy gives a much better basis for analysing the state than a single definition.

For those who are unhappy with typologies or conceptual hierarchies, an alternative approach is simply to analyse the organizational form and sociopolitical bases of the state. For this task, six dimensions seem useful. These comprise:

1. modes of political representation;
2. the internal articulation of the various branches, institutions, and organs of the state;
3. modes of intervention;
4. the social bases of the state considered in terms of specific types of institutionalized compromise among different social forces;
5. the state practices and projects which define the boundaries of the state system and endow it with a degree of internal unity; and
6. the discourses which define the illusory community whose interests and social cohesion are to be managed by the state within the framework of a given historic bloc and hegemonic project (cf. Jessop, 1982, 1983 and 1985).

This list is not intended to be exhaustive but it does provide an initial framework for analysing the state at different levels of theoretical abstraction and complexity and for relating the state to the broader political system and its environing social formation. It also provides an initial conceptual matrix for analysing specific states in crisis and crises of the state form.[7]

It should be noted that my definition does not imply that the state necessarily has a particular class (or gender, ethnic, national, or other) content. Claims of this kind can only be established through detailed analyses of the dialectic between state forms and political practices. The state is a strategically selective terrain which can never be neutral among all social forces and political projects; but any bias is always tendential and can be undermined or reinforced by appropriate strategies. For, within the strategically selective limits established by state structures and operating procedures, the outcome of state power also depends on the changing balance of forces engaged in political action both within and beyond the state.

This does not rule out analyses of the correspondence between different social forms (for example, the value form, the legal form, the state form) in a social formation, nor does it exclude analyses of the structural coupling or co-evolution of such forms in the constitution of specific state systems. That a given state has a typically capitalist form does not imply that it actually functions to reproduce capital accumulation: this can only be established through analyses of the overall impact of state power in relation to specific accumulation strategies in specific conjunctures. In this sense my proposed approach seeks to install political practice and discourse alongside an analysis of state forms and apparatuses at the heart of any serious analysis of the state system.

Indeed, the very contestability and the crucial constitutive role of arguments about the state suggest that state projects are a useful starting-point for theorizing about the state itself. Studies on how this idea emerged already have a long history. Sometimes these take the actual nature of the state and/or its emergence for granted and merely describe how the 'state' concept was developed to describe this new phenomenon. But other studies suggest that the state's genesis, as well as its main forms of organization, depend as much on specific state-building projects as they do on the raw materials to hand. This conclusion should serve as a necessary corrective to more abstract attempts to derive the state from iron laws which operate behind the backs of political agents. It is only when the imperatives of capital accumulation, the audit of war, or the demands of patriarchy (to take three examples) are reflected in specific political projects that states can develop which serve the needs of capital, warfare, or masculine dominance.

The Idea of the State and the State as Idea

Many commentators have noted the close ties between semantic and structural developments in the political domain. Until the seventeenth century the concept of politics was linked to the state and society (rather than to the 'oikos' or private household); but politics was not uniquely coupled with the state as opposed to society or community. Thus civil society was understood as an association of citizens subject to common laws and government; and man was regarded as a political animal (zoon politikon). It was only in the seventeenth century that politics was first linked to the idea of an abstract, impersonal, sovereign state distinct from other parts of society (church, economy, civil associations) and the distinction began to emerge between man in his capacity as private individual and as political citizen (cf. Bobbio, 1985; Dyson, 1980; Entrèves, 1967; Luhmann, 1984; Willke, 1987).

Thereafter the conceptual distinction between state and civil society seems to have developed through four overlapping stages. According to a useful survey by John Keane, these stages can be identified as:

a. a view which counterposed a sovereign, centralized constitutional state standing over its subjects to a series of independent societies which could check its potential to become authoritarian;
b. an anti-statist impulse which called for the strengthening of civil society against the state in the interests of justice, equality, and liberty;
c. a U-turn in which the need for a strong state was stressed to check the paralysis, conflict, and anarchy of civil society; and
d. a renewal of the pluralist approach, in which the self-organization of

civil society was emphasized as a means of resisting encroachment by the state (Keane, 1988: *passim*).

If the concept of state is relatively modern, why did it emerge as and when it did? One possible explanation contrasts the transparency of political life in traditional societies with its abstract form in modern societies. In traditional societies the political system was identified with a specific personage, agency, or institution (the polis, communitas, civitas, regnum, and so on) and it was directly around these that political action was organized. Modern societies are functionally differentiated, each functional subsystem is internally complex, and there is no superordinate subsystem. Thus no single personage, agency, or institution can symbolize or embody the political system: the abstract concept of the state is needed to orient political action and make politics possible. This is reflected in the continued development of discourse about the state. Thus, as the political system becomes institutionally more distinct, the idea of the state becomes more clearly demarcated in relation to religion, education, economy, science, and so on. Likewise, as the political system becomes more complex internally, juridico-political discourse also grows more complex with the development of constitutions, the separation of powers, rules about representation, among other things (Luhmann, 1984: 107–8; cf. Nettl, 1968).

Such analyses go beyond the claim that the idea of the state is just an ideological or conceptual reflection of structural developments in the political system. They suggest that concepts and doctrines about the state play a key role both in the historical development and the juridico-political formalization of the modern state. Thus, whatever the precise origins of the different components of the modern state (such as the army, bureaucracy, taxation, legal system, legislative assemblies), their organization as a relatively coherent institutional ensemble is crucially dependent on the emergence of the concept of the sovereign state. Moreover, since 'the present state' does not exist, the nature of specific states depends on the particular state projects or models of state-building which were undertaken at particular points in time. The distinctive institutional, territorial, and national boundaries of the state and its purposes and activities must be defined and reproduced through discourse about the state and specific projects. Any attempt to theorize the state in abstraction from state projects is bound to lead to formalism and essentialism.

Bringing the State Back in

I have already noted the general resurgence of interest in the state among orthodox social scientists. But there is clearly more than one way to re-import the state as a key factor in analysing societies. Indeed, this is the point at issue between the self-styled 'state-centred' theorists and those whom they accuse of adopting so-called 'society-centred' approaches. Thus Marxist analyses have been loudly condemned for assuming that the form and functions of the modern state are essentially determined by the needs of capital and/or by the dynamic of a class struggle which is essentially located beyond the state. Likewise many orthodox social scientists and historians are criticized for treating the pluralist competition of social forces and/or needs and interests rooted in the organization of society as the decisive causal factors in the dynamic of state policies and power. In contrast 'state-centred' theorists argue that the state is an institutional ensemble or 'structured field of action' with a unique, independent, and central influence in both national and international formations. They claim that there are *sui generis* political processes, interests, and forces which shape its form and functions and that these give the state a genuine and important autonomy in relation to processes, interests, and forces rooted in civil society.

'State-centred' theorists adopt a Weberian conception of the state which emphasizes its distinctive institutional features rather than its articulation with the wider society. They have also emphasized six crucial factors about the state or state system:

1. The geo-political position of different modern states within the international system of nation-states and its implications for the logic of state action.
2. The role of military organization and warfare in the development of the modern state.
3. The *sui generis* powers of the modern state. These are rooted in its capacities to produce and enforce collectively binding decisions in a centrally organized, territorially bounded society and to penetrate, control, supervise, police, and discipline the various subsystems (including the economy), organizations (including capitalist enterprises), and forces (including classes) within its domain.
4. The nature of the state as a distinctive factor in shaping the character of institutions and social forces beyond the state in the economy and civil society.
5. The distinctive interests and capacities of 'state managers' viewed as a social category as well as their room for manoeuvre faced with the pluralistic universe of other forces.
6. The distinctive pathologies of the state system and government (cf. Block, 1977; Nordlinger, 1981; Mann, 1983; Cerny, 1985; Skocpol, 1985; Gurr and King, 1987).

Different 'state-centred' theorists have emphasized different factors but all agree the state is a force in its own right and not just a reflex of civil society. In fact, it enjoys powers of autonomous action which have been neglected by more 'society-centred' theorists. However, while many neo-Marxists have certainly ignored these issues, not all have done so. Indeed others have been accused of 'politicism' precisely because they emphasize the relative autonomy of the state and are held to overlook its determination by the economic instance. Moreover, even a brief review would show that many European Marxists have been concerned with the institutional structure and dynamic of the state and law as well as with phenomena such as militarism and imperialism. One could also dispute how far the pluralist and radical traditions have really neglected the centrality of the state (for a spirited defence of radical power structure research in this regard, see Domhoff, 1985). However, rather than defend Marxist, pluralist, and radical contributions against the state-centred theorists' blanket criticism, it would be better to examine their underlying assumptions.

For, in their eagerness to criticize society-centred analyses, they have failed to distinguish three different sorts of claim about the state. It is not clear whether they are:

a. rejecting the so-called society-centred approach in its entirety and arguing that the state should be the independent variable;
b. bending the stick in the other direction for polemical purposes, one-sidedly emphasizing the importance of the state as a crucial causal factor; or
c. suggesting that a combination of society-centred and state-centred perspectives will somehow provide a complete account of state-society relations.

A little clarity here would greatly help to bring out what is really at stake. However, even if these three claims were more clearly stated, this would not make them any more plausible.

The way in which state-centred theorists distinguish between the two approaches is fundamentally misleading and rests on a 'straw-man' account of the society-centred bias in other studies which deliberately contrasts unfavourably with their own approach. This has unfortunate implications for all three state-centred criticisms. First, if one posits the need to choose between the state and society as the independent variable in social analysis, one implies that both exist as independent entities which are fully constituted, internally coherent, and mutually exclusive and that one always unilaterally determines the other. This would reify and absolutize what is really an emergent, partial, unstable, and variable social distinction and also ignore how the adequacy of an explanation depends on the explanandum. Second, whilst there may be some point in 'bending the stick' for polemical and/or heuristic purposes, polemic as such does not make for good theory and empirical research is never theoretically innocent. It would surely be better to go beyond the dichotomy between state- and society-centred approaches than simply to stress one or other approach for polemical purposes. And, third, in attempting to transcend the dichotomy, it is insufficient simply to combine the two approaches. This would merely reproduce and reinforce the false dichotomy which informs the whole critique. Let me expand on this last point.

Society-centred theorists are alleged to argue that the form and the functions of the state are determined by a logic rooted somewhere in society and/or by the balance of power among societally-based forces. Their state-centred critics argue that the state actually has its own institutional logic and associated interests and activities and/or is a subject in its own right; or else they claim that it is really controlled by state managers, who use this control to advance their own policy preferences and interests. Such views merely reverse society-centred lines of argument and, in so doing, reify the distinction between state and society. This rules out hybrid logics such as corporatism or policy networks; divisions among state managers due to the links between state apparatuses and other social spheres; and other forms of compenetration or overlap between state and society. A false dichotomy is thereby imposed on social analysis in so far as it is suggested that state and society alike are distinct and self-determining, each can be studied in isolation, and the resulting analyses added together to provide a complete account.

In my view, the idea of the state as a social relation offers a middle way between state-centred and society-centred approaches. This view has most recently been advanced by John Hoffman (1988) in his argument that the state is the concentration of relations of power. Following Hegel and Marx, he suggests that the state is the official resumé of civil society and is responsible for maintaining an illusory community of interest in a society divided into a myriad particularisms.[8] Unfortunately Hoffman does not explain how the state 'condenses' relations of power. This is where Poulantzas' claim that the state is a social relation provides more purchase since it suggests that power relations are condensed and materialized in and through the ensemble of institutions and centres of power which comprise the state. In turn this implies, first, that the state apparatus is a strategically selective terrain which has asymmetrical effects on the organization of power; and second, it implies that, within these strategically selective limits, the actual outcome of state power depends on the changing balance of forces engaged in political action both within and beyond the state (for more details, see Jessop, 1985). This provides the crucial theoretical breakthrough for a coherent approach to the state.

Understood in relational terms, a state-centred approach would focus more on how the state shapes social reproduction through its 'infrastructural power' and its strategic selectivity. It would also focus on the distinctive institutional logics of different state forms and specific modes of policy-making: corporatism, parliamentarism, clientelism, pluralism, and so on. And it would specialize in, among other things, the dynamic of the international state system and the organizational logic of militarism, surveillance. All these concerns reflect the influence of the state form as theorized within the relational approach. In turn, a society-centred approach would focus more on the changing balance of forces (including state managers as appropriate) which is condensed in and through the distinct structures and functions of the state. It would also explore the place of state forms in the historic bloc and analyse the linkages among state projects, accumulation strategies, hegemonic projects, and so forth. These concerns reflect the relational theorists' interest in state power and its links to the balance of forces, organization, and strategy. But neither approach could be properly developed without referring to the dialectic between form-determination and the balances of forces – and thus by exploring more systematically the ties between state and society.

The Paradox of State and Society

In rejecting the 'state-centred' account, I have suggested a more relational approach. The state system should be analysed through its compenetration and articulation with the rest of society, and neither should be privileged as an automatic starting point for explanation. Indeed, if the part–whole relation between state and society is taken seriously, the problem should not even be posed in such terms. More interesting is how the state ensemble is related to other institutional orders to constitute a complex social formation and how it contributes to the reproduction of the overall formation of which it is merely one part. This is reflected in the central paradox of the state: although it is merely one part of society, it is charged with securing the overall cohesion of that society.

This primary paradox is reflected in several aspects of 'state–society' relations. First, whilst the state has a key role in defining the identity of the society, its own identity is contested by forces rooted in other spheres. On the one hand, societies do not pre-exist the state system but are constituted in and through state activities; but, on the other hand, forces located beyond it struggle to (re)build the state and redefine its projects. Second, although the state has its own *sui generis* dynamic and strategic capacities so that it is resistant to direct external control, the various spheres of society also have their own *sui generis* logics and capacities which prevent their direct control by the state. This is reflected in a third paradox. For, as the state intervenes more and more in different spheres of society (giving the impression that state power is growing), it undergoes two types of change which undermine its strength (cf. Offe, 1987). On the one hand, its own unity and distinctive identity diminish as it becomes more complex internally, its powers are fragmented among different branches and policy networks, and problems of coordination multiply; and, on the other hand, it depends increasingly on the cooperation of other social forces to secure success for its interventions so that state power is increasingly subordinate to, or interlinked with, external forces. Fourth, even when the state acts in the name of *raison d'état* or invokes states of emergency which suspend normal representative mechanisms, its legitimacy depends on linking state interests and actions to those of society. This means that state and official discourses can never be self-contained: they are always open to disarticulation and disruption by forces beyond the state.

The State and Other Institutional Orders

These remarks suggest that the state cannot be reduced to government. Yet, even when state theorists adopt more inclusive approaches, they still focus too often on its formal, institutional aspects and neglect its substantive, subjective aspects. The latter are crucial to the state's own strategic capacities and the chances of compliance from forces beyond the state (cf. Jaeger, 1979: 53f). The main exception here is Gramsci's account of the 'integral state' – that is, political society plus civil society. Although sometimes criticized for failing to demarcate the state's boundaries (for example, Anderson, 1980), Gramsci was far less concerned with the state apparatus than with state power. For Gramsci the latter was overdetermined by its links to institutions and forces in the broader political system and, indeed, society as a whole. This is why he paid so much attention to the roles of the party system and intellectuals in articulating and mediating the complex relations between political and civil society. It also explains why so many of his concepts deal with subjective elements (commonsense, identity, will-formation, leadership, education) in political life (cf. Jaeger, 1979).

From this perspective, the party system involves far more than electoral strategies and the relations among voters, parties, and leaders. For political parties actively link different spheres of society and different social forces and, in securing the social bases of states, help to constitute specific state forms. In turn, a crisis in the party system is often associated with a crisis in the state – especially if it affects the natural governing party. For the relative operational unity, if any, of the state's powers cannot be derived from constitutional guarantees nor explained as the simple product of the parallelogram of forces on the biased terrain of the state. Its unity results from the exercise of a political leadership concerned to promote and manage a 'party spirit' which gives shape and coherence to the state and links it to a national–popular consciousness which transcends both egoism and group particularism. Thus, for Gramsci, it is in the party that the leaders and the state officials are educated (cf. Migliaro and Misuraca, 1982: 81; Sassoon, 1987: 134–50 and *passim*).

This sort of analysis can be taken further by locating individual parties in the party system as a whole and considering how this in turn relates to the overall institutional structure of the state. For the relations between different parties are crucial for their role in (dis)organizing political forces and developing a collective will. It is the party system which defines the cleavages around which political life revolves and influences the framework in which a national–popular will might emerge. In turn, the institutional matrix of the state influences the form assumed by party systems. Here again we are faced with a complex dialectic. For example, as the executive branch gains power at the expense of parliament, the role of political parties changes and becomes more marginal and other channels for political representation and articulating the political imaginary become more important. Policy networks and functional representation often play a crucial role in political organization and the mass media assume some of the functions traditionally ascribed to the party system in defining the collective will (cf. Poulantzas, 1978).

Once we begin exploring these mediations, it is surprising how varied they can be. Rather than explore them all here it is more important to draw a general conclusion. Unless one examines how state power is realized in and through specific social practices and forces, it could go unexplained or be explained away in terms of structural guarantees and/or functional imperatives. It was the failure of structural Marxism and the capital logic school to explore these mediations which encouraged them to treat the state in capitalist societies as essentially capitalist and to explain this in terms of 'speculative' categories such as determination in the last instance or the state's role as an ideal collective capitalist (cf. Misuraca and Migliaro, 1982: 80). The way to overcome this impasse is through the strategic–relational approach with its emphasis on the continuing interplay between strategies and structures.

Whither State Theory?

By way of conclusion this section proposes six general theses about the modern state[9] and then draws a general conclusion about the nature of research on the state.

First, an adequate account of the state can only be developed as part of a theory of society. The state must be related not only to the broader political system but also to its wider social environment. This does not mean that the state has no distinctive properties and can therefore be fully derived and explained from other factors and forces: for, once constituted historically and characterized by its own distinctive forms of organization and modes of calculation, the state does acquire a logic of its own. But it does mean that, for all its institutional separation and operational autonomy, the state remains part of society and must be related to the wider society. For, if it is true that the distinctive feature of a state system is its concern with the illusory general interest of a divided society and that state power concentrates and condenses power relations within society as a whole, the state can only be understood by examining the emergence of projects to promote the general interest and relating them to the changing balance of forces beyond as well as within the state.

Second, modern societies are so complex and differentiated that no subsystem could be structurally 'determinant in the last instance' nor could any one organization form the apex of a singular hierarchy of command whose rule extends everywhere. Instead there are many different subsystems and even more centres of power. Many of these have developed to an extent which places them beyond direct control by outside forces, the state included. Each is nonetheless involved in complex relations of functional and resource interdependence with other subsystems and is also faced with the problem that it cannot directly control the actions of the other subsystems in its environment. This engenders a paradox in which modern societies reveal both a growing independence and growing interdependence among their parts.

Third, the state is the supreme embodiment of this paradox. Among the various institutional orders in modern societies, it is the state which is responsible in the last instance for managing their interdependence. But, as one institutional order among others, it can only do so through its own institutions, organizations, and procedures. Thus, although the state is empowered to make and enforce collectively binding decisions, its actions in this respect are a specific, selective concentration and condensation of struggles within the overall political system and their success depends on conditions and forces beyond its immediate reach. In this sense, the success of the state depends on its integration into an historic bloc characterized by a non-necessary, socially constituted, and discursively reproduced relative unity. Moreover, although the state is the key site of the illusory community and general will formation, the political imaginary is always selective and inevitably marginalizes some wills and interests.

Fourth, the state must be analysed both as a complex institutional ensemble with its own modes of calculation and operational procedures and as a site of political practices which seek to deploy its various institutions and capacities for specific purposes. Rather than trying to define the core of the state in *a priori* terms, we need to explore how its boundaries are established through specific practices within and outside the state. Moreover, in identifying this core, one is neither claiming that this exhausts the state nor that this core (let alone the extended state) is a unified, unitary, coherent ensemble or agency. Instead, the boundaries of the state and its relative unity as an ensemble or agency would be contingent. It is in this context that we must examine the various projects and practices which imbue the state with relative institutional unity and facilitate its coherence with the wider society.

Fifth, as an institutional ensemble the state does not (and cannot) exercise power: it is not a real subject. Indeed, rather than speaking about the power of the state, we should speak about the various potential structural powers (or state capacities) inscribed in the state as institutional ensemble. How far, and in what ways, such powers (as well as any associated liabilities) are realized will depend on the action, reaction, and interaction of specific social forces located both within and beyond this complex ensemble. In short, the state does not exercise power: its powers (in the plural) are activated through the agency of definite political forces in specific conjunctures. It is not the state which acts: it is always specific sets of politicians and state officials located in specific parts of the state system. It is they who activate specific powers and state capacities inscribed in particular institutions and agencies. And, as in all cases of social action, there will always be unacknowledged conditions influencing the success or failure of their actions as well as unanticipated consequences which follow from them.

Sixth, these structural powers or capacities and their realization cannot be understood by focusing on the state alone – even assuming one could precisely define its institutional boundaries. For, considered as an institutional ensemble rather than a real (or fictive) subject, the state comprises an ensemble of power centres which offer unequal chances to different forces within and outside the state to act for different political purposes. This is what it means to talk about the strategic selectivity of the state system. Moreover, although the state system does have its own distinctive resources and powers, it also has distinctive liabilities as well as needs for resources which are produced elsewhere in its environment. This means that the powers of the state are always conditional and relational. Their realization depends on the structural ties between the state and its encompassing political system, the strategic links among state managers and other political forces, and the complex web of interdependencies and social networks linking the state system to its broader environment.

If we take these general theses seriously, then research on the state should proceed in tandem with more general theoretical and empirical work on the structuration of social relations. This can be justified on various grounds sketched above. Thus, if state theorists continue to define their field of research as the state, this need not suggest that they adopt a reified, fetishistic concept of the state. Instead it could mean that, within the general context of research concerned with the dialectic of structure and strategy, their special field of interest is state power. This would involve research on two main issues. State theorists would focus on the distinctive ways in which the specific institutional and organizational ensemble identified as the state condenses and materializes social power relations and they would examine how the political imaginary (in which ideas about the state play a crucial orienting role) is articulated, mobilizes social forces around specific projects, and finds expression on the terrain of the state. In this context, Marxist state theorists would focus on the connections between state power and class domination. But there is no reason why those interested in other forms of power and domination could not adopt the same strategic–relational approach in their own preferred field of enquiry.

NOTES

This essay has benefited from the comments of Rene Bertramsen, Citlali Rovirosa Madrazo, Rob Stones and Carsten Wiegrefe; my intellectual debts on state theory go back so far and are owed so widely that they cannot all be repeated here.
1. For a useful critique of the failure of mainstream sociology to theorize the state, see Badie and Birnbaum (1983: 25–64).
2. On essential constability, see Connolly (1974).
3. On cluster concepts, see Connolly (1974: 15 ff).
4. Types of state are theoretical constructs which define which forms of political organization might correspond to the basic elements of different modes of production: they provide a point of reference for the analysis of states in specific social formations. Engaging in this sort of theoretical exercise does not imply that every state in a capitalist society will correspond to the capitalist type of state (see Poulantzas, 1973).
5. The most obvious examples of this being the rules governing the declaration of states of emergency and their implications for sovereignty.
6. What is normal and what exceptional can only be defined in relation to a given type of state: in the capitalist type, normality is equated with democratic republican forms.
7. It is within this context, for example, that one could distinguish representational crisis,

institutional crisis, rationality crisis, a crisis of hegemony, legitimacy crisis, and organic crisis.

8.   These influences, Hoffman included, should be clear in my own definition.

9.   These theses complement and amplify my theoretical guidelines for analysing the state (Jessop, 1982), my remarks on the strategic-theoretical approach (Jessop, 1985), my views on autopoietic systems theory and its implications for Marxism (Jessop, 1987), and my comments on structure and strategy from a regulationist perspective (Jessop, 1988). Since they can only be presented very summarily here, interested readers are invited to follow them up in my other studies.

REFERENCES

Alford, R. and Friedland, R. (1985), *Powers of Theory* (Cambridge, Cambridge University Press).

Anderson, P. (1980), 'The antinomies of Gramsci', *New Left Review,* **100**.

Badie, B. and Birnbaum, P. (1983), *The Sociology of the State* (Chicago, Chicago University Press).

Benjamin, R. W. and Elkin, S. L (eds) (1985), *The Democratic State* (Lawrence, Kansas, University of Kansas Press).

Block, F. (1977), 'The ruling class does not rule: notes on the Marxist theory of the state', *Socialist Revolution,* **33**.

Bobbio, N. (1985), *Stato, Societa Civile, Democrazia* (Rome, Einaudi).

Carnoy, M. (1984), *The State and Political Theory* (Princeton, Princeton University Press).

Cerny, P. (1985), 'Structural power and state theory', paper presented at the World Congress of the International Political Science Association, Paris 15–20 July, 1985.

Connolly, W. E. (1974), *The Terms of Political Discourse* (Lexington, Mass., D. C. Heath).

Domhoff, W. G. (1985), "Corporate Liberal" Theory and the Social Security Act: a reply to Skocpol and Quadagno', unpublished typescript.

Dunleavy, P. and O'Leary, B. (1987), *Theories of the State* (London, Macmillan).

Dyson, K. (1980), *The State Tradition in Western Europe* (Oxford, Martin Robertson).

Easton, D. (1981), 'The Political System Besieged by the State', *Political Theory,* **9(3)**, pp 303–25.

Entrèves, J. (1967), *The Idea of the State* (Oxford, Clarendon, 1967).

Evans, P. B., Rueschemeyer, D., and Skocpol, T., (eds) (1985), *Bringing The State Back In* (Cambridge, Cambridge University Press).

Gurr, T. R. and King, D. (1987), *The City and the Local State* (London, Sage).

Hoffman, J. (1988), *State, Authority, Democracy* (Brighton, Wheatsheaf).

Jaeger, M. (1979), 'Von der Staatsableitung zur Theorie der Parteien – ein Terrainwechsel im Geister Antonio Gramsci' in *Eurokommunismus und Theorie der Politik* (Argument-Sonderband AS 44).

Jessop, B. (1982), *The Capitalist State: Marxist Theories and Methods* (Oxford, Martin Robertson).

Jessop, B. (1983), 'Capital accumulation, state forms, and hegemonic projects', *Kapitalistate,* 10–11.

Jessop, B. (1985), *Nicos Poulantzas: Marxist Theory and Political Strategy* (London, Macmillan).

Jessop, B. (1987), 'Theories of autonomy and autpoiesis in economics, law, and the state' in European University Institute, Florence: Working Paper.

Jessop, B. (1988), 'Regulation, post-Fordism, and the state: more than a reply to Werner Bonefeld', *Capital and Class,* **32**.

Keane, J. in idem (ed.) (1988), *Democracy and Civil Society* (London, Verso).

Luhmann, N. (1984), 'Staat und Politik: Zur Semantik der Selbstbeschreibung politischer Systeme' in *Politische Vierteljahresschrift*: Sonderheft, **15**.

Mann, M. (1983), 'The autonomous power of the state', *Archives Européennes de Sociologie,* **25**.

Migliaro, L. R. and Misuraca, P. (1982), 'The theory of modern bureaucracy' in A. Showstack Sassoon (ed.), *Approaches to Gramsci* (London, Writers and Readers).

Nettl, P. (1968), 'The state as a conceptual variable', *World Politics,* **20**.

Nordlinger, E. A. (1981), *The Autonomy of the Democratic State* (Cambridge, Mass., Harvard University Press).

Offe, C. (1987), 'Die Staatstheorie auf der Suche nach ihrem Gegenstand. Beobachtungen zur aktuellen Diskussion', in T. Ellwein *et al* (eds) *Jahrbuch zur Staats-und Verwaltungswissenschaft* (Baden-Baden, Nomos).

Poulantzas, N. (1973), *Political Power and Social Classes* (London, New Left Books).

Poulantzas, N. (1978), *State, Power, Socialism* (London, New Left Books).

Sassoon, A. (1987), *Gramsci's Politics*, 2nd edn. (London, Century Hutchinson).

Skocpol, T. (1985), 'Bringing the state back in' in P. B. Evans *et al.* (eds), *Bringing The State Back In* (Cambridge, Cambridge University Press).

Thomas, G. M. and Meyer, J. W. (1984), 'The expansion of the state', *Annual Review of Sociology,* **10**.

Willke, H. (1987), 'Entzauberung des Staates. Grundlinien einer systemtheoretischen Argumentation' in T. Ellwein *et al.* (eds), *Jahrbuch zur Staats-und Verwaltunswissenschaft* (Baden-Baden, Nomos).

5. Comparative Politics: From Political Sociology to Comparative Public Policy

Jan-Erik Lane and Svante Ersson

INTRODUCTION

Comparative politics as a field of study has attracted a growing interest in recent decades, as reflected in the number of publications and journals and the emergence of new study programmes dealing with different areas of the world. Area specialists claim that cross-national studies are a legitimate concern although area studies are more oriented towards case study analysis than the use of the comparative method. At the same time, the interest in genuine comparative analysis has grown substantially, as modern comparative politics is clearly different from what used to be designated 'the traditional approach' (Sigelman and Gadbois, 1983).

In 1955 R. C. Macridis decisively stated the case against the traditional approach as being: non-comparative, descriptive, parochial, static, and monographic (Macridis, 1955). With some notable exceptions – M. Weber, J. Bryce, H. Finer – comparative politics used to focus on rules or constitutions, displayed a heavy bias towards the major Western countries and also lacked any methodology for the conduct of inquiry. The rejection of the traditional approach was too overwhelming not to change the course of comparative politics. A number of developments within Political Science reinforced the search for new approaches in the comparative analysis of political systems (Bill and Hardgrave, 1973; Wiarda, 1986).

The behavioural revolution implied that behaviour was more important than rules, thus necessitating the systematic collection of large amounts of data about politics in various countries. As data without theory would be blind, the behavioural revolution implied the explicit elaboration of concepts, models and hypotheses. Political sociology carried the claim that the politics of a country could be better understood if its institutions were related to social forces. The emergence of the Third World stimulated a whole new approach to the explanation of the differences between politics and society in rich and poor countries – the modernization theme.

The attack on the traditional approach was no doubt successful. The reorientation of comparative politics resulted in an expansion of comparative politics in terms of theoretical depth and empirical scope, as attempts were made to integrate a growing, but disparate, body of knowledge by means of theory. Since theory without data would be empty, genuine comparative theory was put to more severe tests due to an abundance of new data.

COMPARATIVE APPROACHES

Comparative politics has three major concerns:

1. the interpretation of the relationship between society and politics;
2. the identification of the major types of political systems; and
3. the understanding of the impact of politics on society.

Comparative politics first focused on the input side, political sociology claiming that basic properties of political systems were to be understood against background information about structure and processes in society; thus, it was claimed that political conflict dimensions were structured according to cleavage dimensions in the social structure (Rokkan *et al.*, 1970).

This reductionist approach offset a reaction arguing for the autonomy of politics in relation to social and economic factors. The second stage in modern comparative politics aimed at institutional analysis of the variation of political systems and their constituent parts, such as parties and party systems on their own right (Lijphart, 1968; Sartori, 1969; Sartori, 1976). Central to this were crucial distinctions between different types of democracy, authoritarian rule and modernizing polities.

Finally, the growing interest in the output side of politics within Political Science also affected comparative politics. Why study different political systems, if it was not the case that politics matters for policies? The third stage implied a merger of comparative politics with public policy and political economy, attempting to understand what different political systems do (policy outputs) and actually accomplish (policy outcomes) – this is comparative public policy (Groth, 1971; Heady, 1979; Heidenheimer *et al.*, 1983; Wildavsky, 1986). Figure 5.1 illustrates the major approaches to comparative politics.

Those who emphasize the input side typically refer to the impact of social cleavages, the basic problem being the extent to which the environment determines the polity. The cleavage approach reducing politics to cleavage dimensions in the social structure seems as exaggerated as

INPUT AND SOCIAL CONDITIONS	SYSTEM VARIETY	OUTPUT AND OUTCOME
Cleavages	Democracy	Policy convergence
Affluence	Authoritarianism	Politics matters
Modernization	Party system Legislatures	Economic growth

Figure 5.1   Comparative approaches

institutionalism or the hypothesis that there is no relationship whatsoever between social and economic factors and the political system. But how does one strike a balance between social or economic determinism and political indeterminism, or the *new* institutionalism?

How, in the comparative analysis of the political systems in various countries, can one identify crucial concepts with which to sort out in a careful fashion major system differences and similarities? As the attempt to separate traditional, developing and modern polities failed as a result of the value-loaded nature of these concepts (Almond and Powell, 1966), the distinction between democratic and authoritarian regimes became the fundamental one (Blondel, 1979; Dahl, 1971). However, even if there is unanimity as to the meaning and applicability of the term 'democracy' – some 30 polities in the world – there is disagreement about the properties or indicators that identify a democratic regime. Two very different types of democratic models have been recognized: the Westminster type democracy versus the consensus or consociational type democracy (Lijphart, 1984), but how about the far larger set of non-democratic systems? Today, we have more than 160 polities and there is as yet no agreement about the taxonomy of Third World politics (Clapham, 1985). No doubt, much future comparative research will focus on the set of non-democratic regimes in order to set out how they vary along a few basic dimensions (Perlmutter, 1981). The study of subsystems like political parties or party system and legislatures are truly comparative in the systematic sense (Loewenberg and Patterson, 1979; Janda, 1980). However, much too little has been done in order to come up with some sort of typology of non-democratic systems (Linz, 1975).

The comparative analysis of public policy or political economy has added a new dimension to comparative politics (Rose, 1973; Frey, 1978; Alt and Crystal, 1983; Hedström, 1986; Whiteley, 1986). The basic puzzle regarding the output or outcome side is whether politics, in a broad sense, matters for citizen welfare (Castles *et al.*, 1988). Given the profound structural differences between various states in terms of governmental structures, citizen rights and political party or trade union operations, are these vital distinctions also relevant for the understanding of allocational and redistributional differences? It has been argued that what matters for the scope and character of the welfare system – health, education and social care – is not politics but affluence (Galbraith, 1958; Tinbergen, 1964; Pryor, 1968; Wilensky, 1975). The counterargument is that the strength of the right or the left does mean a difference for the size of the welfare system, or policy outcomes like the rates of unemployment and inflation (Castles, 1978; Schmidt, 1982), or the historical evolution of the state matters, and institutional sclerosis affecting the rate of economic growth causing the decline of nations (Olson, 1982). The intersection between comparative politics and public policy is a new focus on the state or national government. Do characteristics like regime properties matter for policies and outcomes?

More specifically, we shall take a closer look at two widely debated themes in comparative politics. On the input side we shall inquire into the relation between the socio-economic structure and the polity, testing claims about social conditions for democracy. On the output side we will look for a relation between system type and policy outputs or outcomes.

THE POLITY

The concept of a democratic regime is employed to distinguish it among political systems. Sometimes a dichotomy between democratic and non-democratic systems is employed. At other times stable and unstable democratic regimes are referred to. R. Wesson in his 1987 overview speaks of stable, insecure and partial democracies versus limited authoritarianism and absolutism. R. Dahl made a distinction between fully inclusive polyarchies and near-polyarchies. Table 5.1 shows the countries which are typically listed as democratic.

The reduction in the number of democracies reflects both real world developments and disagreement about classification. A true development towards a democratic regime has taken place in Spain since 1975, Portugal as of 1974 and Greece since 1974. The existence of democratic political institutions in Mexico, Venezuela, Colombia, India and the Philippines has been interpreted differently, the basic problem being the somewhat blurred dividing line between stable and insecure democracies, as the debatable classification of Greece in 1967 and 1987 exemplifies.

It is now widely recognized that a more precise modelling of the conditions and consequences of democracy requires quantitative indicators measuring the extent of democracy. There exist a number of measurement indices, applied to a different number of countries:

Table 5.1   *Countries classified as stable democracies*

	Rustow (1967)	Dahl (1971)	Wesson (1987)
USA	X	X	X
Canada	X	X	X
Jamaica		X	
Trinidad		X	X
Barbados			X
Mexico	X		
Costa Rica	X	X	X
Colombia	X		X
Venezuela			X
Chile	X	X	
Uruguay	X	X	
United Kingdom	X	X	X
Ireland	X	X	X
Netherlands	X	X	X
Belgium	X	X	X
Luxembourg	X	X	X
France	X	X	X
Switzerland	X	X	X
Spain			X
Portugal			X
Germany FR	X	X	X
Austria	X	X	X
Italy	X	X	X
Greece	X		
Finland	X	X	X
Sweden	X	X	X
Norway	X	X	X
Demark	X	X	X
Iceland	X	X	X
Lebanon	X	X	
Israel	X	X	X
Japan	X	X	X
India	X	X	
Sri Lanka	X		
Philippines	X	X	
Australia	X	X	X
New Zealand	X	X	X
N =	31	30	28

Note: The ordering follows the ICPSR country code.

1. Cutright's index of political development:
    - legislative branch of government
    - executive branch of government (N = 77)
2. Smith's index of aggregate degree of political democracy:
    - Cutright's index
    - composite index of 19 variables (N = 110)
3. Neubauer's index of democratic political development:
    - percentage of adult population eligible to vote
    - equality of representation
    - information equality
    - electoral competition (N = 23)
4. Jackman's index of democratic performance:
    - number of adults voting
    - competitiveness of party system
    - electoral irregularity
    - freedom of the press (N = 60)
5. Bollen's index of political democracy:
    - press freedom
    - freedom of group opposition
    - government sanctions
    - fairness of elections
    - executive selection
    - legislature selection (N = 113)
6. Vanhanen's index of democratization:
    - competitiveness of party system
    - electoral participation (N = 119)
7. Humana's index of human rights:
    - (N = 96; 98)
8. Gastil's index of freedom:
    - political rights
    - civil rights
    - freedom status (N = 167).

The existence of so many indicators of the concept of democracy reflects its contested nature. However, even if standard indicators on democracy differ conceptually, they covary to a considerable extent in reality. Table 5.2 presents a correlation matrix for indicators measuring the degree of democracy in roundabout the 1960s. The different indices refer to different periods of time: some cover a longer time period whereas others refer to a more specific time reference.

With the exception of Cutright's and Neubauer's indices, there is a high correlation meaning that roughly the same countries are placed in the same

Table 5.2 *Correlations between different measures of democracy (circa 1960)*

	(1)	(2)	(3)	(4)	(5)	(6)	(7)
Neubauer 1940–60s (1)	1.00						
Cutright 1940–60s (2)	.15	1.00					
Smith 1960s (3)	.57	.88	1.00				
Jackman 1960s (4)	.63	.64	.80	1.00			
Bollen 1960 (5)	.57	.70	.83	.84	1.00		
Bollen 1965 (6)	.46	.74	.83	.84	.93	1.00	
Vanhanen 1960s (7)	.58	.66	.82	.79	.80	.76	1.00

Table 5.3 *Correlations between different measures of democracy (circa 1980)*

	(1)	(2)	(3)
Gastil 1980s (1)	1.00		
Humana 1980s I (2)	.90	1.00	
Humana 1980s II (3)	.92	.92	1.00

way around 1960. Whereas we have seven indices for the 1960s, there exist only two genuine indices for the 1970s, one referring to human rights and the other to political participation and competition. They correlate considerably: r = .86. With regard to the 1980s there are three indices measuring, basically, human rights. Again, the substantial intercorrelations between the indices means that the countries are measured in a roughly similar way (Table 5.3).

It must be acknowledged that there is no perfect correlation between the indices, neither within the same time period or between the time periods. This reflects again both real world changes and differences in the measurement of the concept. We may disregard the Cutright and Neubauer indices; Cutright's index has been criticized as involving a stability bias (Bollen, 1979) whereas Neubauer's index only covers 23 countries.

To summarize, we may say that, even though there are differences between the indices, the concept of a democratic regime is empirically unambiguous. When indices are applied to the different time periods, there is a strong correlation, meaning that change in real world democracy is not very large (see Table 5.4). Since we focus on democracy in the 1980s and its causes and consequences, we may therefore employ one

Table 5.4   Correlation between measures of democracy for different periods

	(1)	(2)	(3)
(1) 1980s (Humana)	1.00		
(2) 1970s (Gastil)	.82	1.00	
(3) 1960s (Bollen)	.71	.77	1.00

index of the extent to which a political system has a democratic regime with some confidence, because even if it may be objected that there are other equally justifiable indices, it would not make any practical difference to shift to another.

CONDITIONS FOR DEMOCRACY

It is a basic tenet of political sociology that the structure or dynamics of society has a profound impact on the polity. The similarities and differences of political systems are determined by background factors such as level of affluence, rate of economic development, overall socioeconomic development, cleavages and inequality. Economic and social conditions stand in a causal connection with polity properties such as democracy versus authoritarianism or type of democracy and political stability. The basic problem is to model the relationships between environmental and political system variables and to estimate the strength of the relationships in a body of data. How are we to draw causal inferences about the social and economic sources of political systems given the existence of a set of correlations in a comparative context?

The test of models of the sources of a democratic regime has attracted the interest of a large number of scholars, pointing out the methodological difficulties inherent in an inquiry into the causes of political systems in general and democracy in particular. These difficulties involve the selection of indicators, time slices and countries (Neubauer, 1967; Olsen, 1968; Coulter, 1971; Bollen, 1979; Bollen and Grandjean, 1981); moreover, they also include causal modelling problems (Smith, 1969; Rustow, 1970; Jackman, 1974; Huntington, 1984) and the choice between cross-sectional and longitudinal interpretations.

Taking these difficulties into account, we present correlations from a data set that covers some 120 countries at the following points of time: the 1960s, 1970s and 1980s. We focus on the conditions for the persistence of a democracy, not the conditions for the genesis of a democratic regime in the first place (Rustow, 1970). Is it true that the institutionalization of a democratic regime is strongly affected by the economic, social, cultural or political environment of the political system?

The occurrence of democratic regime properties may be indicated by means of the indices introduced above. Table 5.5 shows the average scores of the extent of democracy in various subsets of countries.

The democratic regime type prevails among the OECD countries, occurs sometimes in the set of Central and South American countries and not often in the set of Asian countries. As expected, the extent of democracy is low in the African set and in the Communist world. An analysis of variance indicates that this country pattern is fairly stable ($E^2 > .5$). Thus, we face one of the fundamental puzzles of comparative politics: why is it the case that democracy as a set of regime characteristics occurs so differently in the countries of the world? Or what conditions are conducive to the institutionalization of stable democratic regime characteristics? A number of factors have been suggested in order to explain this fact.

The Lipset affluence model points to the state of the economy (Lipset, 1959). The level of affluence is said to be a crucial determinant of the persistence of democratic regime characteristics. As countries grow more affluent, their social and political structure would become more diversified making a dictatorship impossible. The affluence model attracted considerable attention as several attempts at empirical validation were made (Cutright, 1963; Smith, 1969; Jackman, 1974) until G. O'Donnell questioned the whole approach (O'Donnell, 1973; 1988). What could a theoretical argument making affluence a sufficient or necessary condition for democracy look like (Usher, 1981)? Let us look at the correlations (Table 5.6)

The overall strong statistical association between level of affluence measured in terms of real GDP (RGDP) per capita and various indices of democracy is not stable in various country subsets. The relationship is particularly strong in the set of OECD countries, but not in other country subsets. Given the empirical evidence, it seems premature to conclude that there is a causal connection between the economy and the polity as suggested by the affluence model (O'Donnell and Schmitter, 1986). If affluence is a necessary condition for democracy, then why is there democracy in India? If affluence is a sufficient condition for democracy, why is there not democracy in Saudi Arabia? If this is the conclusion supported by the data in Table 5.6, then what accounts for the occurrence of democratic regime characteristics?

The modernization models argue that a decisive condition for the persistence of a democratic regime is a so-called modern social structure (Lerner, 1958; Deutsch, 1961). Although it is far from obvious what a

Table 5.5   The world of democracy (average values, E^2)

	OECD	Latin America	Africa	Asia	Social	E^2	Min	Max
1980s (Gastil)	95.2	59.9	19.8	36.5	10.3	.72	0	100
1980s (Humana)	92.0	66.1	47.3	44.1	31.0	.68	13	98
1980s (Humana)	89.2	59.4	53.5	48.0	35.5	.58	17	96
1970s (Gastil)	92.4	51.3	18.7	34.2	6.8	.72	0	100
1970s (Vanhanen)	27.2	7.1	0.5	5.7	0.1	.69	0	42.3
1960s (Vanhanen)	24.2	9.1	1.6	5.9	0.7	.59	0	40.7
1960s (Bollen)	89.8	71.0	56.8	54.6	23.1	.45	10.7	100
1960s (Bollen)	90.2	65.8	44.2	49.9	21.3	.48	5.2	100
1960s (Jackman)	77.0	62.4	41.2	64.2	—	.30	18	90
1960s (Smith)	120.7	105.5	90.8	87.2	94.4	.50	55.8	137.7
1960s (Cutright)	58.0	53.1	—	41.7	47.5	.53	33	66

Table 5.6   The affluence model: democracy and wealth (RGDP/cap)
(Pearson's r)

	Total	OECD	Latin America	Africa	Asia
1980s (Gastil)	.67	.62	.39	.15	.28
1980s (Humana)	.66	.61	.53	.04	.27
1980s (Humana)	.60	.68	.29	.13	.11
1970s (Gastil)	.70	.67	.31	.25	.33
1970s (Vanhanen)	.78	.54	.50	.29	.57
1960s (Vanhanen)	.72	.45	.73	− .00	.63
1960s (Bollen)	.47	.57	.47	.20	.39
1960s (Bollen)	.55	.52	.56	− .02	.42
1960s (Jackman)	.60	.52	.43	− .21	.57
1960s (Smith)	.72	.63	.52	.32	.43
1960s (Cutright)	.72	.74	.39	—	.37

'modern' social structure amounts to – modernity being a value loaded concept – the implication of the modernization theme is that processes of industrialization and urbanization are conducive to democracy. However, since modernization is strongly correlated with level of affluence we would not expect that the modernization models fit the data better than the affluence model. The correlations in Table 5.7 corroborates this conjecture.

Social structure involves more than economics and its derivatives. It has been suggested that culture, more generally, conditions the extent of democracy. One theory focuses on religion or more specifically on the position of Protestantism in the country (Schumpeter, 1942; Lenski, 1963). The model states that the stronger the position of Lutheranism or Calvinism in its various forms, the more stable would be the democratic institutions of a country. Another religious model emphasizes homogeneity in the religious structure of a country predicting that heterogeneity would enhance democratic instability or strengthen an authoritarian regime. Diversity in the social structure may pertain to other characteristics than religion, viz. language or cultural tradition. According to this theory, ethnic heterogeneity would make democracy very difficult due to the explosive nature of ethnic cleavages (de Schweinitz, 1964; Moore, 1966; Wallerstein, 1977). The correlations in Table 5.7 provide some confirmation of these hypotheses.

A different theme in modern comparative politics is to look for the determinants of democracy among more specific political factors. One

*Table 5.7   Democratic conditions: correlations between democracy
indices and social structure factors (1980s, 1970s, 1960s)*

	Humana 1980s	Gastil 1970s	Bollen 1960s
Protestantism	.45	.48	.44
Ethno-linguistic structure: fractionalization	− .28	− .29	− .30
Religious structure: fractionalization	− .14	− .12	− .03
Religious and ethnolinguistic fractionalization	− .23	− .23	− .11
Cultural pluralism	− .43	− .42	− .29
Agricultural employment 1965	− .58	− .52	− .65
Agricultural employment 1980	− .50	− .44	− .57
Introduction of modernized leadership	− .57	− .40	− .60
Effective modernized leadership	− .47	− .39	− .54
Qualified as member of the international system	− .38	− .25	− .43
Period of democratic rule (Hewitt)	.56	.30	.56
Period of democratic rule (Muller)	.59	.68	.64

theory points out the length of experience of a democratic regime and
another theory emphasizes the length of the period of so-called moder-
nized leadership. In general, a segmented social structure would be
conducive to democratic instability (Eckstein, 1966; Rustow, 1970; Dahl,
1971). The status of a democratic regime is a function of how long a time
modern institutions have persisted uninterruptedly. Alternatively, a
democratic regime is a function of time, the longer the time period since
the genesis of democracy the more persistent being the democratic polity.
Again, there is empirical support for these models (Table 5.7).

However, all correlations are of such a moderate strength that much
more research is needed in order to arrive at a theory about the conditions
for democratic continuity. Thus, whichever factor we emphasize, there
will be deviant cases requiring *ad hoc* explanations. Take the religious
models: if a Protestant culture matters, then why are there stable democracies in Japan, India or Italy and France; when religious homogeneity is
highlighted, then how about Switzerland and the Netherlands? On the
other hand, if ethnic homogeneity or cultural diversity matters, then why
are there democracies in Spain, the USA, Canada or India? Moreover, if a
modern social structure – that is, a small agricultural population – is
crucial, then why is there democracy in India and not in East Germany? If

an early nation-building process is a necessary or sufficient condition for stable democracy, then why is there democracy in Greece and Portugal and not in Uruguay? These correlations do not suffice for the derivation of either sufficient or necessary conditions. Future comparative research may wish to distinguish between how democracy arises and how it is sustained over time. Almost certainly, single-factor models have to be replaced by combined ones.

DEMOCRATIC PERFORMANCE

Political systems may be valued for their own sake or for their value as instruments for the accomplishment of social goals. Thus, democracy may be emphasized because it embodies certain values in itself or because its operation leads to social outcomes which are considered desirable. There exists a number of models that offer explanations of the consequences of government operations. These effects of the operation of a polity may relate to either general performance dimensions like polity durability, civil order, legitimacy and decisional efficacy (Eckstein, 1971; Gurr and McClelland, 1971), or to specific policy outputs or policy outcomes. We focus on the theme of *democratic performance*.

The equality model claims that the more democratic a polity is, the greater will be the extent of equality in the distribution of affluence (Lenski, 1966). The economic growth model states that the more democratic a polity is, the lower will be the rate of growth in the economy. The soft state model ties into this model predicting that a more authoritarian regime will be conducive to rapid economic development (Myrdal, 1968). So does the sclerosis model: the longer the time period of institutionalization, the stronger the distributional coalitions and the lower the rate of growth in the economy (Olson, 1982). The inflation model implies that the higher the level of democracy in a country, the higher the rate of inflation (Tufte, 1978). The political violence model argues that the more repressive a regime tends to become, the higher will be the levels of occurrence of political violence (Muller, 1985). Finally, the convergence model implies that political systems, whether communist, democratic or socialist, tend towards the same pattern of state activities: the welfare state. This is a hypothesis about variation in policy outputs which denies that policies differ as a function of the type of regime that rules the country (Tinbergen, 1956; Galbraith, 1967). Finally, there is the war model that states that democracy is conducive to peace (Weede, 1984).

A test of these various models presents serious methodological difficulties concerning data, model specification and estimation techniques

Table 5.8 *Democratic performance: correlations between democracy
indicators and output and outcome indicators
(1980s, 1970s, 1960s)*

	Humana 1980s	Gastil 1970s	Bollen 1960s
GNP/capita growth 1965–80	.17	.19	.01
General government expenditures circa 1977	.05	.07	− .02
Welfare effort 1970s (Estes, 1984)	.53	.53	.41
Education 1970s (Estes, 1984)	.47	.52	.43
Education 1980s (Estes, 1984)	.46	.53	.40
Health 1970s (Estes, 1984)	.52	.59	.45
Health 1980s (Estes, 1984)	.49	.59	.43
Inequality: Gini index	− .43	− .40	− .33
Inequality: Ward (1978)	− .47	− .51	− .37
Inflation 1965–80	− .08	− .10	.10
Inflation 1980–85	− .09	− .05	− .05
War	− .14	.02	− .07

(Banks, 1972; Jackman, 1973; Dick, 1974; Hewitt, 1977; Rubinson and Quinlan, 1977, 1983 and 1984; Bollen and Jackman, 1985). Recognizing these technical problems, we arrive at the correlations presented in Table 5.8.

Democracy delivers, in a direct sense, by offering human rights as parts of the democratic procedures themselves. However, there is empirical support for the theory that a democratic regime delivers indirectly by means of policy outputs and outcomes. Democracies have a more pronounced welfare effort than other types of regimes. The hypothesis that political systems would converge towards a similar pattern of welfare expenditures is not substantiated. The welfare efforts in non-democratic polities have not been sufficient to match those in several democracies, particularly as the Communist welfare system has lagged behind during the last twenty years (Castles, 1986). It also seems to be the case that there is a better likelihood for more equality in the distribution of resources in a democracy. On the other hand, we find no evidence of any impact of democracy on economic growth, size of the state, inflation or war experience. Of course, it remains to be explored whether it is really democracy that counts for these performance indicators or whether some other political variable matters more. Comparative public policy or political economy analyses the problem of policy determinants both within the set of democracies – the variation *within* the set of rich countries – and between democracies and non-democracies – the variation *between* rich and poor countries.

CONCLUSION

As the traditional approach to comparative politics was abandoned in the 1960s due to both substantial and methodological criticism, the volume of cross-national studies has risen sharply, particularly the number of area studies. The efforts at more genuine comparative analysis have also increased (Przeworski and Teune, 1970; Przeworski, 1987). Taking a broad perspective on the variety of political systems, the trend is towards quantitative modelling of the causes and consequences of the political system. A bias still lingers on towards looking in particular at democratic regimes, although democracy is by no means the prevailing regime among the political systems today. It may be predicted that the focus on the conditions for democracy and democratic performance will give away to a broader perspective on various types of regimes, their conditions and policy implications.

The research of the 1970s and 1980s has improved our understanding of the conditions for stable democracy as well as the policy implications of long-term democratic rule, but the basic questions about polity causes and policy determinants are by no means fully answered. Further inquiry is needed in the following areas:

1. a typology of regimes that encompasses the large number of non-democratic political systems;
2. models of the causes of the polity that allows us to make distinctions between the conditions for the introduction or *genesis* of democratic rule, and the conditions for democratic continuity or the *persistence* of a stable democracy;
3. models about policy outputs and policy outcomes that allow us to separate the implications of political system characteristics while controlling for other relevant political factors.

No doubt the development of modern comparative politics will become still more rapid as it is progressively recognized that the patterns of discovery in political science increasingly depend on a comparative approach towards the modelling of relationships between concepts measured by means of indicators or indices to be tested against data assembled on the basis of strategic deliberations. This direction is closely associated with some of the concerns of other disciplines in social science (economics) and has hence enhanced its interdisciplinary contribution, while strengthening its own base.

NOTE

We are grateful to Francis Castles, Arend Lijphart and Aaron Wildavsky for helpful comments on an early draft of this chapter.

APPENDIX: DATA, INDICATORS AND SOURCES

Democracy Indicators

1980s Gastil	N = 120	Gastil, 1987
1980s Humana	N = 112	Humana, 1986
1980s Humana	N = 102	Humana, 1983
1970s Gastil	N = 120	Gastil, 1987
1970s Vanhanen	N = 111	Vanhanen, 1984
1960s Vanhanen	N = 111	Vanhanen, 1984
1960s Bollen	N = 110	Bollen, 1980
1960s Bollen	N = 120	Bollen, 1980
1960s Jackman	N = 58	Jackman, 1975
1960s Smith	N = 109	Smith, 1969
1960s Cutright	N = 74	Cutright, 1963
1960s Neubauer	N = 23	Neubauer, 1967

Input Dimension Indicators

RGDP/cap 1960	N = 112	Summers and Heston, 1984
RGDP/cap 1970	N = 112	Summers and Heston, 1984
RGDP/cap 1980	N = 112	Summers and Heston, 1984
Protestantism	N = 121	Taylor and Hudson, 1972
Religious fragment.	N = 120	Taylor and Hudson, 1972
Ethnolinguistic fragmen-tation	N = 121	Taylor and Hudson, 1972
Religious and ethnic frag-mentation	N = 120	Taylor and Hudson, 1972
Pluralism	N = 107	Haug, 1967
Agricultural employm. 1965	N = 114	World Bank, 1987

Agricultural employm.
1980	N = 111	World Bank, 1987

Modernizing leadership:
introduced	N = 121	Taylor and Hudson, 1972

Modernizing leadership:
in effect	N = 121	Taylor and Hudson, 1972

Qualified as member of
the international system	N = 121	Banks, 1971

Period of democratic rule
(Hewitt)	N = 24	Hewitt, 1977

Period of democratic rule
(Muller)	N = 66	Muller, 1988

Output Dimension Indicators

GNP/capita growth
1965–80	N = 94	World Bank, 1987

General government exp.
circa 1977	N = 77	IMF, 1982
Welfare effort	N = 104	Estes, 1984
Education 1970s	N = 104	Estes, 1984
Education 1980s	N = 104	Estes, 1984
Health 1970s	N = 104	Estes, 1984
Health 1980s	N = 104	Estes, 1984
Inequality: Gini	N = 81	Taylor and Jodice, 1983
Inequality: Ward	N = 97	Dye and Zeigler, 1988
Inflation 1965–80	N = 95	World Bank, 1987
Inflation 1980–85	N = 92	World Bank, 1987
War experience	N = 106	Weede, 1984

REFERENCES

Almond, G. A. and Powell, G. B. (1966), *Comparative politics: a developmental approach* (Boston, Little, Brown).

Alt, J. and Crystal, A. K. (1983), *Political Economics* (Berkeley, The University of California Press).

Banks, A. S. (1971), *Cross-polity Time-series Data* (Cambridge, MA, MIT Press).

Banks, A. S. (1972), 'Correlates of democratic performance', *Comparative Politics*, **4**, pp. 217–30.

Bill, J. A. and R. L. Hardgrave (1973), *Comparative Politics: The Quest for Theory* (Columbus, Merrill).

Blondel, J. (1969), *An Introduction to Comparative Government* (London, Weidenfeld and Nicholson).

Bollen, K. A. (1979), 'Political democracy and the timing of development', *American Sociological Review*, **44**, pp. 572-87.

Bollen, K. A. (1980), 'Issues in the comparative measurement of political democracy', *American Sociological Review*, **45**, pp. 370-90.

Bollen, K. A. and Grandjean, J. (1981), 'The dimension(s) of democracy: further issues in the measurement and effects of political democracy', *American Sociological Review*, **46**, pp. 651-9.

Bollen, K. A. and Jackman, R. W. (1985), 'Political democracy and the size distribution of income', *American Sociological Review*, **50**, pp. 438-57.

Castles, F. G. (1978), *The Social Democratic Image of Society: a study of the achievements and origins of Scandinavian social democracy in comparative perspective* (London, Routledge and Kegan Paul).

Castles, F. G. (1986), 'Whatever happened to the communist welfare state?', *Studies in Comparative Communism*, **19**, pp. 213-26.

Castles, F. G., Lehner, F. and Schmidt, M. G. (1988), 'Comparative public policy analysis: problems, progress and prospects' in F. G. Castles (ed.), *Managing Mixed Economies* (Berlin, Walter de Gruyter), pp. 197-223.

Clapham, C. (1985), *Third World Politics: an introduction* (London, Croom Helm).

Coulter, P. (1971), 'Democratic political development: a systematic model based on regulative policy', *Development and Change*, **3**, pp. 25-61.

Cutright, P. (1963), 'National political development: measurement and analysis', *American Sociological Review*, **28**, pp. 253-64.

Dahl, R. A. (1971), *Polyarchy* (New Haven, Yale University Press).

Deutsch, K. W. (1961), 'Social mobilization and political development', *American Political Science Review*, **55**, pp. 493-514.

Dick, G. W. (1974), 'Authoritarian versus nonauthoritarian approaches to economic development', *Journal of Political Economy*, **82**, pp. 817-27.

Dye, T. R. and Zeigler, H. (1988), 'Socialism and equality in cross-national perspective', *PS: Political Science and Politics*, **21**, pp. 45-56.

Eckstein, H. (1966), *Division and Cohesion in Democracy: a study of Norway* (Princeton, Princeton University Press).

Eckstein, H. (1971), *The Evaluation of Political Performance: problems and dimensions* (Beverly Hills, Sage).

Estes, R. J. (1984), *The Social Progress of Nations* (New York, Praeger).

Frey, B. (1978), *Modern Political Economy* (London, Macmillan).

Galbraith, J. K. (1958), *The Affluent Society* (Boston, Houghton Mifflin).

Galbraith, J. K. (1967), *The New Industrial State* (Harmondsworth, Pelican).

Gastil, R. D. (ed.) (1987), *Political Rights and Civil Liberties 1986-1987* (New York, Greenwood Press).

Groth, A. J. (1971), *Comparative Politics: a distributive approach* (New York, Macmillan).

Gurr, T. R. and McClelland, M. (1971), *Political Performance: a twelve-nation study* (Beverly Hills, Sage).

Haug, M. R. (1967), 'Social and cultural pluralism as a concept in social system analysis', *American Journal of Sociology*, **73**, pp. 294-304.

Heady, F. (1979), *Public Administration: a comparative perspective* (New York, Dekker).

Hedström, P. (1986), 'From political sociology to political economy' in U. Himmelstrand (ed.), *Sociology: From Crisis to Science: Volume 1* (London, Sage).

Heidenheimer, A. J., Heclo, H. and Adams, C. J. (1983), *Comparative Public Policy: the politics of social choice in Europe and America* (London, Macmillan).

Hewitt, C. (1977), 'The effect of political democracy and social democracy on equality in industrial societies: a cross-national comparison', *American Sociological Review,* **42**, pp. 450–64.

Humana, C. (1983), *World Human Rights Guide* (London, Hutchinson).

Humana, C. (1986), *World Human Rights Guide* (2nd edn.), (London, Economist Publications).

Huntington, S. P. (1984), 'Will more countries become democratic?', *Political Science Quarterly,* **99**, pp. 193–218.

IMF (1982), *Government Finance Statistics Yearbook* (Washington, DC, IMF).

Jackman, R. W. (1973), 'On the relation of economic development to democratic performance', *American Journal of Political Science,* **17**, pp. 611–21.

Jackman, R. W. (1974), 'Political democracy and equality: comparative analysis', *American Sociological Review,* **39**, pp. 29–45.

Jackman, R. W. (1975), *Politics and Social Equality: a comparative analysis* (New York, Wiley).

Janda, K. (1980), *Political Parties: a cross-national survey* (New York, Free Press).

Lenski, G. (1963), *The Religious Factor: a sociological study of religion's impact on politics, economics and family life* (Garden City, Doubleday).

Lenski, G. (1966), *Power and Privilege* (New York, McGraw-Hill).

Lerner, D. (1958), *The Passing of Traditional Society: modernizing the Middle East* (New York, Free Press).

Lijphart, A. (1968), 'Typologies of democratic systems', *Comparative Political Studies,* **1**, pp. 3–44.

Lijphart, A. (1984), *Democracies: patterns of majoritarian and consensus government in twenty-one countries* (New Haven, Yale University Press).

Linz, J. J. (1975), 'Totalitarian and authoritarian regimes' in F. I. Greenstein and N. W. Polsby (eds), *Handbook of Political Science: Volume 3 Macropolitical Theory* (Reading, MA, Addison-Wesley), pp. 175–411.

Lipset, S. M. (1959), *Political Man* (Garden City, NY, Doubleday).

Loewenberg, G. and Patterson, S. C. (1979), *Comparing Legislatures* (Boston, Little, Brown).

Macridis, R. C. (1955), *The Study of Comparative Government* (New York, Random House).

Moore, B. (1966), *Social Origins of Dictatorship and Democracy* (Harmondsworth, Pelican).

Muller, E. (1985), 'Income inequality, regime repressiveness and political violence', *American Sociological Review,* **50**, pp. 47–61.

Muller, E. (1988), 'Democracy, economic development, and income inequality', *American Sociological Review,* **53**, pp. 50–68.

Myrdal, G. (1961), ' "Value-loaded" concepts' in H. Hegeland (ed.) *Money, Growth, and Methodology and Other Essays in Honor of Johan Akerman* (Lund, Gleerup).

Myrdal, G. (1968), *Asian Drama I–III* (New York, Pantheon Books).

Neubauer, D. E. (1967), 'Some conditions of democracy', *American Political Science Review,* **61**, pp. 1002–9.

O'Donnell, G. (1973), *Modernization and Bureaucratic-Authoritarianism: studies in South American politics* (Berkeley, Institute of International Studies).

O'Donnell, G. (1988), *Bureaucratic Authoritarianism: Argentina 1966-1973 in comparative perspective* (Berkeley, University of California Press).
O'Donnell, G. and Schmitter, P. C. (1986), *Transitions from Authoritarian Rule: tentative conclusions about uncertain democracies* (Baltimore, The Johns Hopkins University Press).
Olsen, M. E. (1968), 'Multivariate analysis of national political development', *American Sociological Review,* **33**, pp. 699-712.
Olson, M. (1982), *The Rise and Decline of Nations*, (New Haven, Yale University Press).
Perlmutter, A. (1981), *Modern Authoritarianism: A Comparative Institutional Analysis* (New Haven, Yale University Press).
Przeworski, A. (1987), 'Methods of cross-national research, 1970-83: an overview' in M. Dierkes (ed.), *Comparative Policy Research: learning from experience* (Aldershot, Gower), pp. 31-49.
Przeworski, A. and Teune, H. (1970), *The Logic of Comparative Social Inquiry* (New York, Wiley).
Pryor, F. L. (1968), *Public Expenditures in Communist and Capitalist Nations* (London, Allen and Unwin).
Rokkan, S. *et al.* (1970), *Citizens, Elections, Parties: approaches to the comparative study of the process of development* (Oslo, Universitetsforlaget).
Rose, R. (1973), 'Comparing public policy: an overview', *European Journal of Political Research,* **1**, pp. 67-94.
Rubinson, R. and Quinlan, D. (1977), 'Democracy and social equality: a reanalysis', *American Sociological Review,* **42**, pp. 611-23.
Rustow, D. A. (1967), *A World of Nations: Problems of Political Modernization* (Washington, The Brookings Institution).
Rustow, D. A. (1970), 'Transitions to democracy: toward a dynamic model', *Comparative Politics,* **2**, pp. 337-63.
Sartori, G. (1969), 'From the sociology of politics to political sociology' in S. M. Lipset (ed.) *Politics and the Social Sciences* (New York, Oxford University Press), pp. 65-100.
Sartori, G. (1976), *Parties and Party Systems: a framework for analysis* (Cambridge, Cambridge University Press).
Schmidt, M. G. (1982), *Wohlfartsstaatliche Politik und bürgerlichen und sozialdemokratischen Regierungen* (Frankfurt, Campus).
Schumpeter, J. (1942), *Capitalism, Socialism and Democracy* (London, Allen and Unwin).
de Schweinitz, K. (1964), *Industrialization and Democracy* (Glencoe, Free Press).
Sigelman, L. and Gadbois, G. H. (1983), 'Contemporary comparative politics: an inventory and assessment', *Comparative Political Studies,* **16**, pp. 275-305.
Smith, A. K. (1969), 'Socio-economic development and political democracy: a causal analysis', *Midwest Journal of Political Science,* **13**, pp. 95-125.
Summers, R. and Heston, A. (1984), 'Improved international comparisons of real product and its composition, 1950-80', *The Review of Income and Wealth,* **30**, pp. 207-62.
Taylor, C. L. and Hudson, M. (1972), *World Handbook of Political and Social Indicators* (2nd. edn.), (New Haven, Yale University Press).
Taylor, C. L. and Jodice, D. (1983), *World Handbook of Political and Social Indicators* (3rd. edn.), (New Haven, Yale University Press).
Tinbergen, J. (1956), *Economic Policy: principles and design* (Amsterdam, North-

Holland).

Tufte, E. (1978), *Political Control of the Economy* (Princeton, Princeton University Press).

Usher, D. (1981), *The Economic Prerequisite to Democracy* (Oxford, Blackwell).

Vanhanen, T. (1984), *The Emergence of Democracy: a comparative study of 119 states, 1850-1979* (Helsinki, Societas Scientiarum Fennica).

Wallerstein, I. (1977), 'Rural economy in modern world society', *Studies in Comparative International Development,* 12, pp. 29-40.

Weede, E. (1983), 'The impact of democracy on economic growth: some evidence from cross-national analysis', *Kyklos,* 36, pp. 21-39.

Weede, E. (1984), 'Democracy and war involvement', *Journal of Conflict Resolution,* 28, pp. 649-64.

Wesson, R. (ed.) (1987), *Democracy: a worldwide survey* (New York, Praeger).

Whiteley, P. (1986), *Political Control of the Macroeconomy: the political economy of public policy making* (London, Sage).

Wiarda, H. J. (ed.) (1986), *New Developments in Comparative Politics* (Boulder, Colorado, Westview Press).

Wildavsky, A. (1986), *Budgeting* (2nd edn.), (New Brunswick, Transaction).

Wilensky, H. (1975), *The Welfare State and Equality* (Berkeley, The University of California Press).

World Bank (1987), *World Development Report* (New York, Oxford University Press).

6. Politics and Development Studies

Adrian Leftwich

INTRODUCTION

This chapter explores the contribution which Political Science (hereafter Politics) has made to the study of development, or development studies. I shall argue that, despite generating a rich literature on many aspects of Third World politics, the discipline's contribution to the analysis and promotion of *development* has been quite slim, since there are as yet no sets of systematic propositions which might constitute theories of the *politics of development*. I shall suggest that, in its engagement with Third World and area studies, the discipline of Politics to some extent lost its way and even its sense of specialist self-identity through its premature immersion in interdisciplinarity. As a result, the discipline's central preoccupations concerning the role of politics, power and the state were reduced to secondary, dependent and even consequential aspects of the varied patterns and forms of socioeconomic development. Accumulated evidence, however, points firmly to the primacy of politics in developmental processes. For the future, therefore, one of the major tasks for political scientists with development concerns will be to generate a more sustained comparative understanding of the role of politics in development and, in particular, what must now be regarded as a *de facto*, distinctive and unusual subtype of the state, the 'developmental state', and its associated politics.[1] But, first, some clarification of key terms is required.

'POLITICS' AND 'DEVELOPMENT'

Two broad senses of the term 'politics' will be used here. The first refers to politics as a pervasive feature of all social life. It comprises all the activities of cooperation, negotiation and conflict which occur in the course of the use, production and distribution of resources in human communities (Leftwich, 1983). Politics occurs in all groups, institutions and organizations – large or small, formal and informal, private and public – and in the relations between them, at all levels – local, national and international –

whether in or between families, villages, regions, private companies, international corporations, public bureaucracies or governments.

Thus defined, pervasive politics is inextricably implicated in all the processes of development from top to bottom.[2] For whatever else it may be about (Seers, 1979a), 'development' necessarily involves change in the way resources of all kinds are used, produced and distributed – whether these resources be land, time, capital, labour, symbols, influence, status, opportunity or power. When developmental change occurs, those who are involved usually know that there will almost always be winners and losers; thus some will resist and some will encourage such changes. And whatever specialist arguments (in economics, agriculture, hydrology or public health) may be advanced in favour of this policy or that strategy, these will seldom alone determine the result of a dispute about change and its direction. Politics, however, will be central to the outcome, whatever its local form and substantive issues. This is true for all societies, at all levels within them and in the relations between them and the wider world, whether in the ancient Greek world (Croix, 1981), northern Nigeria in the early twentieth century (Watts, 1983), colonial Vietnam (Popkin, 1979) or modern Portugal, Japan, Brazil, Pakistan or South Korea (Jenkins, 1979; Dore, 1978; Evans, 1979; Herring, 1983; Lim, 1986).

The second meaning of 'politics' used here refers to the sources, structure and use of official or public power in a society: that is, how public power is fought over and won, constituted and constrained, legitimated, distributed and used, especially, by the state, and particularly in the economy. To distinguish it from 'pervasive politics', I refer to it simply as public politics or, more sharply, 'state politics'. State politics, then, revolves around the structure, composition, control, role and capacity of the state and its relations with other socioeconomic forces both in and beyond the society, and the kinds of policy which it may generate and deliver. Since the state – whether minimalist or maximalist – is central in development, state politics and development are therefore intimate.

Of course there are close and complex relations between pervasive and state politics, but I shall be primarily concerned here with the latter and its importance in development. For if anything has become clear in the Third World since the 1950s (and long before this elsewhere: for instance in the Aztec empire, Song China and post-Meiji Japan), it is that the character and especially the capacity of the state has been a critical variable in the relative developmental successes and failures which can be identified, *however these are defined* (Gerschenkron, 1962; Supple, 1973; Fitzgerald, 1976; Trimberger, 1977; Evans, 1979, 1987; Bates, 1981; Bardhan, 1984; White and Wade, 1985; Anglade and Fortin, 1987; Chazan *et al.*, 1988).

So much for 'politics': but what of 'development'? The term does not here refer simply to a condition which may be reached, like a plateau, as implied sometimes in early modernization theory (Rostow, 1962; Eisenstadt, 1966). Rather, it denotes a process or set of processes – micro and macro, private and public, national and transnational – which may occur in all societies (Leys, 1969: 11–12). Moreover, the idea of 'development', like progress, bears a heavy normative freight, the definition of which varies dramatically between, say, Marxists and neoclassical liberals. However, most people will agree that, in its contemporary Third World identification, 'development' involves all the methods and processes whereby the level and efficiency of the forces and means of production, their organization and control, can be raised or improved, and their product so distributed as to liberate human beings from vulnerability, hunger, poverty, disease and ignorance. Development – involving politics, markets and states, as well as technical innovations – thus provides an expanding environment of freedom in which people can make choices and take opportunities to advance their individual fulfilment and their collective social accomplishments. It is concerned, as Marx wrote, with '. . . replacing the domination of circumstances and chance over individuals by the domination of individuals over chance and circumstance' (Marx, 1977: 190) or, in Sen's terms, it is a '. . . process of expanding the capabilities of people' through the 'expansion of entitlements' (Sen, 1988: 47).

Since politics, and especially state politics, is thus at the heart of these processes, I shall therefore be concerned here with 'the politics of development'. This must be distinguished from what is sometimes referred to as 'political development', a post-war preoccupation of mainly US behavioural political scientists. They focused on changes in political culture, institutions, participation, and socialization, *inter alia*, often as isolable systems or properties of polities, or even as '. . . the political aspect(s) and consequence(s) of the broader processes of modernization' (Huntington and Dominguez, 1975: 4; Migdal, 1983; Kohli, 1986). The study of the 'politics of development', on the other hand, is concerned more directly with the role of politics, power and especially the state as active agencies or conditions of development, not as passive or dependent consequences of it.

DEVELOPMENT STUDIES

What have been some of the major characteristics of development studies since the 1960s?

Despite notices to the contrary (Seers, 1979b; Apter, 1980; Hirschman,

1981; Lal, 1983), development studies is neither dead nor dying. While often aimed specifically at 'development economics', these pronouncements of imminent or recent death have often sought to sweep both the politics and sociology of development into freshly prepared intellectual graves.

Such funereal views suggest a misunderstanding of the relationship of development studies to the social sciences. In a manner of speaking, development studies *is* social science and social science *is* development studies. One could no more bury the one without burying the other. This is true for the two major analytical traditions in social science, and their variants, the one stemming from liberalism and the other from Marxism. From de Tocqueville, Comte and Adam Smith, through List, Spencer, Marx, Weber, Schumpeter and Keynes, right into the modern era (Karl Polanyi and Barrington Moore Jr., being perhaps the most notable recent theorists), the problem of development has been central to the concerns of social scientists and has provided the underlying agenda of questions in terms of which more detailed studies have been undertaken.

Such questions include: what explains and promotes the structural transformation of societies? What arrangement of factors in the history and socioeconomic, cultural, ideological, political and institutional structure of a society block, or facilitate, such transformations? What classes or social groups represent the major agencies of change or resistance, at different times and places, and why? What conditions promote the accumulation of capital? Can transformative models from one place and time be replicated in another? How is power and decision-making constituted and distributed in a given society; what are the relations between those who wield it and those who do not; and what is the reach and effectiveness of administrative authorities? What have been, can be or should be the respective roles of states and markets, at different times, in the economic life of societies, and what kinds of state and market have been able to do this effectively and why? What is the room for manoeuvre of states in an increasingly internationalized economy and how 'autonomous' can they be of both internal and external interests? What is revolutionary change; when and how does it occur; and is it a sufficient or only a necessary condition for development in some societies? Is there a trade-off between the processes of democracy and development, between freedom and equality, planning and enterprise, respect for civil rights and rapid growth? Is there scope, and if so how, for 'new' values (such as those which feminists and 'greens' espouse) to be institutionalized in the normative, economic, political and legal arrangements of a society?

It is clear that these are the fundamental issues of both the social sciences and development studies. Hence it is important to recognize that they concern not only the 'developing societies' of the Third World, but all societies, although perhaps in different ways (*IDS Bulletin*, December 1977; Toye, 1987b). Thus, if the answers to urgent developmental questions of the last 30 years have not been all that we may have hoped for, this does not mean that development studies is either dead or dying but that, like social science of which it forms the core, it remains very important, very difficult and very relevant to the lives of all people in the contemporary world. And politics, as I have suggested, is central to it.

However, the field of development studies has never been simply a branch of detached academic enquiry. Many of those involved have been profoundly concerned for the plight of poor people in poor societies. And they have often approached their work in the light of wider international political commitments – for example, with respect to anti-imperialist, anti-communist or anti-racist struggles in diverse regional and cold war contexts.[3] This has influenced both the passionate and political character of the field and its debates.

Another characteristic of development studies is that, although it has always advertised itself as interdisciplinary, it has been dominated mainly by economists. The flow of papers, articles, books and theoretical contributions from the discipline of economics has been far greater than any other discipline. As a very simple illustration, a rough count of the major articles published between 1964 and 1987 in the British-based *Journal of Development Studies*, reveals that fewer than 9 per cent of them have concerned the politics of development. The picture has been more positive in international journals like *World Politics, World Development* and *Comparative Politics*, and also in the various area studies journals.

This highlights a further important aspect of development studies. It has often merged with, or been lost in, area studies, a point I shall return to later in connection with the discipline of Politics. However, one unfortunate consequence of this has been the extrusion of development studies and its component disciplines from the mainstreams of the social sciences, and despite the fact, as I have suggested, that they are inextricable.

Another feature of the field has been its strong policy involvement, although this, again, seems to have involved development economists far more than other social scientists, with the partial exceptions of some of those working in public administration (Schaffer and Lamb, 1981) and some rural sociologists. National governments and international development agencies have seldom sought the professional services of political scientists. Moreover, one is hard put to find more than a few papers or reports on the politics of development in the hundreds of World Bank *Staff Papers* and other publications (but see Lamb, 1987). Such agencies seem to have wanted to eliminate, at least officially, the idea of politics from their analytical and policy work. By thus removing politics from 'development', the impression is given of development as a narrowly 'technical' matter, presided over and promoted by qualified professionals. Yet privately, and almost without exception, most national and international development officials will emphatically agree that politics is central and that 'good' projects, policies or programmes may often founder on 'bad' politics. However, one seldom encounters clear analysis of this in the official papers, reports or evaluations. Perhaps, also, developmentally inclined political scientists have preferred to maintain an arms-length and critical stance in relation to such institutional and policy entanglements, although less so in the USA than elsewhere. Some might even point to fiascos such as 'Project Camelot' as justification for distancing themselves from 'official' interventions (Horowitz, 1974). But I think one effect of this has been to distance the discipline from direct research exposure to some of the key problems concerning the role of politics, power and the state in the processes and promotion of development.

Development studies has also been shaped by the rise and fall of different theoretical schools, which have been usefully surveyed elsewhere (for example, see Streeten, 1977; Hirschman, 1981; Preston, 1982; Griffin and Gurley, 1985; Lehmann, 1986). Grossly simplified, these schools might be summarized in the following ways.

Classical Marxism

Submerged for much of the post-war period by the hegemony of the other schools discussed below, classical Marxism in fact represents an alternative model of 'modernization'. The approach can be traced to Marx's fundamental recognition of the historically progressive role of capitalism and, hence, to aspects of colonialism and imperialism as an extension of it. It is expressed in his observation that 'The country that is more developed industrially only shows to the less developed, the image of its own future' (Marx 1976: 91), in his references to the 'idiocy of rural life' (Marx, 1958b: 38), and to his dismissive accounts of the political potential of the French peasantry (Marx, 1958b). But it is especially clear in his essays on India and his savaging therein of the '. . . undignified, stagnatory and vegetative life' of traditional rural society and regimes of 'oriental despotism' which '. . . restrained the human mind, making it the unresisting tool of superstition . . . depriving it of all grandeur and historical energies . . .' (Marx, 1969: 94). No North American modernizer ever excoriated traditional society for being such a brake on human progress and development as did Marx. Understandably uncomfortable for contemporary radicals, and greatly ignored, the essence of this view was temporarily drowned in the ideological wave of fervent 'Third Worldism' and associated relativism which engulfed the left from the 1950s (Harris, 1986; Callinicos, 1987). But in the present decade there are signs that the fundamental postulates of this view are being retrieved, elaborated and applied (Warren, 1980: Kitching, 1982 and 1987; Hyden, 1985; Sender and Smith, 1986; Lubeck, 1987).

Modernization Theory

This had diverse antecedents in nineteenth-century evolutionary theory, in British structural–functionalist anthropology and in the sociological theories of Talcott Parsons. Like classical Marxism before it, modernization theory focused on the largely internal 'obstacles' to development and the mainly external items (capital, technology, skills, institutions, education, values and ideologies) which represented the essence of 'modernity' and whose introduction might transform 'traditional' societies into 'modern' ones, on largely Western models (Almond, 1960). It underplayed the role of politics and the state in promoting socioeconomic development and spawned a substantial literature which was influential in the USA (Huntington and Dominguez, 1975; Kohli, 1986). However, it had less direct impact in the UK, outside economics, being criticized for being naive, teleological, optimistic, mechanistic and often imperialistic (Frank, 1969; O'Brien, 1972; Tipps, 1973).

The Social–Democratic 'Development Consensus' of the 1960s and 1970s.

In so far as one can identify and people such a broad category as this, it has its roots in what Seers called 'colonial economics' (1979b: 707) which lay at the heart of development economics which was in turn profoundly influenced by Keynesian concerns. It questioned the applicability of conventional economic theory and policy to the problems of Third World development and placed strong emphasis on the role of states and especially of planning (Robertson, 1984; Brett, 1987). There were also roots in the study and practice of colonial administration (Hailey, 1957). The analysis of politics and development in the Third World was also influenced by the long tradition in the study of political history, institutions and theory in the UK (Leys, 1969) where, from the 1950s, as elsewhere in Western Europe, it was more open to Marxist (or at least socialist) ideas as these shook themselves free of their frozen identification with the official ideology of the Soviet Union. As such, the 'political' side of the consensus was more descriptive, sometimes constitutional, usually non-theoretical in the grand American tradition, but – politically speaking – came to be often more characteristically anti-imperialist and pro-socialist in the 1960s and after, perhaps because so few traditional 'conservatives' have ever been attracted to the serious study of development.

Dependency and Underdevelopment Theory

Despite its many strands and varieties, this has been a very influential school (Cardoso, 1977). Where both classical Marxists and post-war modernizers asserted the progressive character of capitalist expansion and the West in world history, theorists of dependency and underdevelopment, both neo-Marxist and non-Marxist, asserted the opposite. In one way or another, they countered, the primary causes of underdevelopment, and the main problems in overcoming it, lay in the structure of domination originating and expressed in the unequal historical and contemporary economic, political and social relations between the 'core' capitalist countries and the ex-colonial 'periphery'. With roots in Latin American 'structuralism' (Prebisch, 1962; Furtado, 1964), and partially prefigured in the work of Paul Baran (1957), the main sources and impetus of this approach were in Latin American studies (Frank, 1969; Cardoso and Faletto, 1979; dos Santos, 1970, 1973), but it spread to African and Asian studies (Rodney, 1972; Harris, 1975; Bagchi, 1982). It overlapped and merged with theories of the 'world system', 'core–periphery' relations and 'unequal exchange' associated with the work of Immanuel Wallerstein (1974; 1979), Samir Amin (1977) and A. Emmanuel (1972). Subject to mounting criticism in the 1970s, but also refined and modified in useful ways, dependency theory is now much more heterogeneous and less influential as a general explanation of underdevelopment than it was (Lall, 1975; Amsden, 1979; Palma, 1981; Barrett and Whyte, 1982).

Neoclassical Political Economy

Finally, the 1980s has seen a resurgence of neoclassical theory in political economy with a direct impact on all disciplines in the social sciences and development studies, especially in policy circles under Republican and Conservative administrations in Washington and London. Described as a 'counter-revolution' in development theory (Toye, 1987a), its effects on policy have, for the moment, been far-reaching, although its practical effects have yet to be evaluated. The so-called 'counter-revolutionaries' have assailed the prevailing assumptions and practices of development economists and much development theory in general (Bauer, 1971; Lal, 1983). They have railed against many aspects of aid (Bauer, 1981), against 'state failure', gross policy errors, inefficiencies and corrupt or incompetent regimes, pointing to the catastrophic effects of all this, for instance, on agriculture (Bates, 1981). They have sought policy means, through the leverage of structural adjustment lending for example, to roll back the state in the Third World (and elsewhere), reduce swollen public sectors, dissolve obese bureaucracies, batter down protectionist barriers, allow 'realistic' prices to surface, promote free trade and to proclaim the intrinsic and developmental superiority of free economic agents responding to material incentives in open markets (Please, 1984; Toye, 1987a).

POLITICS AND DEVELOPMENT STUDIES

In the light of the above, how has the discipline of Politics contributed to the analysis of development?

Initially, it needs to be said that its contribution to our understanding of pervasive politics in the Third World has generally been greater than to our understanding of state politics, in development. Across a fascinating range of subjects, in all continents, political scientists have generated a rich and remarkable literature, which is too numerous to mention here. Such work has included studies of nationalist movements and decolonization processes, both peaceful and violent; of peasant and village politics, both conservative and revolutionary; of the structure and relations of post-independence political parties, of party–state relations and one-party states in the process of 'nation-building' in often severely divided plural societies; of militaries, coups and the politics of civil, secessionist, revolutionary and ethnic wars; of the politics of 'socialist' and non-socialist patterns of land reform, rural development and industrialization; of the blare of new official ideologies ranging from Burmese, African and Islamic socialisms to the populist and corporatist nationalisms of Latin America, and new variants of democratic theory and practice from Ghana to Indonesia; of the character of the post-colonial state and of state-society, state–economy, interstate and state–transnational economic and political relations; or bureaucracies and of the generally corrosive character of corruption, clientelism, factionalism and varieties of personal rulership; of the political sociology of class formation and conflict and the complex relations of class, culture, ethnicity, sex and nationality in the politics of the new states – and much more besides.

Despite these contributions, the study of the politics of development has, in many ways, been extruded from the mainstreams of the discipline of Politics, and perhaps at some cost to both. It would not be too grotesque a caricature to say that many mainstream political scientists regard the politics of development as not only an exotic specialism, but almost as a separate (and perhaps even dubious) field beyond the discipline, with its own language, preoccupations, journals and conferences. As a simple illustration of this one can point to the fact that less than 5 per cent of all articles since 1967 in the major UK journal of Politics, *Political Studies* concerned anything remotely to do with the politics of Third World development. The figure for the *British Journal of Political Science* (founded in 1971) is even lower. The special twenty-fifth Anniversary Issue of *Political Studies* in 1975 made no mention of developmental questions at all, apart from a brief comment by Norman Chester that area studies (and international relations) could be '. . . undertaken by those without any basic training in politics and government and in any case they tend to take such people away from the core of our subject' (Chester, 1975: 42). Thus the advances achieved in the areas mentioned above have, in general, neither been assimilated into the fundamental concerns of the discipline of Politics nor been used to expand them. Why?

It may in part be explained by the understandable emigration of developmentally interested political scientists into area studies and away from what Michael Oakeshott (1981) once described as the 'unimaginable dreariness' of the institutional study of politics that characterized the discipline in the 1950s, at least in the UK. Indeed, it was not only dreary but very parochial and limited in comparative reach, providing little basis for the study of either Third World politics or the politics of development anywhere. Even today, the systematic study of comparative politics is not a major teaching or research strength in British universities; so it is hardly surprising that both American and British political scientists with Third World interests (but in very different ways) turned outwards for methods and concepts in sociology and especially anthropology (and only much later economics) in order to grapple comparatively with the fluid and less clearly patterned currents of politics in the Third World (Almond, 1960: 4; Vincent, 1969; Balandier, 1970).

But did this embrace with interdisciplinary area studies involve a loss of identity for political scientists? Was there, for us, a blurring of focus and a drift away from some of the fundamental questions to do with the role of power, politics and the state (and especially state politics) in development? Did a further diaspora of regional and micro specialisms then occur as people branched out into fascinating but diverse research? Was there not, also, an absence of clear, developmentally focused research priorities for Politics in often hastily assembled development studies programmes and in often largely unchartered areas (at least for non-Third World political scientists)? In the early 1970s the British Social Science Research Council's 'Development Studies Panel' found that little of the UK political science research in the Third World was developmentally oriented (SSRC, 1972). Perhaps all this was the result of unresolved dilemmas such as: should our work contribute to the general expansion of knowledge in the area studies tradition? Should it seek to extend the range and grasp of comparative politics (but if so, through which frameworks)? Or should it focus more directly on the role of politics, and especially state politics, in advancing or hindering development? Even when these questions were asked, they were seldom answered. No clear theories of the politics of development thus emerged.

Nonetheless, political scientists produced fascinating studies on many aspects of pervasive politics and indeed sometimes state politics as well, for all the areas mentioned above. But until the 1980s, there were neither frameworks nor priorities which systematically tied the analysis of pervasive or state politics to explicitly developmental problems or, especially, the comparative analysis of the developmental capacities and roles of states and the far-reaching policy implications of these. Too often, the role of the state was either taken for granted (in its planning and developmental responsibilities) or it was dismissed (as decadent or the creature of other class forces). Not uncommonly, the prevailing tone of much writing seemed concerned with allocating blame (internal and external) for developmental failure rather than with exploring analytically the mechanisms and interplay of politics, policy and the state which brought about the generally dismal (although occasionally impressive) performances that were recorded. Perhaps, too, in the 1960s and 1970s, political scientists with Third World interests were also buffeted by the high winds of rapidly changing theoretical perspectives, and especially that of dependency theory which tended to divert attention away from internal factors and state politics, by stressing in practice the hegemony of other internal and external socioeconomic forces. And maybe it has also therefore required the passage of time for the very different developmental records of many Third World societies to suggest the centrality of politics and the character of the 'developmental state' as one of the major variables in development.

However, the many case studies and theoretical accounts which emerged in this period now provide a diverse, but rich, set of building blocks, or growth points, for the future. An interesting aspect of many of these is that they converge on problems which are common to *all societies* and not only the Third World. Hence they promise theoretically important unifying possibilities in Politics, which could help to bring the study of the politics of development back into mainstream concerns, and thus to expand the latter decisively.

Put simply, the integrative flow of world economic and political history has done two things. First, it has helped to undermine residual notions that there might be two entirely distinct 'politics of development' in the developing and developed worlds; second, it has strengthened the claims for a single or 'mono' discipline of Politics – something also being debated in economics (Seers, 1963; Hirschman, 1981; Streeten, 1983; Lipton, 1987). In short, while serving to underline the necessity of interdisciplinary work in development studies, it has also emphasized the crucial contribution which the discipline of Politics can make to the understanding and promotion of development, but only by sharpening its focus on the role of politics and especially state politics in the complex of processes involved. What might these building blocks for the future be?

BUILDING BLOCKS

First, from 'classical' Marxist engagements with development problems has come the important reminder to both dependency theory and the idealism of contemporary Third Worldism that there is no socialist path to socialism. Furthermore, in the short term, as Marx argued, capital accumulation seems inescapably contradictory and brutally disruptive in its long-term 'progressive' character, and capitalist development has also taken a variety of '. . . forms and sequences . . . in the necessarily uneven development of the world system' (Kitching, 1987: 43). More central still, scholars in (or influenced by) this Marxist tradition have stressed that the processes of systematic capital accumulation and industrialization in the modern world have generally occurred most successfully and quickly where states and bureaucratic systems, whether officially socialist or capitalist, have been capable of authoritative, far-reaching and generally effective direction of, or intervention in, the economy. They have done this with or without the cooperation of a national or international bourgeoisie, as the modern histories of Japan, the USSR, the People's Republic of China and South Korea all appear graphically to illustrate (Moore, 1966; Trimberger, 1978; Skocpol, 1979; Johnson, 1982; White, 1984; White and Wade, 1985). And they have done so, almost without exception, with little regard for conventional liberal or socialist conceptions of human rights or civil liberties.

Second, while it is still unfashionable to say this, it is certainly now appropriate to commence a cautious re-evaluation of some insights and implications of modernization theory. There are signs that, knowingly or unknowingly, this is already happening (Hyden, 1985; Booth, 1987; Evans, 1987; Crook, 1988; *IDS Bulletin*, October 1988). Significantly, these contributions focus on the distinctive character and capability of developmental states, their bureaucratic apparatuses and technical reach, and draw strength from Marxist, Weberian and neoclassical perspectives. I do not, of course, refer to the evolutionism of modernization theory nor its idealized identification of 'modernity', 'Westernization' and liberal--democratic capitalism on a simplistic historical continuum. Rather, I refer to the concern of modernization theory for a wide range of character-istics which seem to have been critical factors in the achievements to date of at least some of the more successful developmental states mentioned above, nominally capitalist or socialist, and also historical states of which perhaps the Song dynasty in China (960–1279) would appear to be an interesting example (Bray, 1986). These characteristics in the broad 'political culture' of societies include the degree of private and public role differentiation; the ethos, structure, autonomy and accountability of bureaucratic institutions; and the extent and legitimacy of state authority, its effective reach, technical grasp and general probity. It is worth elaborating this further, if only because the received hostility to moderni-zation theory has itself become like a cage, preventing a more reflective and detached re-evaluation.

While modernization theorists tended to see the development of these characteristics as a consequence of the 'modernizing' process, there now seems strong evidence for seeing them as necessary conditions for effective development. Recent administrative reforms and efforts at 'political modernization' in China illustrate this precisely. There, efforts are being made to promote the depoliticization of the bureaucracy, the separation of the political and economic spheres, the extension of individual and corporate rights and greater measures of accountability in the adminis-tration (White, 1987; 1988).

In short, on grounds of efficiency, both left and right, socialists and liberals, seem agreed about the relentlessly negative effects on develop-ment of varieties of patronage, clientelism, nepotism, factionalism, neo-patrimonialism, 'sultanism', politicization, personal rule, the 'economy of affection' and barely concealed incompetence and 'corruption' in many (but not only) Third World states and their administrative systems (Sobhan, 1979; Jackson and Rosberg, 1982; Bardhan, 1984; Clapham, 1985; Hyden, 1985; Manor, 1987). And on broader moral or political grounds of equity, both liberals and socialists in and outside the Third World abhor the denial of open, secular and democratic processes which so much of patronage politics involves in practice.

Quite simply, all forms of patronage politics and administration involve a systematic blurring of the boundaries between the private and the public in the government and administration of developing societies, or '. . . the privatization of public affairs' (Medard, 1982: 184). More explicitly referring to the Zaïrean state as an extreme example of the syndrome, one writer described it as having become '. . . nothing more than an organization of profiteers whose shared goal was the use of public office for personal enrichment' (Sandbrook, 1985: 112). Modernization theorists (of left or right) would correctly identify all this as the pathological consequence of endemic role diffuseness, and the absence of universalistic and achievement criteria in the politics of decision-making and the allocation of resources.

The central point is that, whatever other internal and external problems and constraints may face a developing society (and there are many), such practices simply sap developmental efforts and preempt the emergence of a developmental state, however minimalist. As modernization theorists might be inclined to point out in the language of ascription/achievement or particularism/universalism and role diffuseness/specificity, such practices remain entrenched in the economic structure, political culture and institutional arrangements of such societies. So long as they do, developmental efforts requiring any significant degree of autonomous state involvement will be thwarted. What we therefore need to know is much more about those factors which may promote or contain the influence of such practices under given conditions and what kinds of political, institutional and administrative reforms are possible which could act to limit their effects (*IDS Bulletin*, October 1988). And perhaps certain aspects of modernization theory would not be a bad starting point, though only one of many.

Third, some of the more deterministic versions of dependency theory engendered a debilitating and pessimistic impossibilism concerning the prospects for, and politics of, national development. They could be read as implying that probably only global revolution (and little less than national revolution) would bring about any effective development in the Third World and elsewhere (Pratt, 1973; Wallerstein, 1979). But national, and certainly international, revolution cannot be had to order and, in any event, as it became apparent from the 1970s onwards that very different developmental records were being attained by different societies, productive debates occurred within the dependency approach. There followed important modifications of it in some path-breaking case studies on, for example, 'associated dependent development' and 'dependent development' in Latin America – especially Brazil (Cardoso, 1973; Evans, 1979) and Kenya (Leys, 1975, 1978, 1980; Kaplinsky, 1980) – focusing essentially on the triadic relations between local capital, the state and foreign capital. These debates and theoretical developments have been extended to other countries, such as Nigeria (Biersteker, 1987; Forrest,

1987; Beckman, 1988) and Korea (Lim, 1985). So, despite its many limitations, dependency theory has been vitally important in emphasizing the nature and legacies of historical and structural forms of domination between industrial and non-industrial societies and the implications these transnational economic and political relations may have for the prospects of autonomous development under the auspices of a developmental state.

Fourth, the resurgence of neoclassical theory and its extension into political analysis, and especially the 'new political economy' of development (Staniland, 1985), has perhaps provided the sharpest of spurs for rethinking a whole range of developmental issues, especially with respect to the function and capacity of the state. Some of the critical studies in this tradition – significantly concerning both the developed and developing world – have been both influential and valuable in their own right (Popkin, 1979; Bates, 1981; Olson, 1982), and I suggest three major points arising from them.

The first point is broadly methodological. As some classical Marxists have done from a different perspective, the new political economists have emphasized the necessity of a unified approach to the explanation of politics (political economy), one whose fundamental postulates and broad analytical approaches may be applied in *all* societies. Their position rests on the assumption that, despite apparently baffling differences in their economic, cultural, institutional and ideological contexts and practices, and despite wide differences in effective choice and opportunity, individuals – wherever they are – protect and promote their own interests, however they define these. Generally speaking, people will choose those courses of action, support those policies, respond to those incentives and engage in such politics which they judge will help to secure those preferences, whether they are Chicago trade unionists or Vietnamese peasants. To ignore this in development theory and practice would be folly.

From this flows the second and substantive contribution of neoclassical political economy. The political trick, developmentally, must therefore be to design policies and establish institutions so that '. . . individual behaviour will further the interests of the group, small or large, local or national . . .'; and to '. . . construct a political order that will channel the self-serving behaviour of participants towards the common good' (Buchanan, 1978: 17). Hence monopolies of economic or political economic power (private or public), cultural practices or state policies which crush, coerce, fail to encourage or do not reward the creative energy of individuals (or groups) upon which the collective good depends, may not only turn out to be more expensive in the long run, but will meet with resistance, avoidance and withdrawal (as in the extreme case of Soviet agricultural policy, 1929–34, or the less extreme case of Tanzanian rural development programmes in the 1970s), and will also endanger and slow down development. Neoclassical theorists blame simplistic statist and planning obsessions in development theory and practice and point to often suffocating public sectors which have served to generate monopolistic and unaccountable bureaucracies accumulating their own vested interests, sometimes in alliance with other classes, such that they are now often incapable of implementing developmental reform, least of all their own. They therefore diagnose a general epidemic of 'state failure' and look to the forces of competition, the market, greater accountability and participation in both private and public sectors for the antidote, a view which is in some respects consistent with certain aspects of contemporary democratic theory (Dahl, 1985).

Third, what these neoclassical political economists have in fact forced on to the analytical and policy agenda is not the 'either-or' question of 'markets or states'. That, of course, is too simplistic, because their sometimes rather extreme dismissal of states as *necessarily* incompetent and corrupt has simply failed to recognize the more important point that while some states (both historical and modern) have been like that, others (the effective developmental states) have not. Likewise, whatever it may have done for growth, the unleashing of market forces has commonly produced a grossly uneven developmental effect, to say the least. The really significant question for Politics, therefore, concerns the ways in which different relations of markets and states have combined to advance or impede development at different times and, crucially, the role of state politics in mediating and organizing those relations. This is widely recognized by many outside the school (Bardhan, 1984; Rubin, 1985; Sandbrook, 1985; Manor, 1987).

Finally, then, it is clear that all these building blocks contribute, implicitly or explicitly, to a reconsideration of the character, role and capability of the state in development, whether it is nominally on the 'left' or 'right'. They concern especially questions to do with its historical provenance, economic environment, cultural context and constitutional structure; its social basis, legitimacy and authority; the internal and external constraints on it; its political accountability, will and relative autonomy; its involvement in, and relations with, the market; and its technical grasp and administrative competence in pursuit of clearly defined developmental goals.

These concerns incorporate, but also reach beyond an older tradition in the study of the Third World state (for instance, Myrdal, 1968; Alavi, 1972; O'Donnell, 1973; Saul, 1974; Fitzgerald, 1976; Collier, 1979). They also merge with new developments in the analysis of the state–economy relationship in mainstream Politics and Political Sociology, and also the question of 'relative autonomy', which has generated a burgeoning literature for both industrial and Third World societies (Poulantzas, 1973; Stepan, 1978, 1985; Nordlinger, 1981; Hamilton, 1982; Jessop, 1982; Evans *et al.*, 1985; Hall, 1986; Kohli, 1987).

CONCLUSIONS

What, briefly, might be some of the important areas for future work?

Political scientists with general Third World interests in either the area studies or comparative politics traditions will, of course, want to continue the rich and varied work carried out in the spheres of both pervasive and state politics. But those with more precise developmental concerns may want to focus sharper attention around a narrower band of issues, of which there are many. But, given the urgency of helping to eliminate the worst enduring features of poverty, hunger, disease and the general unpredictability of existence for the majority of people in the Third World, I think that there are three central problems which need special attention and which are the proper and specialist concern of the discipline of Politics. They are:

1. the appropriate balance between state and market at different times in developmental processes and sequences; the ways in which any given balance between state and market may advance or frustrate development; and especially the role and capacity of state politics in shaping this;
2. the prospects for national development in an increasingly international economy and the role and capacity of states in mediating between sub-national, national and international interests; and
3. the tensions between developmental and democratic priorities and processes at different times and in different circumstances and, again, the role of the state in this.

These points require elaboration.

First, despite the current fashion for promoting competitive market forces in more and more areas of economic and social life everywhere, the history of post-war Third World development makes it quite clear that the role of the state and especially a 'developmental state' is absolutely central, as are its relations with the private sectors (internal and external) and other states. In almost every major area of developmental concern – land reform, agrarian change, capital accumulation, education, the 'informal sector', relations with foreign capital and aid donors, for example – the role of the state is central. But few societies in the Third World seem to have been able to generate and sustain 'developmental states' which are capable of acting decisively in these and other areas.

A major task for Politics, therefore, is the detailed comparative analysis of the historical and contemporary forms of this kind of state under different regimes and international environments. Some valuable preliminary comparative work has been done, some of the best of it by historical and political sociologists (Myrdal, 1968; Skocpol, 1979; Trimberger, 1978; White, 1984; White and Wade, 1985; Evans *et al.*, 1985; Evans, 1987), but not enough of this focuses specifically on the conditions for, and forms of, developmental states. The way forward will therefore require detailed comparative work across space and time.

Second, such work will have important policy implications, since it will also need to explore comparatively the compatibility between the capability or given state and administrative systems, on the one hand, and certain developmental policy objectives on the other. It may be that some states, at certain times, are incapable or relatively less capable of pursuing and securing certain kinds of developmental policy objective and, hence, perhaps 'state capacity' should be seen as a significant variable in the formulation of development policy.

Third, within this broad framework of priorities, there is need for comparative research into specific institutional innovations in rules, cultures and procedures at all levels in public and private administrative systems. This will need to be sensitive to the characteristics and traditions of different societies and yet still seek to combine developmental drive with accountability, flexibility with purpose, and incentives with stability.

In the broader sphere of pervasive politics (but with profound implications for the state politics of development), more comparative studies are needed of the political sociology of class formation and especially the complicated patterns in which identities of class, caste, culture, ethnicity, nationality, sex, region and religion work with and against each other, and their effects on development. It will be valuable to revisit some of the sophisticated work done on pluralism in the late 1960s and early 1970s. Specifically, we need to know how these social and political forces act to shape the structure and character of developmental states and how in practice they influence the formation, implementation and impact of development policy. In short, what are the historical, cultural and social conditions for the emergence of developmental states? And, conversely, what have been the objectives and effects of the policies of such states on class formation and politics?

As we approach the turn of the century, the struggle for development against the offensiveness of poverty and oppression is no less urgent than it was 30 or 100 years ago. Few people still believe that it will be possible to build a New Jerusalem in the tropics but, if first best solutions remain beyond reach, the search must be for those means which can yield effective second, or even third, best ones.

The forms and possibilities of both pervasive and state politics, the structures of public power and the character and capacity of the state are as central to this as they are to the discipline of Politics. By pursuing these and other issues in research and teaching, political scientists will both contribute to the study and promotion of development, and also help to bring these questions firmly back into the mainstreams of the discipline of Politics. This is where they belong as part of the great tradition of enquiry into the fundamental issue of all politics in its inextricable and interdisciplinary involvement in the economic and social affairs of societies: how, as human beings, do we live together and how might we do so, while seeking simultaneously to promote the collective welfare of all and the individual fulfilment and potential of each? The practical answer to this question anywhere will lie in devising appropriate and necessarily shifting strategic balances between the public and the private, the state and the market, structure and freedom, rights and responsibilities, planning and enterprise, constraint and liberty. That is politics; that is development.

NOTES

I am very grateful to David Held, Chris Allen and Isabelle van Notten for their valuable comments on an early draft of this chapter, although the responsibility for its argument remains my own.
1. The precise origin of the term 'developmental state' is not clear, but the idea has been around in different forms for a while. Myrdal used the idea of a 'strong' or 'hard' state in his work on India; O'Donnell elaborated the idea of the 'bureaucratic authoritarian' regime for some Latin American societies; White refers to the role of the 'pervasive' state in socialist industrialization; and Chalmers Johnson uses the term 'developmental state' explicitly in his account of MITI in Japan, as have a number of other social scientists discussing East Asia and Africa (Myrdal, 1968; O'Donnell, 1973; White, 1984; Johnson, 1982; *IDS Bulletin*, April 1984). The idea does not refer simply to an 'authoritarian' state which may generate little developmental momentum, such as Haiti under the Duvaliers or Zaïre under Mobutu. See also Deyo (1987).
2. In an important survey of Third World socialist industrialization, Gordon White uses the term 'pervasive' to refer to a pattern of measures taken by a state to intervene actively and directly in '. . . processes of industrial investment, production and circulation, eliminating or circumscribing the autonomy of economic actors' (White, 1984: 100). I use the term in a different sense here.
3. A good instance of the influence of Cold War politics on development theory is reported by Howard Wiarda. A seminar series at Harvard in the early 1980s was attended by some members of the original SSRC Committee on Comparative Politics (USA) which promoted a flood of modernization literature in the 1960s. Some of them agreed that one of their objectives in promoting theories of political development had been to counter the appeal of Marxism in developing countries (Wiarda, 1985: 16).

REFERENCES

Alavi, H. (1972), 'The state in post-colonial societies: Pakistan and Bangladesh', *New Left Review,* **74**, July–August.

Almond, G. A. (1960), 'A functional approach to comparative politics' in G. A. Almond and J. S. Coleman (eds), *The Politics of the Developing Areas* (Princeton, New Jersey, Princeton University Press).

Amin, S. (1977), *Imperialism and Unequal Development* (Brighton, Harvester).

Amsden, A. (1979), 'Taiwan's economic history: a case of étatisme and a challenge to dependency theory', *Modern China* **5(3)**.

Anglade, C. and Fortin, C. (1987), 'The role of the state in Latin America's strategic options', *CEPAL Review,* **31**, April.

Apter, D. (1980), 'The passing of development studies', *Government and Opposition,* **15(3–34)**, Summer–Autumn.

Bagchi, A. K. (1982), *The Political Economy of Development* (Cambridge, Cambridge University Press).

Balandier, G. (1970), *Political Anthropology* (London, Allen Lane).

Baran, P. A. (1957), *The Political Economy of Growth* (New York, Monthly Review Press).

Bardhan, P. (1984), *The Political Economy of Development in India* (Oxford, Basil Blackwell).

Barrett, R. E. and Whyte, K. M. (1982), 'Dependency theory and Taiwan: analysis of a deviant case', *American Journal of Sociology* **87(5)**, March.

Bates, R. C. (1981), *Markets and States in Tropical Africa* (Berkeley, University of California Press).

Bauer, P. T. (1971), *Dissent on Development* (London, Weidenfeld and Nicholson).

Bauer, P. T. (1981), *Equality, the Third World and Economic Delusion* (London, Methuen).

Beckmann, E. (1988), 'The post-colonial state: crisis and reconstruction', *IDS Bulletin* **19(4)**.

Biersteker, T. J. (1987), 'Indigenization and the Nigerian bourgeoisie: dependent development in an African context' in Paul M. Lubeck (ed.), *The African Bourgeoisie* (Boulder, Lynne Rienner).

Booth, D. (1987), 'Alternatives in the restructuring of state–society relations: research issues for tropical Africa', *IDS Bulletin* **18(4)** October.

Bray, F. (1986), *The Rice Economies. Technology and Development in Asian Societies* (Oxford, Basil Blackwell).

Brett, E. A. (1987), 'States, markets and private power in the developing world: problems and possibilities', *IDS Bulletin,* **18(3)**, July.

Buchanan, J. (1978), 'From private preferences to public philosophy: the development of public choice' in J. Buchanan *et al. The Economics of Politics* (London, Institute of Economic Affairs).

Callinicos, A. (1987), 'Imperialism, capitalism and the state today', *International Socialism,* **2(35)**.

Cardoso, F. H. (1973), 'Associated–dependent development: theoretical and practical implications' in A. Stepan (ed.), *Authoritarian Brazil: Origins, Policies and Future* (New Haven, Yale University Press).

Cardoso, F. H. (1977), 'The consumption of dependency theory in the USA', *Latin American Research Review,* **12(3)**.

Cardoso, F. H. and Faletto, E. (1979), *Dependency and Development in Latin America* (Berkeley, University of California Press, 1979).

Chazan, N. *et al.* (eds) (1988), *Politics and Society in Contemporary Africa* (London, Macmillan).

Chester, N. (1975), 'Political studies in Britain: recollections and comments' *Political Studies,* **23(2–3)**, June–September.

Clapham, C. (1985), *Third World Politics. An Introduction* (London, Croom Helm).

Collier, D. (ed.) (1979), *The New Authoritarianism in Latin America* (Princeton, Princeton University Press).

Croix, G de Ste. (1981), *Class Struggle in the Ancient Greek World* (London, Duckworth).

Crook, R. C. (1988), 'State capacity and agricultural development in post-colonial Africa: the Ivorien case', unpublished paper delivered at Political Studies Association Conference, Plymouth, April.

Dahl, R. A. (1985), *A Preface to Economic Democracy* (Cambridge, Polity).

Deyo, F. C. (1987), 'Introduction' in F. C. Deyo (ed.), *The Political Economy of the New Asian Industrialism* (Ithaca, Cornell University Press).

Dore, R. (1978), *Shinohata. A portrait of a Japanese Village* (New York, Pantheon).

dos Santos, T. (1970), 'The structure of dependence', *American Economic Review* **60(2)**.

dos Santos, T. (1973), 'The crisis of development theory and the problems of dependence in Latin America' in H. Bernstein (ed.), *Underdevelopment and Development* (Harmondsworth, Penguin).

Eisenstadt, S. N. (1966), *Modernization, Protest and Change* (Englewood Cliffs, Prentice-Hall).

Emmanuel, A. (1972), *Unequal Exchange: a study in the imperialism of trade* (New York, Monthly Review Press).

Evans, Peter B. (1979), *Dependent Development* (Princeton, Princeton University Press).

Evans, Peter B. *et al.* (eds) (1985), *Bringing The State Back In* (Cambridge, Cambridge University Press).

Evans, Peter B. (1987), 'Class, state and dependence in East Asia: lessons for Latin America' in F. C. Deyo (ed.), *The Political Economy of the New Asian Industrialism* (Ithaca, Cornell University Press).

Fitzgerald, E. V. K. (1976), *The State and Economic Development: Peru since 1968* (Cambridge, Cambridge University Press).

Forrest, T. (1987), 'State capital, capitalist development and class formation' in Paul M. Lubeck (ed.), *The African Bourgeoisie* (Boulder, Lynne Rienner).

Frank, A. G. (1969), *Latin America: underdevelopment or revolution* (New York, Monthly Review Press).

Furtado, C. (1964), *Development and Underdevelopment: a structural view of the problems of developed and underdeveloped countries* (Berkeley, University of California Press).

Gerschenkron, A. (1962), 'Economic backwardness in historical perspective' in his *Economic Backwardness in Historical Perspective* (Cambridge, Mass., Harvard University Press).

Griffin, K. and Gurley, J. (1985), 'Radical analyses of imperialism, the Third World and the transition to socialism: a survey article', *Journal of Economic Literature* **23(3)**, September.

Hailey, (Lord) (1957), *An African Survey* (Oxford, Oxford University Press).

Hall, P. (1986), *Governing The Economy* (Cambridge, Polity).

Hamilton, N. (1982), *The Limits of State Autonomy* (Princeton, Princeton University Press).

Harris, N. (1986), *The End of the Third World* (London, I. B. Tauris).

Harris, R. (ed.) (1975), *The Political Economy of Africa* (New York, Wiley, 1975).

Herring, R. (1983), *Land To the Tiller, The Political Economy of Agrarian Reform in South Asia* (New Haven, Yale University Press).

Hirschman, A. O. (1981), 'The rise and decline of development economics' in his *Essays in Trespassing. Economics to Politics and Beyond* (Cambridge, Cambridge University Press).

Horowitz, I. L. (1967), *The Rise and Fall of Project Camelot* (Cambridge, Mass., MIT Press).

Huntington, S. P. and Dominguez, J. I. (1975), 'Political development' in F. I. Greenstein and N. Polsby (eds), *Handbook of Political Science*, vol. 3 (Reading, Mass., Addison-Wesley Publishing Company).

Hyden, G. (1985), *No Shortcuts To Progress. African Development Management in Historical Perspective* (London, Heinemann)

IDS Bulletin **9(2)** (December 1977), 'Britain: A case for development?'

IDS Bulletin **15(2)** (April 1984), 'Developmental states in East Asia: capitalist and socialist'.

IDS Bulletin **19(4)**, (October 1988), 'Adjustment and the state: The problem of administrative reform'.

Jackson, R. H. and Rosberg, C. G. (1982), *Personal Rule in Black Africa* (Berkeley, University of California Press).

Jenkins, R. (1979), *The Road to Alto* (London, Pluto).

Jessop, B. (1982), *The Capitalist State* (Oxford, Basil Blackwell).

Johnson, C. (1982), *MITI And The Japanese Economic Miracle* (Stanford, Stanford University Press).

Kaplinsky, R. (1980), 'Capitalist accumulation in the periphery: The Kenyan case re-examined', *Review of African Political Economy,* **17**.

Kitching, G. (1982), *Development and Underdevelopment in Historical Perspective* (London, Methuen).

Kitching, G. (1987), 'The role of a national bourgeoisie in the current phase of capitalist development: some reflections' in Paul M. Lubeck (ed.), *The African Bourgeoisie. Capitalist Development in Nigeria, Kenya and the Ivory Coast* (Boulder, Lynne Rienner, 1987).

Kohli, A. (ed.) (1986), *The State and Development in the Third World* (Princeton, Princeton University Press).

Kohli, A. (1987), *The State and Poverty in India* (Cambridge, Cambridge University Press).

Lal, D. (1983), *The Poverty of Development Economics* (London, Institute of Economic Affairs).

Lall, S. (1975), 'Is "dependence" a useful concept in analysing underdevelopment?', *World Development,* **3(11–12)**, November–December.

Lamb, G. (1987), *Managing Economic Policy Change: Institutional Dimensions*, Discussion Paper 14 (Washington, DC, The World Bank).

Lehmann, D. (1986), *Dependencia: an ideological history*, IDS Discussion Paper 219 (Brighton, Institute of Development Studies).

Leftwich, A. (1983), *Redefining Politics: People, Resources and Power* (London,

Methuen).

Leys, C. (1969), 'Introduction' in C. Leys (ed.), *Politics and Change in Developing Countries* (Cambridge, Cambridge University Press).

Leys, C. (1975), *Underdevelopment in Kenya* (London, Heinemann).

Leys, C. (1978), 'Capital accumulation, class-formation and dependency: the significance of the Kenyan case' in R. Miliband and J. Saville (eds), *Socialist Register 1978* (London, Merlin).

Leys, C. (1980), 'What does "dependency" explain?', *Review of Political Economy* (17).

Lim, H. C. (1985), *Dependent Development in Korea, 1963–1979* (Seoul, Seoul National University Press).

Lipton, M. (1987), 'Development studies: findings, frontiers and fights', *World Development* 15(4).

Lubeck, P. M. (ed.) (1987), *The African Bourgeoisie. Capitalist Development in Nigeria, Kenya and the Ivory Coast* (Boulder, Lynne Rienner).

Manor, J. (October, 1987) 'Tried, then abandoned: economic liberalization in India', *IDS Bulletin,* 18(4).

Marx, K. and Engels, F. (1958a), 'The Communist Manifesto' (1848), in *Selected Works*, vol. 1 (Moscow, Foreign Languages Publishing House).

Marx, K. (1958b), 'The Eighteenth Brumaire of Louis Bonaparte', (1852) in *Selected Works*, vol. 1 (Moscow, Foreign Languages Publishing House).

Marx, K. (1969), 'British Rule in India' (1853) in *Karl Marx on Colonialism and Modernization* edited by S. Avineri (New York, Doubleday).

Marx, K. (1976), *Capital,* vol I (Harmondsworth, Penguin).

Marx, K. (1977), *Selected Writings* edited by D. McLellan (Oxford, Oxford University Press).

Medard, J-F. (1982), 'The underdeveloped state in tropical Africa: political clientelism or neo-patrimonialism?' in C. Clapham (ed.), *Private Patronage and Public Power* (London, Pinter, 1982).

Migdal, J. (1983), 'Studying the politics of development and change: the state of the art' in Ada Finifter (ed.), *Political Science. The State of the Discipline* (Washington, DC, American Political Science Association).

Moore, B. (1966), *Social Origins of Dictatorship and Democracy* (Boston, Beacon Press).

Myrdal, G. (1968), *Asian Drama* (Harmondsworth, Penguin).

Myrdal, G. (1970), 'The "soft state" in underdeveloped countries' in P. Streeten (ed.), *Unfashionable Economics: essays in honour of Lord Balogh* (London, Weidenfeld).

Oakeshott, M. (1981), 'The study of politics in a university' (1961) in his *Rationalism in Politics and Other Essays* (London, Methuen).

Nordlinger, E. A. (1981), *On the Autonomy of the Democratic State* (Cambridge, Mass., Harvard University Press).

O'Brien, D. C. (1972), 'Modernization, order and the erosion of a democratic ideal', *Journal of Development Studies* 8(3), July.

O'Donnell, G. A. (1973), *Modernization and Bureaucratic Authoritarianism: studies in South American politics* (Berkeley, University of California Press, 1973).

Olson, M. (1982), *The Rise and Fall of Nations* (New Haven, Yale University Press).

Palma, G. (1981), 'Dependency and development: a critical overview' in D. Seers (ed.), *Dependency Theory. A Critical Re-assessment* (London, Pinter).

Please, S. (1984), *The Hobbled Giant. Essays on The World Bank* (Boulder, Westview Press).

Poulantzas, N. (1973), *Political Power and Social Classes* (London, New Left Books).

Popkin, S. (1979), *The Rational Peasant. The Political Economy of Rural Society in Vietnam* (Berkeley, University of California Press).

Pratt, R. B. (1973), 'The underdeveloped political science of development', *Studies in Comparative International Development, 8*.

Prebisch, R. (1962), 'The economic development of Latin America', *Economic Bulletin for Latin America, 7(1)*.

Preston, P. W. (1982), *Theories of Development* (London, Routledge and Kegan Paul).

Robertson, A. F. (1984), *People and the State. An Anthropology of Planned Development* (Cambridge, Cambridge University Press).

Rodney, W. (1972), *How Europe Underdeveloped Africa* (London, Bogle-L'Ouverture).

Rostow, W. W. (1962), *The Stages of Economic Growth* (Cambridge, Cambridge University Press).

Rubin, B. (1985), 'Economic liberalization and the Indian state', *Third World Quarterly, 7(4)*, October.

Sandbrook, R. (1985), *The Politics of Africa's Economic Stagnation* (Cambridge, Cambridge University Press).

Saul, J. S. (1974), 'The state in post-colonial societies: Tanzania' in R. Miliband and J. Saville (eds), *The Socialist Register, 1974* (London, Merlin).

Schaffer, B. B. and Lamb, G. (1981), *Can Equity Be Organized?* (Farnborough, Gower).

Seers, D. (1963), 'The limitations of the special case', *Bulletin of the Oxford Institute of Economics and Statistics, 25(2)*, May.

Seers, D. (1979a), 'The meaning of development' in David Lehmann, (ed.) *Development Theory. Four Critical Case Studies* (London, Cass).

Seers, D. (1979b), 'The birth, life and death of development economics', *Development and Change, 10*.

Sen, A. (1988), 'Development: Which way now?' in C. K. Wilber (ed.), *The Political Economy of Development and Underdevelopment* (4th edn.), (New York, Random House).

Sender. J. and Smith, S. (1986), *The Development of Capitalism in Africa* (London, Methuen, 1986).

Skocpol, T. (1979), *States and Social Revolutions* (Cambridge, Cambrige University Press).

Sobhan, R. (1979), 'Perspectives on Corruption', mimeo (Bergen), July.

SSRC (Social Science Research Council) (1972), *Development Studies at British Universities and Research Institutes*, Report of SSRC Development Studies Panel, 1970–72, chaired by Dr E. R. Leach (London, SSRC).

Staniland, M. (1985), *What is Political Economy?* (New Haven, Yale University Press).

Stepan, A. (1978), *The State and Society: Peru in comparative perspective* (Princeton, Princeton University Press).

Stepan, A. (1985), 'State power and the strengths of civil society in the southern cone of Latin America' in P. B. Evans *et al.* (eds), *Bringing the State Back In*

(Cambridge, Cambridge University Press).

Streeten, P. (1977), 'Development ideas in historical perspective' in K. M. Hill (ed.), *Toward a New Strategy for Development*, Rothko Chapel Colloquium (New York, Pergamon Press).

Streeten, P. (1983), *Development Dichotomies*, IDS Discussion Paper 187 (Brighton, Institute of Development Studies, 1983).

Supple, B. (1973), 'The state and the industrial revolution' in C. Cipolla (ed.), *The Fontana Economic History of Europe III* (London, Collins/Fontana).

Tipps, D. C. (1973), 'Modernization theory and the comparative study of societies: a critical perspective', *Comparative Studies in Society and History,* **15(2)**.

Toye, J. (1987a), *Dilemmas of Development* (Oxford, Basil Blackwell).

Toye, J. (1987b), 'Development studies and change in contemporary Britain', *World Development,* **15(4)**.

Trimberger, E. K. (1977), 'State power and modes of production: implications of the Japanese transition to capitalism', *Insurgent Sociologist,* **7**, Spring.

Trimberger, E. K. (1978), *Revolution From Above: military bureaucrats in Japan, Turkey, Egypt and Peru* (New Brunswick, NJ., Transaction Books).

Vincent, J. (1969), 'Anthropology and political development' in C. Leys (ed.), *Politics amd Change in Developing Countries* (Cambridge, Cambridge University Press).

Wallerstein, I. (1974), *The Modern World System* (New York, Academic Press).

Wallerstein, I. (1979), *The Capitalist World Economy* (Cambridge, Cambridge University Press).

Warren, B. (1980), *Imperialism. Pioneer of Capitalism* (London, Verso, 1980)

Watts, M. (1983), *Silent Violence: food, famine and peasantry in northern Nigeria* (Berkeley, University of California Press).

White, G. (1984), 'Developmental states and socialist industrialization in the Third World', *Journal of Development Studies,* **21(1)**, October.

White, G. (1987), 'The Leninist state under threat? The politics of economic reform in China', *IDS Bulletin,* **18(4)**, October.

White, G. (1988), 'Administrative reforms in post-Mao China', *IDS Bulletin,* **19(4)**, October.

White, G. and Wade, R. (eds.) (1985), *Developmental States in East Asia*, IDS Research Report 16 (Brighton, Institute of Development Studies).

Wiarda, H. J. (ed.) (1985), *New Directions in Comparative Politics* (Boulder, Westview).

7. Public Administration: Lost an Empire, Not Yet Found a Role?

Christopher Hood

INTRODUCTION: TRADITIONAL PUBLIC ADMINISTRATION

Public administration – the study of institutional arrangements for provision of public services[1] – is a subject which has often been declared to be in a condition of chaos and decline. A babel of tongues, a subject in intellectual crisis, a 'cause for discontent' (Ridley, 1972), 'a subject matter in search of a discipline' (Charlesworth, 1968: 2) – these are some of the more polite verdicts on the state of public administration over the past 20 years or so. What I want to suggest is that public administration today is in the position summarized by Dean Acheson's famous comment on Britain after the Second World War – of having lost an empire and not yet found a role (*Oxford Dictionary of Quotations*, 3rd edn. 1979: 1).

Traditional Public Administration

As an intellectual structure, traditional public administration never had the coherence of, say, mainstream economics. It always lacked the properties which make an analytic approach readily teachable and applicable – that is, a distinguishing set of 'hard core' non-falsifiable assumptions (Lakatos, 1970), often linked to some compelling analogy founded in reason and nature, such as the head and the body, thought and action, sun and planets (Bobrow and Dryzek, 1987: 10; Douglas, 1987). Within public administration, there are several rather different mainstream traditions: for example, a Continental European tradition focusing on the legal analysis of the use of public power, a British tradition of pragmatic analysis based mainly on history and philosophy, and an American tradition with more ambitions to science and more fully articulated normative principles.

However, each of these different traditions did have some features in common. Perhaps the nearest that they got to a Lakatosian non-falsifiable 'hard core' was a shared focus on the system of government bureaucracy as the proper starting-point for analysis – particularly public bureaucracy in its 'classic' form as specialized disciplined hierarchies financed by general fund allocations from a stable and productive tax system. In practice, public administration meant government (especially local government) administration (Spann, 1979: 16), and the task of the discipline of public administration was to describe that system and to aim to improve it.

If there was a 'crude analogy' linked to this 'hard core', it is perhaps the ancient and beguiling eighteenth-century image of institutional arrangements as machinery (cf. Parry, 1963: 182), with the implication that public administration was a form of design science, concerned to match a knowledge of properties of materials to an understanding of context, or at least a species of engineering concerned with ways of keeping the various different parts of the machine in smooth synchronization.

The elaborative theories that developed within this framework included:

- extensions of J. S. Mill's classic argument in *Representative Government*, that executive government performs best when particular policy responsibilities are monopolized by a single bureau which can be held accountable for their discharge, and where public officials are appointed on professional merit rather than elected or appointed on political criteria (Mill, 1910: 331–46);
- development of the traditional German public law argument (crystallized in Max Weber's famous essay on bureaucracy, first written about 1911 [see Gerth and Mills, 1948: 196–244] but going back almost a century before that) that executive government performs best when it is organized in military style, in single-command hierarchies holding one person responsible at each level of oversight;
- development of Woodrow Wilson's classic (1887) argument that honest government is best achieved by lifetime career service and democratic government is achieved by drawing a line between what counts as 'politics' or policy and what counts as 'administration';
- development of early twentieth-century arguments about good business management practices – systematic specialization of work, reporting and planning techniques for running large bureaucracies under centralized control from the top, good 'human relations' practices (cf. Dunsire, 1973: 87–106).

Outside the USA, however, theoretical elaboration in public administration was fairly limited up to the 1960s, and there was no very distinct methodology which marked the discipline of public administration off from other forms of social inquiry. The normal method of analysis was by historical case study, often based more on shrewd common sense than explicit theory. The overwhelming need was seen to be for basic description of the functioning and evolution of public bureaucracies in a situation when little of the structure was effectively mapped. (Such mapping was particularly important in the UK, lacking as it did any comprehensive set of legal/constitutional principles for the organization of public enterprises: the study of British public administration in large part emerged as the effort to map out the 'chaos' of a century's 'random' development, as in the work of the Webbs.)

What did make public administration, particularly in its US variant, somewhat distinctive from some of the more detached branches of political science was its concern for reform and practical applicability, rather than for explanation and prediction alone. Traditional concerns were with the removal of corruption and dishonesty in administration, with making bureaucracy legally and politically responsible, with drawing effective geographical and functional boundaries between the responsibilities of different public bodies, and with raising bureaucratic competence. The traditional recipe for this consisted, *inter alia*, of extra training, more specialization, a more legal–rational style and removal of jurisdictional overlap between bureaucracies (see Ostrom, 1974).

This traditional structure had some real intellectual weaknesses. But academic public administration commanded respect and some degree of influence over government organization, especially in the USA and in continental Europe. It appeared to have something practical to contribute to public service organization, particularly in an era when bureaucratic growth seemed inexorable and solutions to social problems by the adoption of non–market 'public administration' methods seemed inevitable and were taken for granted.

THE LOST EMPIRE? DEVELOPMENTS OVER THE PAST TWENTY YEARS

Over the past 20 years, the discipline of public administration has changed dramatically, and the traditional approach has become less influential in practice according to observers such as Self (1986). Both changes perhaps reflect the end of post-1945 Keynesian era confidence about social engineering, the onset in the mid-1970s of the first serious attempts since the 1930s to cut back public spending and staffing, and the fact that separate specialisms took the ground and the initiative in particular areas –

such as town planning, public health, social work – leaving public administration to reflect on the generic problems of public service provision.

During the past two decades, at least six different types of theoretical development have taken place. These can briefly be labelled the policy approach, the organizational sociology approach, the neo-Marxist approach to the analysis of the state, the critical or philosophical approach, the public management approach and the public choice approach. I shall discuss the first four quite briefly and devote most space to the latter two, since they have most claim to have captured public administration's former empire.

The Policy Approach

One important departure from traditional public administration orthodoxy since the late 1960s has been the continuing development of the 'policy approach' – an approach which takes generic policy programmes, processes, choices or outcomes as its focus of analysis, not institutional design. The policy approach divides loosely into professional approaches concerned with ways of improving public policy by better analytic techniques – particularly welfare-economic ways of determining 'optimum policy' by a form of cost–benefit analysis – and into academic approaches concerned with better descriptions, explanations and predictions of how the policy process works (see Jenkin, 1978; Bobrow and Dryzek, 1987). Much of the latter kind of work is, in essence, an elaboration of the bureaucratic–politics models expounded by Braybrooke and Lindblom (1963) and Allison (1971). The aim is to try to explain how policy processes work in ways that make fairly conservative assumptions about how altruistic, rational and farsighted the actors in the policy process are. A good recent example of work in this vein is Bendor and Moe's adaptive model of bureaucratic politics (1985 and 1986).

Both of these approaches were showing signs of intellectual fatigue by the 1980s. Professional approaches to improving public policy by better information systems and by cost–benefit techniques had failed to demonstrate dramatic pay-offs, despite the obvious desirability of some touchstone of 'rationality' to guide analysis. The 'better information' approach is notorious for the unreality of its assumptions about human cognitive and group processes; and the cost–benefit approach, despite its ingenuity in approaching revealed preferences, has no effective way of dealing with the interpersonal comparison of utility problem which dogs any utilitarian approach to policy (Self, 1975). The academic 'policy approach' was beginning to come under attack as a glorification of US bureaucratic politics, lacking a dimension of constitutional analysis and providing no real explanation of where policy ideas come from, how they come to be dominant and how they came to be modified (see Sabatier, 1987; Douglas, 1987).

Organizational Sociology

A second development, particularly in the 1970s, came from the then expanding field of organizational sociology, which purported to offer theory explaining the structure and behaviour of all formal organizations. In the eyes of organizational sociologists, traditional public administration is merely 'normative Weberianism', properly to be conceived as part of a larger, more 'scientifically' oriented discipline of organization studies. In the 1960s and 1970s the 'contingency' approach, which sought to relate formal organizational structures to factors such as size, technology and environment by the use of quantitative measures and regression analysis, became the dominant paradigm in organizational sociology (see Blau and Schoenherr, 1971; Kast and Rosenzweig, 1973). This was seen to have important implications for the analysis of public administration (see Pitt and Smith, 1981; Hood and Dunsire, 1981) and found its way into public administration textbooks and research agendas.

Again, by the 1980s, the contingency approach had lost much of its lustre, partly because attempts to link contingencies to structure produced inconclusive results and partly because the conventional methodology of the contingency approach was seen as unsuited for handling symbolic action and organizational power processes (see Pollitt, 1984). The field of organizational theory fragmented into a variety of different approaches – for example, 'corporate culture' approaches, 'population ecology' approaches, 'institutional' approaches and the radical organization theory approach (see Clegg, 1975).

Neo-Marxist State Theory

Traditionally, public administration had little to do with Marxist or neo-Marxist ideas, partly because Marxist theory did not have much to say about state bureaucracy or public service provision, and what it did say was pitched at a very general level. However, the emergence since the Second World War of more detailed attention by neo-Marxists to the structure and functioning of state institutions (cf. Dunleavy and O'Leary, 1987: 236) has laid some foundations for the development of radical and Marxist approaches to public administration (Dunleavy, 1982). An example is Dearlove's (1979) account of the reorganization of British local government in the 1970s as prompted by a 'need' to take control of the local state out of the hands of the working class. Another is Fainstein and Fainstein's (1980) analysis of US bureaucracies, whose successes they attribute to the extent to which there is a 'supportive' class environment and whose failings they attribute to 'a state structure in which the central government cannot direct economic production and does not even control the means of public administration' (Fainstein and Fainstein 1980: 290).

One development which was important to the new approach was Castells' (1977) influential 'collective consumption' analysis of urban public services, with its argument that state provision of services tends to generate collective protest activity in a way that private market provision does not. Another was O'Connor's (1973) 'dual state' thesis, arguing that the state faces contradictory pressures in its role of promoting capital accumulation and of legitimating the social system. Writings such as these generated a new research agenda which led Marxist scholars more closely into the detailed study of public bureaucracies and institutions – the empire once monopolized by traditional public administration.

Marxist analysis has the appeal of seeming to offer an explanation of public service institutions and processes which is deeper than that attempted by traditional public administration, by seeking to put it into a context of 'fundamental' social forces (see Pinch, 1985: 144). The approach, of course, has 'applicability' only in the context of radical politics. There are well known problems of teleology and falsifiability in explanation, and difficulties – familiar to traditional public administration – of matching general theory with the intractable variety and historical specificity of real-life cases.

Critical or Philosophical Approaches

As noted above, traditional public administration in the USA tended to follow Woodrow Wilson's argument that elected politicians should set the goals, and appointed administrators should carry them out. By the 1950s this was widely regarded as an unsatisfactory description of the real-life demarcation of roles between elected officials and administrators, but it nevertheless survived as a normative doctrine for democratic administration (Thompson, 1976: 117). However, by the late 1960s, even that normative doctrine started to come under attack.

One form of attack came from the 'New Public Administration' in the USA in the late 1960s (Marini, 1971). The New Public Administration approach claimed that values such as equity and equality should be paramount in public administration, and that administrators should not simply obey whatever goals elected officials choose to set. The New Public

Administration movement was short-lived and its doctrines soon came under attack as a formula for élitism and a politically irresponsible bureaucracy. However, the traditional formula is a useful starting-point for a philosophical analysis of the moral dilemmas faced by administrators as individuals, and the 1970s were an 'ethics decade' in public administration, according to Kernaghan (1980), with increased input from political philosophy – for example, in the work of Hodgkinson (1978).

The latter approach is less vulnerable to traditionalist criticism than the New Public Administration approach, and in some ways represents a return to an older 'philosophic' strain of public administration (Thomas, 1978). The 'ethics' approach seems to be set to grow, but it nevertheless faces the familiar dilemmas of political philosophy, such as the proliferation of conflicting value bases (notably utility and rights), and the difficulty of bringing 'clean' philosophic analysis to bear on complex linkages of issues (cf. Bobrow and Dryzek, 1987: 112–14).

Public Management

One of the important areas in which traditional public administration has 'lost an empire' is through the increasing acceptance of private business management theory and practice in public organization. Perry and Kraemer (1983) have usefully crystallized this trend by writing of 'public management' as a merger of the normative orientation of the old public administration tradition with the instrumental approach of business management (see also Overman, 1984; Eliasson and Kooiman, 1987).

The public management approach has found readier acceptance among public administration practitioners than any other discussed here, perhaps because the élite ranks in public bureaucracies like to take the private business executive as a role model: for example, Martin (1983: 34ff) has shown from survey evidence that managers in US public bureaucracies are mainly influenced by private-sector management textbooks rather than by traditional public administration texts.

Dominant as the public management approach to public administration may be in practice, it has some inherent weaknesses. First, it might be questioned whether the business-management approach to public administration is really a 'professional' one at all, in so far as a profession involves arrangements for *systematic and cumulative* additions to the knowledge of the profession through *published* writing and research (Wilson, 1968: 30). The managerial approach has not yet provided us with a clear set of principles on which to organize public services, built up from cumulative case study and capable of telling us under what circumstances we should prefer principle A rather than principles B, C or D. This approach has not advanced administrative theory beyond the collection of incompatible proverbs, which Herbert Simon complained about forty years ago (cf. Simon 1958: 20–44). To that extent it has no intellectual superiority over the old orthodoxy in public administration.

Second, the control techniques drawn from the management of large private corporations are notorious for the bizarre and unwanted results which they produce when introduced into public bureaus. This happens because of the observer paradox, the inherent difficulty of transferring private-sector control techniques, and because traditional public bureaus are implicitly built on a quite different management theory. In the management theory of the classic bureau, direction from the top is by direct political oversight, with ever-changing priorities (so there are no stable objectives), and control is effected by a very dense structure of procedural rules buttressed by legal review procedures and constant political scrutiny. In such a structure, there is little room for either middle management 'rights to manage' in resource allocation or 'human relations'. In fact, the traditional public bureau structure is an implicit denial of the idea that for any organization to function there must be a class of managers separated from those who actually do the work, except at top level.

When 'middle managers' are introduced into such a structure, following business management practice, it often turns out that there is not much for them effectively to do (especially when cutbacks are in train) except to interpret and enforce the flow of regulations coming down from the top (Martin, 1983). This is not exactly the heroic decision-making role that managers are assumed to play in the business management textbooks. Indeed, rather than resulting in lower costs and more effective performance, it can easily result in increased frustration among everyone – both the managers themselves and the front-line workers who tend to see middle management as parasitic and self-serving.

The introduction of measured performance controls, linked to individual and organizational rewards, also tends to produce bizarre and counterproductive results. There seems to be an ineluctable Gresham's Law of performance appraisal in public administration, in which the measurable drives out the important, and producing the right statistics for the record means ignoring important, but unmeasured, aspects of service provision. For example, performance-linked pay is not a new concept in public administration (it was used for centuries to reward tax collectors and many other types of officials) but it raises real difficulties of crafting measures that are reliable, objective (rather than based on prejudice or corruptible judgement of superordinates) and valid (particularly where there are multiple goals, multiple organizations, team activity, multiple factors capable of affecting the goal). That is why many traditional performance-linked reward systems were abandoned, and why classic public bureaucracies were traditionally controlled by input or throughput rather than by output measures. Many of the 'pathologies of public policy' identified by Hogwood and Peters (1985) arise from the skewing effect of performance measurement. For example, many writers on police organization attribute typical pathologies of police behaviour (such as patrol abandonment, brutality with suspects, fabrication of evidence) to a management system which is built upon the productivity measure of crime clear-up rates (see Jones, 1980). As Downs and Larkey (1986: 3) point out, if all that was needed to make public administration efficient was to remake government in the image of the private sector, the problem would have been solved a century ago when this strategy was applied to US city governments.

Public Choice

As was shown earlier, traditional public administration was intellectually underdeveloped. It failed to provide a way of determining by *a priori* reasoning *under what circumstances* public bureaucracies could be expected to outperform other institutional arrangements. This was a serious defect. For an administrative 'principle' to be of any value, there must be a means of locating its limits – the objection which J. S. Mill justly raised to Chadwick's principle of 'competition for the field' (see Crain and Ekelund, 1976). Nor did traditional public administration marshal evidence unambiguously demonstrating the superior performance of public bureaucracies as service providers in terms of efficiency or service quality. Both of these failures left the traditional approach very exposed to the attacks of the public choice school from the 1960s.

From the 1950s, economists (mainly in the USA) rediscovered institutional economics, and this generated a form of theory about public administration which ran quite counter to the traditional orthodoxy. Instead of the traditional recipe for better bureaucratic government, the argument led to a preference for consumer choice rather than producer monopoly, for smaller-scale rather than larger-scale service, for service provision through organizations other than classic public bureaucracies, and for services financed by user charges rather than from allocations from a general fund budget. A landmark in the development of this approach was Ostrom's (1974) attack on the traditional Weber–Wilson orthodoxy in favour of a public choice approach.

From this viewpoint, orthodox public administration had failed to deal seriously with either allocative or X-inefficiency in public bureaucracies

(Albrow, 1970: 64). It began by assuming that not all bureaucrats were self-regarding opportunists, perhaps because the modern theory of bureaucracy was brought to birth in European societies where the élite ranks of the bureaucracy were part of an 'officer class', with group solidarity based on ideologies of *noblesse oblige*, Christian service or racial supremacy. But when large public bureaucracies developed in societies like the USA, with a general culture of individualism, self-help egalitarianism, opportunistic entrepreneurship, the effects of exploitation of the system by self-regarding opportunists became only too clear. Indeed, perhaps it was because the old faith was a European transplant thinly rooted in American soil that it crumbled so quickly and unresistingly before a fairly ill-developed alternative.

The theory of public administration that developed from the 'economics of bureaucracy' school laid strong emphases on the disadvantages of 'monopoly bureaus' and argued that there is no logical reason why the provision of many public services must be carried out by public bureaucracies, in the sense of hierarchies of salaried officials under direct day-to-day political oversight by elected public officials. Only in comparatively modern times has that institutional form been adopted even for services which are defining to government, such as defence, tax collection and police services.

The 'economics of bureaucracy' school thus concentrated on institutional arrangements which as far as possible established rivalry and consumer choice: by voucher schemes rather than mandatory allocation; by cash transfers rather than services in kind; by provision of services on the basis of competitive performance contracts or franchises rather than permanent public bureaucracies; by small-scale monopolies rather than large-scale monopolies; by user charges rather than tax-based financing for services other than pure public goods; and by local-level service provision which enabled consumers to 'vote with their feet'.

As a justification of some important administrative trends in the USA, the UK and other countries over the past decade or so, this school is rather more 'mainline' in terms of its practical (if implicit) acceptance than orthodox public administration. It has undermined some of the traditional assumptions built into academic public administration, to the point of now constituting a major alternative academic approach to the subject.

However, this approach has some well known limitations (cf. Bobrow and Dryzek, 1987). It undoubtedly exposed an Achilles' heel in traditional public administration by starting from the assumption that both producers and consumers of public services were self-regarding opportunists and showed how this could produce major potential inefficiencies in communications in long hierarchies, in relationships between budget allocators and departments making claims on the budget, in institutions where lack of ownership transferability exempts the directorate from built-in punishment for operating other than at least cost, or where general-tax-based finance encourages consumers to use more of the service than they would choose to do if given the money cost rather than the services in kind.

But 'efficiency' is not the only criterion for judging institutional arrangements for public service provision: or to put it differently, efficiency depends on context (see, for example, Wilenski, 1986: 57–8, 154–65). Other criteria include the limitation of corruption and dishonesty, the exclusion of certain groups or individuals from the ability to exert power, and the preservation of social order. Specifically,

1. side-payments which reduce technical efficiency may be needed to keep a political system going. Hidden bribes needed to keep the system going are 'system maintenance costs' in the currently unfashionable jargon of functionalist Political Science. Narrower notions of 'efficiency' can only operate in the context of a reasonably orderly and predictable political environment, and the cost of creating and maintaining that environment cannot be ignored.

2. Restrictions on transferability of property rights, by definition, create allocative inefficiency, but the alternatives are sometimes worse. For example, the economist's preference for conveying benefits to particular citizens in monetary terms rather than in kind, on standard allocative efficiency grounds has important political and administrative consequences. First, it loads the political scales by reducing the level of benefit that a democratic process is likely to agree to, since the beneficiaries in such a situation are consumers only, rather than a coalition of consumers and producers, and since no account is taken of the preferences of those bearing the cost as to how the benefits are to be spent. Second, it puts the whole weight of any redistributive process on the tax and transfer system, even though all experience testifies to the administrative difficulty of using taxes alone as an effective redistributory mechanism.

    Similarly, there are political drawbacks to allowing unlimited play to the free transferability of property rights in the production units of public services: opposition to such transfer does not always reflect the 'capture' of political decision-makers by producer group interests. Some potential owners of producer units in public administration – indeed, those to whom the assets would be most valuable – are politically unacceptable. Just as gun licensing in many countries is intended to put a bar on the transfer of lethal weapons into the hands of criminals, to whom those weapons would be most valuable (thus creating allocative inefficiency in a strict sense), so the 'defining' services of the state – arms, justice, finance, foreign affairs, police – are inappropriate for unrestricted ownership transfer. In fact, there could be efficiency gains from international or national trade in public administration under the conventional economic gains-from-trade analysis. But, for at least some types of public services, the criterion of efficiency becomes secondary to other political considerations.

3. The argument that franchising or contracts under periodic contract renewal rules will provide services more efficiently than public bureaucracies never subject to competition depends on the assumption that the regulatory or contract awarding process will itself be relatively honest and efficient. It assumes, for instance, that: inefficient (high cost/low service) providers will in fact be replaced by more efficient producers at franchise renewal time; that franchises will be taken away from obvious non-performers; that franchisees will not seek opportunistically to renege on their contracts at politically strategic moments; that there will, or can be, a genuine arms-length political relationship between regulator and regulatee. The extreme weakness of such assumptions are obvious enough to anyone who has studied the real-life history of franchising for public services or of regulated monopolies, so rife with extortion and bribery; those weaknesses can indeed be derived from the *very same* institutional economics paradigm which has often been used to show the imperfections of public bureaucracy provision of public services.

4. Efficiency depends on the creation and maintenance of a general social climate of honesty and fair dealing, which may itself involve some efficiency costs. It is perilous to assume that the natural state of business enterprise is honesty, fair dealing and competition. Classical economists, like Adam Smith, were very well aware of inherent tendencies to concentration, cartelization and dishonesty in the business world. Given that simple regulatory activity may be insufficient to keep such tendencies in check, it may be necessary for government to go into business itself to preserve competition or to promote honesty among traders. Even if this means a high-cost mode of supply partially underwritten by the taxpayers, that 'inefficiency' has to be set against collective costs of the 'public bad' of generalized dishonesty and monopoly.

The benefits of activities not related to efficiency in the narrow sense – keeping the system going, excluding politically illegitimate groups from the ability to exercise the public power, limiting corruption and preserving a general climate of honesty – are impossible to compute, and perhaps harder to identify than the narrower efficiency costs of such measures. But they have been powerful spurs to the growth of public bureaucracies in the past, and their importance is likely to become much more visible to the extent that public choice prescriptions are carried into effect.

FINDING A ROLE: POSSIBLE NEW DIRECTIONS

The argument here is that traditional public administration has to some degree 'lost an empire' through a loss of initiative to subject specialists, through a plethora of different approaches causing a loss of coherence, particularly through the rise of managerialist and public choice approaches to the subject. If that is true, what is the proper role for academic public administration today? If academic public administration did not exist, would it be necessary to invent it?

The argument developed above indicates that none of the challenges described above completely supplants the need for academic public administration, and in fact many of them suggest ways in which public administration can be re-invigorated. Three elements seem particularly important: the need for better frameworks and metalanguages; the need for juxtaposition and integration of different analytic paradigms; and the need for independent contribution to the debate on privatization and deregulation. These are discussed below.

The Need for Better Frameworks and Metalanguages

The fragmentation of the subject into many specialist subdisciplines makes it particularly important to develop overall frameworks, metalanguages and perspectives for the understanding of administrative structures and processes. That role certainly cannot be fulfilled by private sector-based corporate management theory, since it lacks the wider 'system' focus which is distinctive to traditional public administration, and lacks any constitutional dimension. It is therefore most useful in relation to the organization of those 'programmable' aspects of public service provision, and for dealing with the parts rather than with the whole. Further, it has no intellectual edge over old-style public administration, in the sense of being more coherent or having more predictive power.

The intellectual tools which are needed for the development of better overall frameworks for the understanding of public service provision are thus unlikely to be importable from private-sector management theory.

They need to come from intellectual spheres which are broad enough to be comprehensive in coverage, to be capable of cutting across specialist subfields and identifying what is generic and what is special. Paradigms which meet this criterion include cybernetics (approaching administrative systems as if they were environment-sensing computer programs), economics (approaching administrative systems as incentive structures in the face of self-regarding opportunism) and institutional theory (approaching administrative systems as formal rule structures), rhetoric (the analysis and classification of deliberative arguments – particularly applicable to public administration since its characteristic form of argument is what Aristotle called enthymeme, a maxim followed by a reason).

Indeed, its established taxonomic character ought to be one of the strengths of traditional public administration: what is curious is how little these concerns have been developed. A well developed body of ideas about public service provision should be concerned with developing distinctive metalanguages for understanding public service provision – that is, a way of looking at the picture as a whole. What I mean by this is a comprehensive and systematic way of identifying choice among organizational types, coupled with theory about the circumstances in which one type of organization might be preferred to another, with a cumulatively developing body of supporting studies. Such work is a prerequisite for a real 'design science', yet orthodox public administration was traditionally weak in just the area where the distinctive analytic thrust of Public Administration should, above all, be developed.

The Need for Juxtaposition, Dialogue and Integration of Different Analytic Paradigms

Given the multitude of approaches to public administration, as indicated above, it is important to do more to develop 'test sites' in which alternative approaches to understanding administrative phenomena are identified, juxtaposed and tested.

Here there is a significant role for academic public administration. There is a need simply to keep cataloguing and juxtaposing the various different approaches as they develop; for example, even now, there are still relatively few textbooks that include an account of the public choice approach as well as of the traditional approach. Beyond that, there is a need to undertake comparison, juxtaposition and synthesis of different ways of understanding or predicting patterns of public service provision – for example, alternative ways of looking at law enforcement.

This can bring important pay-offs. For example, the greatest value of institutional economics to the student of public administration is its potential power to locate the limits of ideas about privatization and deregulation in the way that orthodox public administration could not do. Until now, the economics-based paradigm has been used principally to expose the many inefficiencies and other problems inherent in classic public bureaucracies, but that paradigm can also be used to show the limitations of alternative forms of provision.

Take the now-familiar argument that, in classic public bureaucracies, self-regarding producers will try to convert budgetary funds and other assets into 'private' benefits – pay and pensions, a leisurely job, and perks of all kinds. Given their vulnerability to such tendencies, it is part of the rule structure of classic bureaus that their activities are subject to heavy audit procedure, that decisions on matters such as pay, pensions, grading, thickness of office carpets, and so on are centralized and fixed. In fact, the form of enterprise most vulnerable to the kind of self-regarding behaviour that the 'economics of bureaucracy' school identify are enterprises which are *not* classic bureaucracies – non-classic bureaucracies such as publicly owned trading enterprises or enterprises set up in the form of companies, trusts and associations. The latter form of enterprise does not involve a rigid system of rules designed to prevent the enterprise's members from converting public assets to their private advantage, because the law of such bodies is built on the assumption that such tendencies will be kept in check by other means – such as challenge from a membership, by the operation of the capital market or by competition in the product market, or by the predominance of other-regarding motivations, in the case of charitable organizations. However, where such enterprises are merely public bureaucracies 'in mufti' as it were, and where the assumptions about control which are built into the law of their organizational form do not apply, we can expect the effects of their members' self-regarding opportunism to be far more marked than in the case of classic public bureaucracies.

In short, the 'economics of bureaucracy' school itself furnishes the basis for an argument against providing public services in private-sector guise in circumstances where there is no genuine product or capital market competition, where the directorate is not subject to control by a membership, or where motivations for service are not other-regarding. Ironically, these are precisely the circumstances in which the insights of the 'economics of bureaucracy' school about the effects of opportunism are likely to apply most – not the circumstances of the classic bureau in which the theory was first developed. Few real-world cases where the operation of a service has passed from classic public bureaucracy to non-classic bureaucracy or to private-sector organizational forms are invulnerable to this kind of producer–group exploitation.

Similarly, the institutional economics approach helps us to identify the limits, as well as the possible advantages, of contracting out public services rather than directly providing them by public bureaucracies. The very same institutional economics which points out the vulnerability of classic public bureaucracies to opportunism and information distortion tells us something about the limitations of a contract relationship. Williamson (1975) has shown that, in circumstances of high uncertainty coupled with limited rationality (such that all possible contingencies cannot feasibly be specified in a performance contract) and small numbers coupled with self-regarding opportunism (such that there are not large numbers of buyers and sellers for the product in question), performance contracting has no obvious benefits over direct employment. Now many public services do have precisely those characteristics of high uncertainty and small numbers of potential buyers and sellers, and this may explain why contracting out for such services can be unsatisfactory.

In fact, the 'economics of bureaucracy' school contains within itself just what old-style public administration lacked – the elements of a theory locating the limits of privatization and deregulation. What is needed is a new public administration which brings together the contributions of both the 'economics of bureaucracy' and the traditional approach.

The Need for Independent Contribution to the Debate on Privatization and Deregulation

A third challenge to academic public administration lies in the changing context in which public administration operates today – particularly the prevailing context of privatization, corporatization and deregulation. Such changes give much greater salience to the subject which traditional public administration devoted itself to study, by changing who *gets* what, who *pays* what, and who *does* what in the provision of public services; and this has the effect of 're-agendizing' classic questions about the institutional arrangements appropriate for the performance of public services.

Now, it is impossible to witness the public debates on these matters without being struck by the shallowness of argument on both sides (to the point where it is not only facile but vicious); the lack of any historical dimension; the ignorance of what past thinkers have had to say about these issues (or perhaps deliberate misrepresentation, as in the case of Adam Smith's ideas about administration), the rhetorical style of argument (incorporating familiar fallacies such as 'proof' by selective illustration, correlation as cause, *post hoc ergo propter hoc, ipse dixit*); and the fact that virtually all contributors to the debate on both sides are blatantly *parti pris*.

Much of that is inevitable. But academic public administration must shoulder part of the blame for failing to contribute an effective and credible independent view to the debate. Too many academic commentators with a public administration background have approached the debate in terms of substantive defences of the broad *policies* now under attack – such as welfarism, Keynesianism, egalitarianism – rather than by commenting on the administrative and constitutional theory aspects of these changes. No respectable and tightly argued defence of the 'old orthodoxy' in administrative theory terms has yet been offered. Old-style public administration seems to have chosen to die in the dark. The traditionalists have been silent even on the issue that is dearest to their hearts, namely the traditional recipes for politically responsible and corruption-free government.

Such changes create a need for independent research on factors affecting public service performance and for careful argument and debate about alternative modes of organization rather than bred-in-the-bone assumptions. They also create a need for public administration academics to reexamine the ABC of their subject and the intellectual tools of their trade.

Intellectually, this reopening of questions once taken for granted can do nothing but good, since it brings a field of study which had been fairly torpid back into the centre of the political agenda. It also provides a challenge for public administration academics to justify the need for public administration as a distinct academic field of study. Above all, it provides a stimulus to provide better arguments about the circumstances in which one organizational form of provision is to be preferred to another or others, and to produce better studies which throw light on the consequences of choosing one form of provision rather than another.

NOTES

I am grateful to Andrew Dunsire and Martin Painter for comments on an earlier draft of this paper, and to Adrian Leftwich for editorial guidance.
1. For a fuller discussion of the meaning(s) of the terms 'institutional arrangements' and 'public services' see *The Blackwell Encyclopaedia of Political Institutions* (ed. V. Bogdanor), (Oxford, Blackwell 1987), pp. 504–7.

REFERENCES

Albrow, M. (1970), *Bureaucracy* (London, Pall Mall).
Allison, G. (1971), *Essence of Decision* (Boston, Little, Brown).
Bendor, J. and Moe, T. M. (1985), 'An adaptive model of bureaucratic politics' *American Political Science Review,* **79**, pp. 755–74.
Bendor, J. and Moe, T. M. (1986), 'Agenda control, committee capture and the dynamics of institutional politics', *American Political Science Review,* **80**.

Bobrow, D. B. and Dryzek, J. S. (1987), *Policy Analysis by Design* (Pittsburgh, University of Pittsburgh Press).

Blau, P. M. and Schoenherr, R. A. (1971), *The Structure of Organisations* (New York, Basic Books).

Braybrooke, D. and Lindblom, C. (1963), *A Strategy of Decision* (New York, Free Press).

Castells, M. (1977), *The Urban Question* (London, Arnold).

Charlesworth, J. C. (ed.) (1968), *Theory and Practice of Public Administration* (Philadelphia, American Academy of Political and Social Science/American Society for Public Administration).

Clegg, S. (1975), *Power, Rule and Domination* (London, Routledge and Kegan Paul).

Crain, W. M. and Ekelund, R. B. (1976), 'Chadwick and Demsetz on competition and regulation', *Journal of Law and Economics,* **19**.

Dearlove, J. (1979), *The Reorganisation of British Local Government* (Cambridge, Cambridge University Press).

Douglas, M. (1987), *How Institutions Think* (London, Routledge and Kegan Paul).

Downs, G. W. and Larkey, P. D. (1986), *The Search for Government Efficiency: from hubris to helplessness* (Philadelphia, Temple University Press).

Dunleavy, P. (1982), 'Is there a radical approach to public administration?', *Public Administration,* **60**.

Dunleavy, P. and O'Leary, B. (1987), *Theories of the State* (London, Macmillan).

Dunsire, A. (1973), *Administration: the word and the science* (London, Martin Robertson).

Dunsire, A. (1978), *Control in a Bureaucracy: the execution process, Vol 2* (Oxford, Martin Robertson).

Eliasson, M. and Kooiman, J. (eds) (1987), *Managing Public Organizations* (London, Sage).

Fainstein, S. S. and Fainstein, N. I. (1980), 'The political economy of American bureaucracy' in C. Weiss and A. H. Barton, *Making Bureaucracies Work* (Beverly Hills, Sage).

Gerth, H. H. and Mills, C. M. (1948), *From Max Weber: essays in sociology* (London, Routledge and Kegan Paul).

Hodgkinson, C. (1978), *Towards a Philosophy of Administration* (Oxford, Blackwell).

Hogwood, B. and Peters, B. G. (1985), *The Pathology of Public Policy* (Oxford, Clarendon).

Hood, C. C. and Dunsire, A. (1981), *Bureaumetrics* (Farnborough, Gower).

Jones, J. M. (1980), *Organizational Aspects of Police Behaviour* (Farnborough, Gower).

Jenkins, W. (1978), *Policy Analysis* (Oxford, Martin Robertson).

Kast, F. E. and Rosenzweig, J. E. (1973), *Contingency Views of Organization and Management* (New York, Science Research Associates).

Kernaghan, K. (1980), 'Codes of ethics and public administration: progress, problems and prospects', *Public Administration,* **59**.

Lakatos, I. (1970), 'Falsification and the methodology of scientific research programmes' in I. Lakatos and A. Musgrave (eds), *Criticism and the Growth of Knowledge* (Cambridge, Cambridge University Press).

Marini, F. (ed.) (1971), *Toward a New Public Administration: the Minnowbrook*

Perspective (Scranton, Chandler).

Martin, S. (1983), *Managing Without Managers* (Beverly Hills, Sage).

Mill, J. S. (1910), *Representative Government* (London, J. M. Dent and Sons).

O'Connor, J. (1973), *The Fiscal Crisis of the State* (New York, St Martin's Press).

Ostrom, V. (1974), *The Intellectual Crisis in American Public Administration* (rev. edn.), (Alabama, Alabama University Press).

Overman, E. S. (1984), 'Public management: what's new and different?', *Public Administration Review,* **44**.

Parry, G. (1963), 'Enlightened government and its critics in eighteenth century Germany', *The Historical Journal*, **6(2)**.

Perry, J. L. and Kraemer, K. L. (1983), *Public Management: public and private perspectives* (Palo Alto, Calif., Mayfield Publications).

Pinch, S. (1985), *Cities and Services: the geography of collective consumption* (London, Routledge and Kegan Paul).

Pitt, D. C. and Smith, B. C. (1981), *Government Departments: an organisational perspective* (London, Routledge and Kegan Paul).

Pollitt, C. (1984), *Manipulating the Machine* (London, Allen and Unwin).

Ridley, F. F. (1972), 'Public administration: cause for discontent', *Public Administration,* **50**.

Sabatier, P. (1987), 'Knowledge, policy-oriented learning and policy change: an advocacy coalition framework', *Knowledge Creation, Diffusion Utilization,* **8(4)**.

Self, P. (1975), *Econocrats and the Policy Process* (London, Macmillan).

Self, P. (1986), 'What's gone wrong with public administration?', *Public Administration and Development,* **6**.

Simon, H. A. (1958), *Administrative Behavior* (2nd edn.) (New York, Macmillan).

Spann, R. N. (1979), *Government Administration in Australia* (Sydney, Allen and Unwin).

Thomas, R. (1978), *The British Philosophy of Administration* (London, Longman).

Thompson, V. A. (1976), *Bureaucracy and the Modern World* (Morristown, NJ, General Learning Press).

Wilenski, P. (1986), *Public Power and Public Administration* (Sydney, RAIPA/Hale and Iremonger).

Williamson, O. E. (1975), *Markets and Hierarchies* (London, Collier Macmillan).

Wilson, J. Q. (1968), *Varieties of Police Behavior* (Cambridge, Mass., Harvard University Press).

8.   Weight or Lightness? Political Philosophy and its Prospects

John Horton

What then shall we choose? Weight or Lightness? (Kundera, 1984)

INTRODUCTION AND SCOPE

Political philosophy is apparently flourishing: within a decade and a half of Peter Laslett's assertion that 'political philosophy is dead' (Laslett, 1956: viii) the publication and reception of John Rawls', *A Theory of Justice* (1971) provided seemingly conclusive evidence that the obituary had been premature. The subsequent publication of several substantial works have confirmed its vigour. The proliferation of journals, monographs, textbooks and such like is a superficial, but reliable, indicator of the sheer quantity of political philosophy currently being produced. In what follows I shall be concerned first to offer a brief account of the development of political philosophy from the mid-1950s to the present. Second, I shall provide some indication of the kind of work that is currently undertaken by political philosophers. I shall then say something about the relations between politics and philosophy more generally which make political philosophy a particularly precarious and ambiguous undertaking. This will provide the background to a discussion of some recent developments which embody a more ambivalent, even sceptical, attitude to the aims and ambitions of much contemporary political philosophy. I shall conclude with a few highly speculative and inconclusive remarks about the possible future development of political philosophy.

Before undertaking a brief review of the recent history of political philosophy it is necessary to make a few preliminary comments about the limited scope of what follows. First, the focus of attention will be directed at Anglo-American political philosophy. I shall have nothing to say about non-Western political philosophy, and continental political philosophy will be touched upon only in so far as one significant development of recent years has been a *rapprochement* between some European and Anglo-American philosophers. The point of view adopted, however, will be one from very much within the Anglo-American tradition. A second limitation will be that the discussion will not directly concern itself with all the important developments even within Anglo-American political philosophy and, in particular, it will ignore that cross-fertilization with other disciplines and theoretical traditions which has been one significant feature of recent years. The two omissions which are most serious in this respect are, fortunately, to some extent dealt with in other essays in this volume.[1] First, there is the enormous growth of welfare economics and social choice theory in which there has been a fruitful interaction between economics, ethics and political philosophy. Second, there is the perhaps more surprising emergence of 'analytical Marxism' in which the tools and techniques of analytical philosophy have been applied to the articulation and development of Marxist social theory.

A final limitation is that the primary focus of attention will be very much on the work of writers such as Rawls, Nozick, Dworkin, Ackerman and Gewirth whose writings will be regarded as representative of the most ambitious strand of Anglo-American political philosophy (Rawls, 1971; Nozick, 1974; Dworkin, 1977; Ackerman, 1980; Gewirth, 1978, 1982). This is not intended to reflect an evaluative judgement on my part of the relative worth of this work. Rather it is motivated by a recognition that it is such work that generates most discussion, is most frequently cited and is widely perceived as being typical or characteristically expressive of the aims, style and methods of contemporary analytical political philosophy. Even the political temper of their writings, which despite enormous differences, can meaningfully, if very broadly, be described as 'liberal' is fairly representative of the range of much contemporary political philosophy – from libertarianism to social democracy and non-Marxist socialism. Inevitably all these judgements and generalizations are very rough and ready and highly approximate but hopefully they provide a preliminary delimitation of the following discussion.

PHILOSOPHY, POLITICS AND POLITICAL PHILOSOPHY

In sketching the recent history of Anglo-American political philosophy and its reviving fortunes, the notorious remark of Laslett's with which this essay began is an obvious point at which to take up the narrative. Although with the benefit of hindsight it is easy to dismiss Laslett's pronouncement, two points in his defence ought to be made. First, it was always a more equivocal judgement than it has sometimes been presented since, in context, the claim was qualified and the full conclusion was expressed more ambiguously as 'for the time being anyway, political philosophy is dead'. Death, of course, does not have that kind of temporal structure and the two parts of the claim stand in an uneasy relationship, each, at least partially, undermining the other. Second, if death, precisely because of its finality, was simply an inapt metaphor then the sense of political philosophy as something barren, moribund and empty that Laslett intended to convey, was a largely accurate description of it in the mid-1950s.

Developments in the academic study of both philosophy and politics were antithetic to political philosophy: both subjects had been deeply influenced by the aggressive positivism of the 1920s and 1930s. Positivism, especially in the extreme form of logical positivism (Ayer, 1971, originally published 1936), effectively denied any place for political philosophy. For if the only meaningful statements were either empirical hypotheses, the province of the sciences, or logical truths, the business of formal logic, there was nothing left to constitute such subjects as aesthetics, ethics and political philosophy. On this view, what passed as political philosophy was mostly a declaration of preferences or the mere expression of attitudes. On the other hand, the more valuable parts were really empirical claims about political processes and institutions which ought to be tested and assessed by an empirically rigorous Political Science. While logical positivism proved something of a passing fashion, it did leave an enduring legacy. Its remorseless scientism had an important effect upon the development of Political Science in the USA where there was a widespread and self-conscious effort to displace political philosophy with a study aspiring to the status of the natural sciences and supposedly modelled on their methods; an effort which met with considerable institutional success. Furthermore, the linguistic philosophy emerging from Oxford which superseded logical positivism offered only a marginally more sympathetic context for political philosophy. While not denying the possibility of political philosophy, its reduction of philosophy to an examination of the ordinary use of words, whatever its value elsewhere in philosophy, did little to stimulate political philosophy, draining it of imagination, creativity and depth.[2] This is clear in the prime exemplar of linguistic analysis in political philosophy, *The Vocabulary of Politics* (Weldon, 1953), a depressingly banal book, which interprets political disagreements as resting on either verbal confusions or unresolved empirical disputes.

Thus the cumulative impact of intellectual developments within philosophy and political studies was, by the mid-1950s, such as to issue in an extremely attenuated and trivialized conception of political philosophy. It was not implausible to believe that the alleged refreshing rigour of the new philosophy had actually induced *rigor mortis* in political philosophy. Furthermore, other social and intellectual developments tended to reinforce this apparent demise: the Cold War, the supposed end of ideology, post-war reconstruction and the sheer terrifying awesomeness of the previous 30 years which had climaxed in the concentration camps, world war and the atomic bomb. For political philosophy, the period from the First World War to the early 1960s seemed largely barren and tending to exhaustion. Of course, it is possible to exaggerate this picture: for example, in the two decades prior to the 1960s there had been interesting and significant work by political philosophers largely uninfluenced by linguistic philosophy such as Collingwood, Popper, Hayek, Arendt and Oakeshott (Collingwood, 1942; Popper, 1945; Hayek, 1944, 1960; Arendt 1958a and 1958b; Oakeshott, 1962). However, although the work of these philosophers had its enthusiastic admirers it had little sustained impact on the inert state of political philosophy. In addition, in the USA, Leo Strauss and his pupils kept alive a rather idiosyncratic and esoteric conception of political philosophy but one which had the status of little more than a marginal cult within the wider philosophical community (Strauss, 1953). How then was political philosophy resurrected from such an apparently terminal condition?

THE REVIVAL OF POLITICAL PHILOSOPHY

The explanation of the revival of political philosophy is more obscure and uncertain than the reasons for its decline. Much had to do with the changing political and cultural climate: the emergence of the counter-culture of the 1960s, the maturing of a new generation with no direct experience or memory of the Second World War, the growth in higher education and, perhaps most of all, the fierce political controversy occasioned by American involvement in the Vietnam War. More interesting from the point of view of this essay, although perhaps initially less causally significant, were developments within philosophy and political studies. In the case of Political Science, the increasingly obvious sham of its 'scientific' pretensions, its complacent ethnocentricity and its complicity with American imperialism did much to undermine its credibility. Yet more important were developments within philosophy, especially in the USA where most of the leading figures in the resurgence of political philosophy in the late 1960s and 1970s emerged from philosophy departments or philosophically inclined law departments. At this time the locus of philosophical innovation decisively shifted from Oxford to the USA, where it has subsequently remained. The conception of philosophy as linguistic analysis, concerned with puzzles arising from lack of attention to the details of ordinary language was superseded by a more traditional conception, concerned to develop comprehensive philosophical theories supported by rigorous abstract arguments and aiming to resolve genuine problems. More specifically, though, how did these developments relate to the rejuvenation of political philosophy?

Oversimplifying greatly, I offer two principal suggestions. First, the political, social and cultural changes in which disagreements about values came to the fore created the conditions in which political philosophy could be perceived once again to have an important adjudicative role to play. Second, the developments within philosophy restored to political philosophy the aspirations and methods through which it might hope to play such a role. As a result, the revitalization of political philosophy took the form primarily of developing theories, of more or less comprehensiveness, through which disputes about political values could be mediated and arbitrated. In this respect Rawls' work is typical. Through the use of the theoretical construct of 'the original position', an account of justice is developed which subsumes apparent conflicts of political values within a more deeply rooted, consensually-based and philosophically justified theory. Similarly, despite their differing styles and conclusions, Nozick and Dworkin try to derive substantive and comprehensive political theories from such apparently widely shared premises as that every individual has rights to life, liberty and property or the equal moral worth of each person.

The aspiration of such work is to provide a philosophically compelling account of a political theory which will largely resolve the apparently endemic conflicts of political values. It seeks more than either the clarification of such disputes or their retrospective historical interpretation, aiming rather to discover or construct through philosophical argument secure foundations for political values. In this respect at least, such work is clearly at home in the Western tradition of political philosophy which, since its origins with Socrates and Plato, has had this as one of its principal motivations. This is a point I shall pursue later but before doing so it is necessary to characterize more fully the present state of political philosophy.

There are at least three strands in contemporary political philosophy which are especially worth distinguishing. First, as has already been indicated, there are writers such as Rawls, Nozick, Dworkin, Ackermann, and Gewirth, all of whom are concerned to articulate the philosophical foundations of a particular moral and political theory. All, as it happens, would describe themselves as 'liberals' but from my point of view this is less important than something they share with utilitarians, who may or may not be liberals, namely, an understanding of the task of political philosophy as the discovery or construction of the foundations of political value. Although there are differing emphases among these philosophers, to a greater or lesser extent they all share the ambition of demonstrating or conclusively justifying their theories in terms of first principles; they all assign the crucial role in this process to abstract philosophical argument; and more ambivalently, they all seek to show that their theories have a general validity which transcends any very particular set of socio-historical circumstances.[3] This kind of political philosophy I shall refer to as 'foundationalism' and it has been central to recent developments often feeding or providing a background to other kinds of work.

A second style of political philosophy is more piecemeal but often, though not invariably, parasitic upon the first. This 'applied philosophy' starts from particular problems: issues such as the justification of punishment, civil disobedience, reverse discrimination, war, toleration and such like and proceeds to assess them in the light of a particular moral theory or in terms of some general political principles (for example, Acton, 1969; Singer, 1973; Goldman, 1979; Walzer, 1977; Mendus, 1988). Usually the philosophical apparatus brought to this task derives from some more fundamental moral or political theory and concepts such as rights, utility, justice in terms of which the discussions characteristically take place frequently presuppose some, perhaps unstated, underlying general political theory.

The third strand in contemporary political philosophy exists in an ambiguous relation to the other two and includes writers such as Sandel, Taylor and MacIntyre (Sandel, 1982; Taylor, 1985; MacIntyre, 1981, 1988). These philosophers are largely critical of foundationalism and, in contrast, place much greater emphasis on the unavoidable contingency and historicity of moral and political values. Yet, although critical of foundationalism, they write in a style and manner not altogether different from those they criticize and they are recognizably part of the same philosophical community. I shall have more to say about foundationalism and its critics shortly but, before so doing, I want to say something of a very general nature about the activities of politics and philosophy which provides a context for those remarks.

POLITICS AND THE ROLE OF POLITICAL PHILOSOPHY

The relationship between politics and philosophy has historically been an uneasy one: the quarrel between politics and philosophy goes back at least to the Greeks and has never been convincingly settled. The Platonic aspiration for philosophers to usurp the position of politicians, however reluctantly, or the sense that the political philosopher knows best, has been a recurrent feature of the history of political philosophy. Politicians, although sometimes seduced by the lustre of political philosophy, have understandably thought differently for the most part. Philosophy is usually regarded by politicians as either unworldly or dangerous, whereas political philosophers are often impatient of the contingency and compromise of political life. Politicians are inclined to be dismissive of the idea that they might have anything to learn from philosophers: philosophers are frequently contemptuous of the way politics is characteristically conducted. I shall suggest that, at least in part, these antagonisms are not altogether surprising and are to be explained in terms of the characteristic differences between the activities of politics and philosophizing. Political philosophy has often been like a marriage between two ill-matched suitors in which a fleeting infatuation is soon regretted in the predictably uneasy and uncertain relationship that follows. Later, I shall pursue the suggestion that there is a continuing tension between the demands of philosophy, forever implicated in the aspiration to timelessness, truth and certainty, and those of politics, a perpetual realm of precariousness, accommodation and contingency. If the philosopher is forever seeking a place in the sun, politics seems always to exist in the darkness of the cave. I shall begin by saying a little more about this conflict between politics and philosophy.

It is impossible to characterize the Western tradition of philosophy, or even political philosophy, in a way which is both inclusive and informative. However, it is possible to identify some features which seem central to that tradition, even though some philosophers inevitably will be either marginalized or excluded. Philosophy has most commonly been understood as the pursuit of general truths about the human condition and our experience and knowledge of it. Philosophers have variously attempted to develop theories to explain our most basic beliefs, ideas and concepts; to undermine prejudice and bigotry; and to distinguish systematically truth from falsity. What is it to know something? What is a logically valid argument? Is there a God? What is the good life? These are all questions which have been of more or less recurrent concern within philosophy.

Political philosophy has mostly been concerned with a range of questions arising from the nature of the good life. What is the best form of political arrangements? How, if at all, should persons be governed? What is the proper relationship between individuals and the polity of which they are members? These are three questions, or perhaps three different ways of asking the same question, which have been central to that part of philosophy concerned with politics. They easily lead into questions about law, coercion, freedom, justice, equality, authority, democracy, rights and obligations. Virtually all political philosophy has centred around one or more of these concepts. Most has been concerned to devise or discover the most appropriate set of political arrangements in which human beings will flourish. Furthermore, most has been conducted on the assumption that, whatever its difficulties, this is an intelligible project for political philosophy to pursue. The governing idea has been that politics as an activity should ultimately be made to conform to the principles and theories articulated by the political philosopher. These have been persisting and widespread, though not universal, features of the Western tradition of political philosophy.

The nature of politics is a deeply contested issue: both at theoretical and practical levels. Any characterization, therefore, will to some extent be controversial (Leftwich, 1984). At one extreme are views which see politics as almost coextensive with the whole of human activity while at the other are conceptions of politics as a highly specific and limited activity. Since my interest is not primarily to articulate or defend a particular theoretical understanding of politics I wish to sidestep such disputes so far as is possible. While there are many activities which are only disputedly political there are also some which are more or less indisputably so. Most of those activities have to do with the deciding, implementing and enforcing of the arrangements through which a society manages its affairs: fundamental disagreement and the exercise of political power are among their persistent features. These activities are characteristically highly contingent, circumstantial, ameliorative and precarious. Furthermore, whereas philosophy tends to terminate in a set of propositions or a theory, politics terminates in action: politics is a practical endeavour, philosophy is speculative reflection. Of course this contrast should not be overdrawn. Any political activity will involve some element of reflection while most philosophy involves reflection upon something outside of itself. Yet some such distinction as that outlined seems well founded in the self-understandings of both philosophers and politicians.

CONTEMPORARY RESPONSES

One impatient, but commonsense, response to this antithesis between politics and philosophy is to concede that politics and philosophy are fundamentally different but to deny that this gives rise to any interesting problems or difficulties. There are, however, two possible directions from which doubt about the adequacy of this overly sanguine response might arise. The first raises the question of whether politics is an activity peculiarly resistant to the aspirations of philosophical reflection. The second asks about the relationship between the theories or conclusions of

philosophy and the activities of politicians. I shall briefly discuss each of
these sources of scepticism about contemporary political philosophy and
will then link these to a more general scepticism towards some of the
deepest aspirations of Western philosophy. Taken together, I shall suggest
these considerations constitute a genuine challenge to the proclaimed aims
and methods of much contemporary political philosophy. In so far as
these considerations have been taken seriously it has been among those
political philosophers critical of foundationalism and it is from among
them, I shall suggest, that the most interesting developments in political
philosophy may be expected, although it also has to be admitted that the
foundationalist endeavour is likely to persist undeterred.

One source of scepticism about political philosophy has recently been
expressed with unusual candour by David Lloyd Thomas. He writes:

> One of the most disturbing things about books on political philosophy is that
> their authors are apt to present arguments for positions they believe in. One
> does not find an author of socialist persuasion explaining how (disconcerting
> though this was) he found himself led by reason to the conclusion that the rights
> of private property must be upheld come what may. The conclusions of books
> on political philosophy are apt to turn out surprisingly congenial to the political
> dispositions of their authors, given that they are supposed to be based on
> considerations that any reasonable person could accept. (Lloyd Thomas, 1988:
> vii)

Of course, this claim should not be exaggerated: some political philosophers have at least claimed to have changed their political convictions in
the light of philosophical arguments. Furthermore, this phenomenon is
hardly specific to political philosophy, indeed not only is a tenacious
adherence to theoretical positions common in all areas of philosophy, but
if recent work in the history and sociology of science is to be believed, then
even in the most objective and disinterested of enquiries, the natural
sciences, prejudice, presumption and such like play an important role (for
example, Kuhn, 1970; Feyerabend, 1975, 1978). However, allowing for
these qualifications, it seems to be almost paradigmatically true that
political convictions precede philosophical argument. The latter usually
takes the form of a *post hoc* justification of a prior political position
determined by, and on the basis of, beliefs, influences and feelings other
than the philosophical argument which is supposed to justify it. Furthermore, Rawls' method of 'reflective equilibrium' or 'constructivism' seems
to concede something to this view, although precisely how much is unclear
and disputed.

Most foundationalists, however, have been reluctant to go even that
far, rejecting the Rawlsian methodology as a Trojan horse in the foundationalist citadel on the grounds that it leaves too little room for serious

philosophical argument. Such an observation, though, is clearly double-edged. One possible response is that the proper inference to be drawn is simply that there is little room for philosophical argument so construed. Such political philosophy might still have its uses, as ideology or rhetoric for example, but this would be precisely to deny its status as political *philosophy* in the eyes of its practitioners. Of course this argument does not take the form of trying to demonstrate an *a priori* impossibility. Rather, it begins from the prosaic observation that philosophical argument never does play a foundational role, leading to doubt, in the light of this fact, whether it is appropriate to think that it can do so. It is reinforced, however, by the connected and equally prosaic observation that foundationalist philosophers disagree among themselves in both their arguments and conclusions. Thus the supposedly logically compelling arguments of political philosophy only infrequently persuade others than the author of their validity. This too must be an embarrassment to any conception of political philosophy as a rigorously argumentative pursuit of truth. For, although some disagreement might be expected, such pervasive, persistent, widespread and seemingly ineliminable disagreement must call into doubt some of the grander ambitions of foundationalist political philosophy.

A second source of scepticism about contemporary political philosophy has its roots in a similarly unsophisticated observation to the first, although it comes from a rather different direction. It is expressed by John Dunn discussing theories of justice such as Rawls in the following terms:

> A theory of social justice is a fine thing, a good thought in a naughty world. But it is the naughty world which has to be dealt with. As we look around that world . . . theories of social justice sit very lightly on it and shape in practice very little of it indeed. (Dunn, 1986: 24)

Here the claim is that political philosophy exists at such a distance from the concerns of practical politics that its relevance to political activity is so tenuous as to be nearly non-existent. Political philosophy here appears as a series of argumentative and conceptual webs which have little to do with political life as it is lived and experienced. It provides neither understanding of, nor guidance for, political practice. On this account, political philosophy is insufficiently sensitive or attentive to the realities of politics. In Dunn's view what is lacking from contemporary political philosophy is a theory of prudence, 'a theory adequate to the historical world in which we *have* to live' (Dunn, 1985: 189; also Dunn, 1979). Unfortunately, Dunn gives not the slightest indication of what a philosophical theory of political prudence might look like. Indeed, there must be at least the suspicion that political prudence is not something that will admit of a philosophical theory although it would probably be going too far to claim that nothing of a theoretical and philosophical nature can be said about political prudence (for example, Beiner, 1983). Nevertheless, the most likely and obvious general pronouncement is that a substantial part of political prudence will consist of circumstantial judgement which, by its very nature, is largely resistant to abstract theorizing. However, none of this undermines Dunn's initial observation that the relationship between contemporary political philosophy and practical politics is such that the former, however conceptually and argumentatively sophisticated, is largely a politically irrelevant fantasy in the face of the latter.

Thus, whereas the first line of argument casts doubt upon the *philosophical* credentials of political philosophy, the second calls into question its relevance to *politics*. One mistaken response would be to draw comfort from these arguments by claiming that they are mutually inconsistent: the first presenting political philosophy as political preference or ideology masquerading as philosophy, the latter claiming that philosophical rigour is pursued at the expense of political purchase. However, though they can be represented as contradictory in this way it is also quite possible to combine the two lines of objection.

One philosopher who apparently does so is Richard Rorty. He argues both that philosophy, including political philosophy, is not the disinterested pursuit of timeless truth and that the theories of political philosophers have little to contribute to the understanding or guidance of political practice. Indeed, simplifying greatly, on Rorty's view it is philosophy's misunderstanding of itself as the disinterested pursuit of timeless truth that largely accounts for its practical irrelevance. Rather than articulating some objective, independent foundations for political value, Rorty sees the reconstructed task of political philosophy more discursively. 'The real issue', he writes, 'is between those who think our culture, or purpose, or intuitions cannot be supported except conversationally, and people who still hope for other sorts of support' (Rorty, 1982: 167). What should be important 'is our loyalty to other human beings clinging together against the dark, not our hope of getting things right' and this requires us 'to accept the contingency of starting-points . . . to accept our inheritance from, and conversation with, our fellow-humans as our only source of guidance' (Rorty, 1982: 167). In short, conversation must replace the search for foundations. The value of most traditional political philosophy is at best merely as an aid 'in thinking through our utopian visions' (Rorty, 1987: 569).

Rorty's conception of political philosophy rests not merely on a scepticism specific to political philosophy but, as implied, on a radical scepticism about the point and value of the mainstream tradition of

Western philosophy more generally. It is a scepticism deriving from the fact that, in Kolakowski's words:

> . . . among questions that have sustained the life of European philosophy for two and a half millennia not a single one has ever been solved to our general satisfaction. (Kolakowski, 1988: 1–2)

However, whereas for Kolakowski 'the search for the ultimate foundation is as much an unremovable part of human culture as the denial of the legitimacy of this search' (Kolakowski, 1988: 27), Rorty looks forward to what he calls a 'post-Philosophical culture' in which 'men and women felt themselves alone, merely finite, with no links to something Beyond' (Rorty, 1982: xlii–xliii). He seeks a culture of pluralist *jouissance*, although he is clear that this is a distant aspiration which has 'no relevance to the question of what is to be done here and now: what concrete measures will further human solidarity' (Rorty, 1987: 572), and it is this question which it is more profitable to discuss.

It is for these reasons Rorty identifies his approach with pragmatism and contrasts the pragmatist understanding of philosophy with what he sees as the dominant tradition of 'Philosophy'. What differentiates them is, he claims,

> . . . *whether philosophy should try to find natural starting-points which are distinct from cultural traditions, or whether all philosophy should do is compare and contrast cultural traditions.* . . . The intuitive realist thinks there is such a thing as Philosophical truth because he thinks that deep down beneath all the texts, there is something which is not just one more text but that to which various texts are trying to be 'adequate'. The pragmatist does not think there is anything like that. He does not even think there is anything isolable as 'the purposes which we construct vocabularies and cultures to fulfill' against which to test vocabularies and cultures. But he does think that in the process of playing vocabularies and cultures off against each other, we produce new and better ways of talking and acting – not better by reference to a previously known standard, but just better in the sense that they come to *seem* clearly better than their predecessors (Rorty, 1982: xxxvii).

Thus, for Rorty, political philosophy needs to redirect its attention away from the 'big questions' of justice, truth and freedom towards a more pragmatic, conversational endeavour to reconcile ourselves one to another and to think concretely about whatever specific problems confront us; in short to substitute for a metaphysics of absolute conceptions, the ameliorative aspirations of liberal politics. However, when examined more closely, the politics of Rorty's pragmatism are worryingly vague. The frequent resort to an undefined, yet likeminded, 'we' and the conception of political philosophy as conversation are suspiciously cosy.

They seem precisely to ignore the facts of fundamental ideological disagreement and the centrality of power and coercion in politics which any serious thought about politics, whether or not it is called 'philosophical', must acknowledge. In short, 'conversation' is a dangerously inadequate metaphor: while apparently politicizing political philosophy by detaching it from any realm of metaphysical absolutes, Rorty simultaneously depoliticizes it through a metaphorical evasion of some of the inescapable realities of political life.

Rorty might be thought of as being on the extreme of those political philosophers such as MacIntyre, Sandel and Taylor who are critical of foundationalism. However, the dangers of categorization immediately become clear in considering this both politically and philosophically heterogeneous grouping. It may seem that all they have in common is that they are anti-foundationalists and, even in that respect, there are some significant differences, although these will not be elaborated here. However, there is also a more positive feature of their approaches which they largely share. This is the belief that political philosophy might be understood as a necessarily and essentially historically and culturally situated activity. All would agree with Rorty that political philosophy has at least to start from the circumstances and conditions of its own engagement and more importantly that it can never entirely transcend its own historical and cultural specificity. All give particular prominence to a conception of community and a community is always an historically specific entity.

However, at this point agreement ends, for there are significant differences between these philosophers in their understandings of the present situation of the West. Where MacIntyre sees an incoherent babble of conflicting or incommensurable traditions, Rorty envisages a playful pluralism (at least in prospect) and Sandel sees more unity and coherence than either of them. From one point of view, these differences are unimportant for the argument developed here, since this is not concerned with specific conclusions or arguments within political philosophy. From another point of view, however, some of these differences are symptomatic of a more relevant and deeper ambiguity within anti-foundationalism. For, in so far as its emphasis is upon the community as the essential condition of political philosophy, it seems to depend upon some substantial and coherent sense of there being a community within which the political philosopher is embedded. Yet, in so far as the critique of foundationalism also derives in part from a perceived breakdown of community in the contemporary Western world, and in Rorty's case at least, draws on post-modernist theorizing, it comes close to denying the very conditions of the possibility of political philosophy it proclaims. It is this tension, and the possibilities it harbours for political philosophy that I shall explore by briefly examining Kundera's metaphors of lightness and weight.

POSSIBILITIES FOR POLITICAL PHILOSOPHY

The search for the philosophical foundations of political value is from an anti-foundationalist perspective weighed down by the metaphysical baggage it carries with it; burdened by Justice, Freedom, Equality, Rights and such like and anchored by Truth. In contrast, metaphysically, anti-foundationalism travels light. Yet, as Sandel has argued in his critique of modern liberal theorizing, in social and political terms it is liberal foundationalism with its 'unencumbered self' which travels light, and anti-foundationalism which is heavy with the historical and cultural specificity of a particular community and tradition. However, this sense of community itself seems ethereal when the understanding of the present is couched in terms of the fragmentation of its culture, its moral heterogeneity and the incommensurability of its forms of life. In political terms, this lightness issues in a tension between a suspiciously coercive conservatism of nostalgia for a time of organic unity and shared values, and the politically ineffective emptiness of the ever-open horizons of a playful pluralism. The situatedness of the political philosopher so central to the critique of foundationalism seems displaced either into a largely mythical past or a perpetual present scarcely more locatable than the *sub specie aeternitatis* of foundationalism. Correspondingly, the associated conceptions of political philosophy are in danger of being reduced either to the vain pursuit of an irrecoverable past entombed in a dead discourse or the quasi-solipsistic inconsequentiality of an endless monologue masquerading as a conversation. In short, political philosophy is either weighed down by a past which gave it life but which is no longer adequate to comprehend the present or is floating lightly free from any recognizable reality, constrained, if at all, only by the conceit of the political philosopher.

If, then, the pretensions of foundationalism are put aside what remains? Anti-foundationalism seems uncertain as to its answer, being clearer in what it rejects than what it has to put in its place. Perhaps in some sense political philosophy cannot amount to more than the stories we tell ourselves to make sense of, and give significance to, some inescapable features of the human predicament. But it is not clear that this is either a worthless or dispensable activity, nor that it need lack rigour or standards of persuasiveness. That it is never-ending; that there are no right answers or last words; that the world often goes on pretty much as it does whatever political philosophers may have to say about it may be dispiriting from some point of view, but if political philosophy has no ultimate truth to convey, no final consolation to offer, then this need not be a cause for embarrassment or apology. It is only on the assumption that foundationalism is a feasible project that we should be disappointed by its failure. But the failure of that project may not have quite the radical implications that critics such as Rorty insinuate. That political philosophy does not have the use that many of its practitioners believed it to have is not to say that it has no use. The always unfinished business of making sense of ourselves and our situation is part of what it is to be a reflective being: it is also one of the deepest motivations for philosophy. The tradition of political philosophy may itself be open to reinterpretation in these terms. Or rather, the extent of such a possibility is not simply settled by a rejection of foundationalism and remains something to be explored.

The disingenuousness of foundationalism, however, does raise the issue of how long, in good faith, we can carry on in the same way pretending that we have not heard the news of its demise. What a reconstructed political philosophy might look like remains an open question. However, it will need to accommodate both the critique of foundationalism and the fundamental facts of disagreement and the exercise of power as continuing features of our political experience for the foreseeable future. Metaphysical lightness must not lead to political lightheadedness, but nor must the weight of our particularity and our history overwhelm our political imagination. In terms of the metaphors of weight and lightness there is no one choice to be made.

NOTES

An earlier version of this paper was read to the Political Theory Workshop at the University of York and I am much indebted to the discussion it received on that occasion. I am particularly grateful for their comments to David Edwards, Maurice Glassman, Joanna Hodge, Adrian Leftwich, Christopher Megone, Susan Mendus, Glen Newey and Peter Nicholson.

1. See the essays by Alex Callinicos and Albert Weale; see also, for example, Roemer (1986) and Bonner (1986).
2. One closely related area where linguistic philosophy did seem to have a more beneficial effect is legal philosophy (for example, Hart, 1961).
3. Other political philosophers share most, but not all, of these beliefs (see, for example, Raz, 1986; Walzer, 1983). It then becomes a complex question how far they can be properly understood as 'foundationalists'.

REFERENCES

Ackerman, B. (1980), *Social Justice and Liberal State* (New Haven, Yale University Press).

Acton, H. B. (ed.) (1969), *The Philosophy of Punishment* (London, Macmillan).

Arendt, H. (1958a), *The Origins of Totalitarianism* (New York, The World Publishing Company).

Arendt, H. (1958b), *The Human Condition* (Chicago, University of Chicago Press).

Ayer, A. J. (1971), *Language, Truth and Logic* (Harmondsworth, Penguin).

Beiner, R. (1983), *Political Judgement* (London, Methuen).

Bonner, J. (1986), *Politics, Economics and Welfare* (Brighton, Wheatsheaf Books).

Collingwood, R. G. (1942), *The New Leviathan* (London, Oxford University Press).

Dunn, J. (1979), *Western Political Theory in the Face of the Future* (Cambridge, Cambridge University Press).

Dunn, J. (1985), *Rethinking Political Theory* (Cambridge, Cambridge University Press).

Dunn, J. (1986), 'What is living and what is dead in the political theory of John Locke' unpublished paper presented to the Morrell Political Theory Conference, University of York.

Dworkin, R. (1977), *Taking Rights Seriously* (London, Duckworth).

Feyerabend, P. (1975), *Against Method* (London, New Left Books).

Feyerabend, P. (1978), *Science in a Free Society* (London, New Left Books).

Gewirth, A. (1978), *Reason and Morality* (Chicago, University of Chicago Press).

Gewirth, A. (1982), *Human Rights* (Chicago, University of Chicago Press).

Goldman, A. I. (1979), *Justice and Reverse Discrimination* (Princeton, NJ, Princeton University Press).

Hart, H. L. A. (1961), *The Concept of Law* (London, Oxford University Press).

Hayek, F. A. (1944), *The Road to Serfdom* (London, Routledge and Kegan Paul).

Hayek, F. A. (1960), *The Constitution of Liberty* (London, Routledge and Kegan Paul).

Kolakowski, L. (1988), *Metaphysical Horror* (Oxford, Basil Blackwell).

Kuhn, T. S. (1970), *The Structure of Scientific Revolutions* (2nd edn.), (Chicago, University of Chicago Press).

Kundera, M. (1984), *The Unbearable Lightness of Being* (London, Faber and Faber).

Laslett, P. (1956), 'Introduction' in P. Laslett (ed.), *Philosophy, Politics and Society*, First Series (Oxford, Basil Blackwell).

Leftwich, A. (ed.) (1984), *What is Politics?* (Oxford, Basil Blackwell).

Lloyd Thomas, D. A. (1988), *In Defence of Liberalism* (Oxford, Basil Blackwell).

MacIntyre, A. (1981), *After Virtue* (London, Duckworth).

MacIntyre, A. (1988), *Whose Justice? Which Rationality?* (London, Duckworth).

Mendus, S. (ed.) (1988), *Justifying Toleration* (Cambridge, Cambridge University Press).

Nozick, R. (1974), *Anarchy, State and Utopia* (Oxford, Basil Blackwell).

Oakeshott, M. (1962), *Rationalism in Politics* (London, Methuen).

Popper, K. (1945), *The Open Society and its Enemies* (London, Routledge and Kegan Paul).

Rawls, J. (1971), *A Theory of Justice* (Oxford, Oxford University Press).

Raz, J. (1986), *The Morality of Freedom* (Oxford, Oxford University Press).

Roemer, J. (ed.) (1986), *Analytical Marxism* (Cambridge, Cambridge University Press).

Rorty, R. (1982), *Consequences of Pragmatism* (Brighton, Sussex, Harvester Press).

Rorty, R. (1985), 'Solidarity or objectivity?' in J. Rajchman and C. West (eds), *Post-Analytic Philosophy* (New York, Columbia University Press).

Rorty, R. (1987), 'Thugs and theorists: a reply to Bernstein', *Political Theory,* **15**.

Sandel, M. (1982), *Liberalism and the Limits of Justice* (Cambridge, Cambridge University Press).

Singer, P. (1973), *Democracy and Disobedience* (London, Oxford University Press).

Strauss, L. (1953), *Natural Right and History* (Chicago, University of Chicago Press).

Taylor, C. (1985), *Human Agency and Language, Philosophical Papers* (2 vols), (Cambridge, Cambridge University Press).

Walzer, M. (1977), *Just and Unjust Wars* (Harmondsworth, Penguin).

Walzer, M. (1983), *Spheres of Justice* (Oxford, Martin Robertson).

Weldon, T. D. (1953), *The Vocabulary of Politics* (Harmondsworth, Penguin).

9. International Relations

Steve Smith

This chapter focuses on the subfield of international relations, which has historically been rather more separate from the main body of writing and teaching about politics than has been the case with the other subfields dealt with in the other chapters of this book.* The chapter will first examine the developments and achievements of the area since the late 1960s; second, it will look at the problems that have emerged in the subject as it has developed since the late 1960s; finally, it will point to the new directions and focal points for the next decade or so. It will be particularly interesting to see if this final section indicates that international relations is moving any closer to the concerns of the other areas of Politics, which is a theme that I will return to in the concluding part of the chapter.

INTRODUCTION

As an introduction, we need to say a little about two issues: first, why the subject has developed rather separately from the mainstream of Politics; second, what aspects of the subject of international relations will be dealt with in this chapter. On the first point, it is worth recollecting that the modern discipline of international relations only came about as a direct response to the First World War. Up until that time the issues now dealt with in the subject had been the concern of a number of disciplines – most notably law, history, economics and philosophy. It was only with the horrific and seemingly unintended events of the period between 1914 and 1918 that academics began to speak of a distinct and separate discipline of international relations. This new discipline was recognized by the establishment of the first chair in the subject, at Aberystwyth in 1919. It was also an explicitly campaigning discipline, dedicated to preventing the recurrence of war. Believing the First World War to have been the result of misunderstanding, it stressed the need to enlighten and mediate. This phase lasted until the events of the late 1930s demolished any remaining belief in this Idealist conception of the international system. Since then, the subject has been dominated by a conservative and somewhat pessimistic theoretical view known as Realism. This was severely challenged by the behaviouralists in the 1950s and 1960s; indeed, many of them thought that they had indeed replaced Realism, but the fact of the matter is that Realist assumptions have dominated the subject for the last 40 years.

International relations has developed in ways that mirror (and usually lag behind) those that have occurred in the other areas of the discipline, but the separateness of the subfield has been one of its most noticeable features. It, like other subfields of Politics, has its own journals and conferences, but it also has its own professional organization (in the UK the British International Studies Association; in the USA the International Studies Association). More concretely, the subject is often taught in separate departments of international relations, in which there are specialists in international economics and law as well as international politics. This is a degree of separateness that does not really typify other areas of Politics.

Turning to the areas to be covered in this review, it is obvious, given what has just been said about the interdisciplinary nature of the subject, that it is impossible to summarize the trends and developments in each of the areas within international relations. Instead, the chapter will focus on the mainstream theoretical work within the subject. This means omitting the details of debates in areas such as international organizations, strategic studies and foreign policy analysis, and instead means concentrating on those debates and trends of which any academic working within the subject would have to take account. In short, we will focus on the central debates within the core theories of international relations.

DEVELOPMENTS AND ACHIEVEMENTS IN INTERNATIONAL RELATIONS SINCE THE 1960s AND 1970s

What then have been the major developments in the subject since the late 1960s? At the most general level, there has been a major movement away from the heady days of behaviouralism. The 1960s was very much a decade in which positivism, narrowly defined, ruled the subject. The major methodological debates of the 1960s became increasingly concerned with the relative merits of various ways of manipulating data, and it was taken as given that this new international relations bore little resemblance to the Realism it was said to replace. Most importantly, it was taken for granted that those engaged in studying international relations were involved in studying regularities of behaviour, with the aim of creating a general theory. All work that was not moving towards this end was seen as essentially irrelevant, belonging to the old, and failed, school of traditionalism. As one of those in the forefront of this movement put it in 1969: 'The war is clearly over. Many traditionally trained scholars are beginning to tool up . . . there is no longer much doubt that we can make the study of international relations into a scientific discipline worthy of the name' (Singer, 1969: 85–6).

This type of assumption dominated virtually all of the theoretical work coming out of the USA in the late 1960s, so much so that those engaged in this approach to the subject could think of themselves as having won a war, in much the same way as Singer indicated above. This view was not completely accepted, and certainly not in the UK where a strong reaction to the claims of the behaviouralists was led by figures such as Hedley Bull, Martin Wight and Fred Northedge (see Butterfield and Wight, 1966; Bull, 1966, and Northedge, 1976a). Nevertheless, the behaviouralists dominated the subject in the USA and therefore dominated the literature worldwide: international relations, to use Stanley Hoffmann's words, has been very much an American social science (Hoffmann, 1977).

Since the late 1960s, this concentration on a positivist conception of the subject has come under increasing attack. Not only have the traditionalists continued to bemoan the lack of achievements, as well as the pretensions of the behaviouralists but, more importantly, there have been major reservations expressed about the advantages of positivism by some of the major theorists in the subject. Put simply, the positivists ran up against the age-old problem of induction – namely that there is no automaticity about the transformation of data into theory. Having received mass funding for quantitative research in the 1960s and early 1970s, the behaviouralists failed to deliver the goods. Their data collections rarely led to new findings, let alone theory. Now, some behaviouralists would argue that theory *per se* was never the main goal, and that the whole purpose of behavioural international relations research was to unearth data that could be used to test theory; but this is simply to return to the kinds of claim made for behaviouralism in the 1960s. What is far more important is to note that the subject moved radically away from a naive behaviouralist epistemology during the mid- to late 1970s.

In virtually all areas of the subject, attention turned away from the search for general theory to a concentration more on middle-range theory. Thus, whereas the 'key' works of the 1960s focused on general theory, the 1970s saw an emphasis on less ambitious theory. There remained the fascination with quantitative approaches, and the basic elements of the behaviouralist creed were still evident, but the assumption that moving from data collection to theory was an automatic, and straightforward, activity disappeared. To take just one example, in the area of foreign policy analysis the 1960s were dominated by the search for general theory, with the works of Modelski (1962), Snyder, Bruck and Sapin (1962), and especially Rosenau (1966, 1967, 1969, 1974) being the core theoretical statements. Each saw the task of constructing a general theory of foreign policy behaviour as the goal of the subject, and each saw a clear route to creating such a general theory.

Contrast the methodological assumptions of these works with the main works of the 1970s and 1980s. Not only did the leader of the general theory approach, Rosenau, confess that the subject was in disarray (1976a), just after having pronounced that the subject was now in a state of Kuhnian 'normal science' (1976b), but the most important works published were all concerned with a much less ambitious claim. The key works of Allison (1971), Janis (1972, 1982), and Jervis (1976) all sought to explain, by a case-study approach, some aspects of the foreign policy behaviour of some states. There was no indication that such an account would apply to all states, nor to all aspects of foreign policy behaviour. These were middle-range theories, and they did not claim that general theory was the goal. Not surprisingly, these middle-range theories led to a large amount of follow-up work, such that each has now established an impressive and theoretically powerful area of explaining foreign policy behaviour.

A similar story could be told in many of the main areas of international relations theory. Indeed, by the mid-1970s the subject was involved in a lengthy debate over the appropriateness of the scientific route to enquiry generally, and the utility of quantitative methods more specifically. Excellent examples of this debate can be found in Sullivan (1976), Hoole and Zinnes (1976), and Zinnes (1976). Each of these books reviews the achievements of quantitative international relations research, and, while Sullivan and Zinnes tend to summarize the state of the subject, the essays in Hoole and Zinnes are more critical: the book consists of a set of papers looking at the achievements of the four main quantitative projects ('Correlates of War', 'Dimensionality of Nations, 'Inter-Nation Simulation', and the '1914 Project'). The essays are bleak reading for anyone who had, or has, faith in the quantitative route to theory. In each case the project had been in existence for between 10 and 20 years, yet none had achieved much in the way of consistent findings, let alone theory. One has to say that, nearly 15 years later, the picture has not greatly altered.

This retreat away from full-blown behaviouralism does not mean either that the subject is no longer dominated by behaviouralist methods or that there is no search for general theory in the current literature. Behaviouralism continues to be the dominant methodology, but there is no longer the assumption that there is a single road that leads inexorably to theory. This search for theory continues, but there are a number of routes being followed. What makes the story of the rise and decline of positivism in international relations more easy to understand is the critical point that, despite the claims of the leaders of the movement, behaviouralism was only concerned with issues of methodology. The behaviouralist revolution in international relations never really involved theory. This seems like heresy to the behaviouralists whose own view of their work stressed their massive opposition to the assumptions of the traditionalists. Yet, in truth, the behaviouralists tended to accept the theoretical assumptions of traditionalism.

This has been most clearly exposed by John Vasquez in his 1983 book, *The Power of Power Politics*. In this study, Vasquez indicates that the vast majority of the behaviouralists' work was carried out within the theoretical assumptions of the Realist paradigm. Put simply, behaviouralists tended to accept the three central assumptions of Realism: that states were the dominant actors in international relations; that there was a sharp divide between domestic and international politics; and that there was a hierarchy of interests, with military–security issues at the top and economic issues at the bottom. Despite their beliefs to the contrary, then, behaviouralists tended to have no theoretical differences with Realists. This explains why no major breakthroughs in theory resulted from quantitative research.

Therefore, in contrast to many portrayals of the subject during the last two decades, the implication of this analysis is that there has been a great deal of theoretical continuity, despite much methodological noise. The fascination with disputes about method has masked fundamental agreement about theory. In this light, Realism continues to dominate the subject. This has been confirmed by recent studies, as well as by the vast amount of detailed examination of the issue in Vasquez's book (see, for further examples, Alker and Biersteker, 1984, and Holsti, 1985).

MAJOR THEORETICAL ISSUES SINCE THE LATE 1960s

Given this overview of developments at the general level of methodology and theory, what have been the most important theoretical debates? Not surprisingly, the most important theoretical issues have concerned challenges to the Realist view of international politics. Taking the three defining features of Realism noted by Vasquez, there have been debates within each of these. To a large extent these debates have occurred in response to what were seen in the USA as the major issues of international relations in the 1970s. At the risk of great oversimplification, these could be summarized as the rise of détente (which many saw as a new equilibrium in superpower relations, one that removed war as a policy option), combined with a massive increase in the importance of economic issues.

The East–West divide was seen as being replaced by a North–South divide, and economic issues were replacing military issues as the central aspects of international politics. Furthermore, in this new North–South economic world, the dominant actors were often not states. This led to a large body of opinion challenging the Realist orthodoxy about the central theoretical issues of the subject.

The first area of debate concerned the role of the state. Once the central military contest between the USA and the USSR was perceived as moving off centre-stage, those military conflicts that remained tended to involve at least one non-state actor. Similarly, once international relations was seen as more economic than military in character, then the actors involved were often non-state actors. The debate was one between state-centrism and transnationalism. The key publications in this debate were the 1972 study edited by Keohane and Nye, and the 1976 *Web of World Politics* study by Mansbach Ferguson and Lampert. The latter went so far as to claim that the state was no longer involved in the majority of international transactions. This debate over the role of non-state actors such as multi-national companies and revolutionary groups persisted through the 1970s, with powerful counterattacks coming from state-centric scholars such as Bull (1977) and Northedge (1976b). A good summary of the debate is found in Maghroori and Ramberg (1982).

There is no need to elaborate on this debate since it is, in many ways, the most important debate in international relations theory. There seems no way in which the subject will transcend the rival views, and there now seems to be agreement within the discipline that one of the most important theoretical issues within the subject concerns the role of state and non-state actors.

The second area of the Realist orthodoxy to be challenged has been that of the domestic–international divide. The point at issue here is the extent to which it is possible to distinguish between the domestic and external environments of states. If one can distinguish between them, then it allows powerful models of state behaviour to be developed by using notions of system–unit relations. If states are indeed closed units, then it is possible to construct models and theories of behaviour which introduce notions of systemic causation. At this point, international relations theory begins to mean something rather specific, as the internal attributes of states (such as ideology, political system, economic system, culture, and values) can be treated as exogenous. It was this distinction between external and domestic environments that gave Realism such theoretical power. It could claim to be a theory of the behaviour of all types of states, and not be prone to the type of ethnocentrism that pervaded its main theoretical rival, Idealism.

However, this assumption has come under severe challenge since the 1960s. Of course, no Realist ever assumed that the actual external and domestic environments could be so easily separated, only that this was possible analytically. By the early 1970s, even this assumption seemed unwarranted given the dominant issues to which states had to respond. These were primarily economic in character, and, as such, not only involved actors that were not states, but also seemed to render obsolete any pretence that the external and internal environments could be distinguished analytically. There were two aspects of this argument. The first was that the process of modernization altered the structure of world society such that there were no longer obvious behavioural divides between the domestic and the international environments. As Morse (1976) has argued in probably the most influential statement of this viewpoint, the process of economic modernization has transformed international society such that the traditional distinction between domestic and foreign affairs has broken down.

A second strand of thinking about this issue has been summarized under the term 'interdependence'. According to this line of argument, most clearly discussed in Keohane and Nye (1977) and Cooper (1968), the increasing percentage of GNP represented by foreign trade has created a situation in which economies have become increasingly sensitive and vulnerable to events in other economies. This increasing interdependence results in a situation in which it becomes analytically impossible to distinguish between domestic and international politics: there is no longer a neat divide between the two environments, and therefore systemic accounts of international politics become more problematic.

The final area of the Realist paradigm that has come under attack is the related one of the hierarchy of interests. It was this that made it possible to develop a power politics model of international relations. Accordingly, power was a fixed phenomenon, which meant the same thing to every international actor. Moreover, the most important aspect of power was the military dimension, thus making it possible to distinguish between high and low politics. The existence of such a distinction made it straightforward for Realists to talk of their theory as objective and not susceptible to subjective factors. However, once it is accepted that economic issues are centre-stage, then this distinction between high and low politics loses its coherence. When, to coin Richard Cooper's phrase, 'trade policy is foreign policy' (1972: 18), then it is clear that there is no objective measure of power and this results in serious problems for the Realist paradigm. Rather, as Mansbach and Vasquez (1981) have argued, the power politics model gets replaced by an issue politics model.

Together, these three areas of challenge to the Realist model have constituted the main theoretical battleground since the late 1960s. But, it must be noted that this challenge has been severely attacked in turn. The obvious empirical reason for this attack was the return to the 'good old days' of the Cold War in the early 1980s. In many ways the early 1980s resembled the 1950s and 1960s more than the 1970s. The East–West divide again seemed to be the central issue in world politics, and the actors were states. Not only this, but the rise of economic issues did not lead to the erosion of state power in these areas; on the contrary, states soon became more heavily involved. Not only do they wish to avoid giving up sovereignty or control, but their populations call for their governments to act to protect them from the deleterious effects of international economic forces.

The reaction to the transnationalist challenge has been most visible in two areas. The first is in the literature on international political economy, which has been the most important area of development in the theory of the subject in the last decade. Developing out of the recognition that economic issues were rising in importance (although Marxist writers would argue that they have never been unimportant), international political economy (IPE) has sought to explain the patterns of international politics that result from economic interaction. In the literature, the debate has centred around the concept of regime, the argument concerning how the international economy remains stable in the absence of a hegemonic power. Reflecting much of the discussion surrounding the decline of the US economy, the regime literature has sought to explain stability without a hegemon. The key works in the debate are Krasner (1983) and Keohane (1984). Within the IPE literature, the other main strand has been that of the world systems theorists, such as Wallerstein (1974, 1980), who seek to explain the development of international politics by the development of the world economy.

The more general response to the transnationalist challenge has been the rise of an approach dubbed Neo-realism. If the transnationalist challenge was the central theoretical debate of the 1970s, then the subject has been fixated with Neo-realism in the 1980s. One strand of Neo-realism has already been discussed – namely, the attempt to introduce economics into the Realist account of world politics. This has been done by those IPE scholars who seek to explain international economics by reference to the behaviour of states. A classic example of this is Krasner's 1978 study *Defending the National Interest*. The more important aspect of Neo-realist thought has developed around the 1979 book by Kenneth Waltz, *Theory of International Politics*, in which the author seeks to develop a truly systemic account of international relations. He attacks existing systemic theories as being reductionist and argues that a truly systemic account would explain international relations by reference to only three factors: the organizing principles of the system (hierarchy or anarchy); the functional differentiation between the units of the system (do they carry out the same functions or do they perform different functions?); and the distribution of capabilities between the units. Waltz argues that international systems are always anarchic and that the units (states) carry out identical functions; therefore, the only criterion by which international systems can be distinguished concerns the distribution of capabilities – are they multipolar or bipolar?

Waltz's attempt to construct a systemic account of international relations has led to a number of responses, the most important of which have been published as a collection edited by Keohane (1986). These responses concentrate on whether he has distinguished between unit-level and system-level causes; on whether his assumptions about the sources of systems change can actually account for that change; and whether he too can avoid reductionism. This is, at the time of writing, still the major debate in the subject.

In addition to these general theoretical debates within the subject, there have been a number of developments in the various subfields that make up the discipline. Broadly speaking, the last two decades have seen a decline in the literature in the area of integration studies, as well as a review of the ethical dimensions of strategic studies. In the 1970s, the growth subfields were peace studies, ecology and international political economy and, in the 1980s, Neo-realism and critical theory. Above all, however, the subject has been trying to explain the relationship of developments in the 1970s to the immediately preceding and following decades. Therefore, all subfields have been working within the overarching theoretical issues discussed above.

PROBLEMS EMERGING SINCE THE LATE 1960s

The next area addressed by this chapter concerns the limitations of the way in which the subject has developed since the late 1960s. Broadly speaking, we can identify seven main problems and anomalies in the field. The first of these is that the field has continued to be very ethnocentric. It is a US social science, with the second largest professional grouping of scholars being in the UK. This Anglo-American dominance of the literature, reflecting also the dominance of the English language, has led to the dominance of Anglo-American values and policy concerns. Put simply, the agenda that the subject has set up reflects the interests of just one part of the world. Of course, many scholars from countries other than the USA and the UK have been involved in the professional debate, but it is vital to note that they have only rarely been able to put other items on the agenda. Lukes' third view of power applies to the academic world as well! In many respects, the problem of specifically US interests dominating the subject can at least be observed and accounted for. More problematic is the fact that the theoretical debate has been overwhelmingly determined by US policy concerns. The theory of the subject, therefore, has responded to a very specific notion of the most pressing and important issues in world politics, and this has produced a subject that treats some issues as *the* central ones to be explained by theory. International relations has become a hegemonic discipline reflecting the policy agenda of the hegemon.

A second limitation is that the debate about method has never really been resolved. By this I do not simply mean that there continue to be a number of different approaches but rather that the subject seems never to have decided whether it is a science or not. Now, this may well be true of all social sciences, as well as all other areas of Politics, but the behavioural revolution in the USA has resulted in a subject that remains wedded to a positivist route to theory, without any notion of what theory really involves. Similarly, those scholars who are basically historians seem increasingly drawn in to the language of theory. Writers such as Alex George, John Gaddis, Deborah Larson, Paul Kennedy and Paul Lauren have all written excellent histories, but each has utilized international relations theory explicitly. Maybe this is not so much a limitation as an area of intersection, but the worry persists that each set of scholars approaching the intersection does so with a very different set of theoretical assumptions. In short, the subject continues to be heavily divided about method, with little in the way of attempts to bridge these divides or to address the subject from a number of theoretical perspectives.

The third area of concern results from the second, and this is that the subject has not been very cumulative. What we have is a number of research frameworks, or paradigms, with little debate between them, and no real sense of an emerging comprehension of the subject. The research frameworks have their own journals, and professional meetings, and seem unable to speak to one another. In a Kuhnian sense, the subject is in a pre-paradigmatic state.

A fourth problem is that there has been a marked tendency for the subject to omit considerations of values in its discussions. The great problem of the behaviouralist legacy was an almost total concentration on that which could be measured. When the world of understanding and knowledge is restricted to such a narrow agenda, many critical issues get ignored. These issues are precisely those that have been central to other areas of Politics, most notably political theory. There was a revival of an explicit concern with values in the 1970s, under the aegis of movements such as the World Order Modelling Project, and the Club of Rome, as well as the whole peace studies movement, but all too often these were dismissed by those in the mainstream as failing to address the 'real' world. By and large, the subject has continued to stress the realities of power, and has contended itself with speaking 'truth' to power rather than talking in terms of morality. The other side of this coin is that the subject has, especially in the USA, become obsessed with policy relevance, and with consultancy rather than scholarship.

The fifth problem is that the state has remained the central unit of analysis without recognizing that the state has undergone fundamental transformations in the last few decades. In this light, it is simplistic to claim that the age-old 'laws' of international politics can apply in the late 1980s in the same way that they did (if they ever did) in the 1900s. Furthermore, the subject has continued to address an agenda of power politics whereas the actual policy concerns of states are much more to do with economic issues. Such a focus not only defines the subject in a particular way but also defines the space within which non-state actors can operate. The implication of this is that the subject has never really come to terms with the relationship between economics and politics: these aspects of the subject are dealt with by rather distinct research communities, often proceeding as if the other did not exist. This, of course, has been a problem that has historically bedevilled work in Politics generally, but the events of the last decade or so in international relations have made it particularly salient for that discipline. In many ways it has become the central debate in the subfield, with competing research communities offering distinct accounts of international relations from various positions based on conceptions of the economics–politics relationship.

A sixth anomaly is that international relations scholars have tended to ignore the domestic politics of states. What happens within a state is often treated as exogenous. Similarly, the subject has proceeded without taking much notice of what is happening within the area of comparative politics. The very real tension that this reflects is that international relations theory is at its most powerful when all states are treated as if they are essentially the same. The empirical picture is, of course, that the two areas of political activity are completely intertwined, but accepting this analytically has tended to make it very difficult to develop theory.

Finally, there is the issue of the extent to which the international system is a system; in other words, there remains a very real question over whether or not the behaviour of states can be explained by seeing them as units in a system. On the one hand, the notion of a power politics system makes it difficult to explain the development of aspects of a global community or society; on the other, systems forces do seem to overwhelm ideology and other transnational movements. Nonetheless, there are many examples where the behaviour of states is determined by domestic events. The problem is that there seems no way of combining the causal processes operating at the systemic and at the unit levels. As David Singer pointed out in 1961, there *is* a level of analysis problem in international relations.

THE FUTURE

If these are the problems that the subject is facing, what are the subject areas comprising the principal areas for development in the next decade? One obvious answer would be that the subject will need to address the seven problems noted immediately above, but this is a rather too hydraulic model of the sociology of knowledge. Also, many of these problems may well be endemic to the subject. Instead, I shall briefly list the six main areas which I think will prove to be the most important developmentally in the coming decade.

The first is a new area for development, and is that of feminism and international relations. The fundamental challenge posed by feminist thinking to Politics generally has emerged in the last 10 years or so, but in international relations it is only in the last year or two (and this is being written in August 1988) that the topic has been addressed. The feminist perspective will be dismissed by many scholars as completely irrelevant to the 'real' issues of international politics, but this simply misses the point. What feminists have to say about the subject is not confined to how many women are in the profession or in the policy-making community, nor is it confined to examining issues of gender or discussing 'women's issues'. Rather, the major contribution that feminism really can make is to discuss the values and methods that dominate international relations. As such, the feminist challenge is not so much a narrow one about specifically 'women's' concerns, although there clearly are such issues; rather it is more a critique of the dominance of male values and notions of enquiry in the subject.

To give just a few examples, what is this thing called 'the state'? Is it a body in which all persons are citizens, or is it a male state? Is the resort to war a male phenomenon, reflecting different patterns of socialization for males as distinct from females, or does it reflect an inherent set of male characteristics? What have feminists to say about the central concept of international politics, power: is this a gender-specific notion of power? What about crisis behaviour: do men tend to get locked into acts of aggression, being unwilling to 'back down', and do they tend to reject attempts to compromise? More saliently, is the very logic of decision-making in international relations one that reflects certain sets of assumptions about the world and how to be 'successful' in it, and are these values male as distinct to female? Is the logic of enquiry in international relations a male scientific one, stressing control, power and domination, or does it reveal more holistic conceptions of reality?

These are merely illustrative of the kinds of questions and challenges that feminist writers can pose to the orthodoxy of the subject, and are certainly not an attempt to define the content of their critiques. The central point is simply that the subject has been very much a male one, and therefore I believe that feminists have much to say about the assumptions and values that inform the study, and practice, of international relations. Feminist writers will face considerable opposition from the discipline, ranging from the hostile to the more likely response that the approach has nothing to say about the 'real' world. The more time that feminists are able to spend on the substantive issues rather than having to defend themselves against charges of irrelevance, then the more they will be able to challenge and transform the subject. It will be interesting to see what the state of play is in the other areas of the discipline with regards to the receptiveness to feminist arguments.

A second, and related, area for development is that of critical theory and international relations. This has been a growth area for the last decade, but in my view it remains one of the most fruitful and important areas for future development. As with feminism, it seeks to challenge the assumptions of the subject, by pointing out the silences that it does not address. Writers such as Robert Cox (1983), Richard Ashley (1984), Rob Walker (1987) and James Der Derian (1987) have already written extensively on this subject, but the challenge for critical theorists remains to write in a way that does address the issues dealt with in the mainstream of the subject, and which does engage in those debates. At present, the critical theorists remain 'voices off'. Together with the feminists, they have the prospect in the next decade of radically enlivening and restructuring the discipline.

The third area also challenges the dominance of the orthodoxy. This is that the subject needs to become much less hegemonic. It has to develop discourses and languages of debate that do not treat the concerns of countries outside the Anglo-American community as both peripheral, and, anyway, much like the concerns of the central actors. The subject needs to be international, and open to a variety of agendas, focal points, and logics and methods of enquiry.

The fourth aspect of the subject that is a major area for development in the next decade involves the linkage between international economics and international politics. This is probably a problematic intersection for many areas of Politics, but in international relations it has well developed research frameworks dealing with the two sets of issues – for example, international political economy, foreign policy analysis, and strategic studies. There is an evident need for scholars working in these areas to read each other's work and to try to address the central research questions of other research traditions. The literature on IPE does seem to be moving towards this, as does much Neo-realist work, but there is a long way to go before the separate frameworks concentrating on economics and politics can discuss the same set of issues. Of course, it may be that such an overlap is impossible, since the different research communities are indeed discussing different worlds.

Fifth is the development of work linking the explanation of the policy-making process within the state to the foreign policy behaviour of states. This involves building on the work undertaken on the decision-making system, most promising of which is the work on the impact of bureaucratic politics, group-think and belief systems on foreign policy. But it also requires much more consideration of two hitherto neglected aspects of policy-making: first, there needs to be much more attention paid to the implementation process. Until now, most foreign policy models and theories have concentrated on policy-making as if that is foreign policy behaviour. Clearly it is not, and the impact of the process of implementation has only recently been appreciated in the literature. Second, those models that do look at decision-making need to try to integrate the various middle-range accounts. All too often these are used in combination, whereas in fact they involve mutually exclusive assumptions. Most important in this enterprise is the linking of mechanistic models of behaviour, such as bureaucratic politics, with accounts of how actors see the world.

Finally, there remains the really central area for further examination – namely, the relationship between unit-level and system-level causes of unit behaviour. This has already been commented on above, but it is still the critical, even defining, issue of the subject. This is not some naïve call for an overarching theory, nor is it a claim that the level of analysis problem can be 'solved' or transcended. But it is vital that work continues to try to isolate the various causal processes involved at the different levels of analysis and, at the very least, to remember that international relations is caused by processes at more than one level.

This chapter started by commenting that the subject of international relations has been rather more separated from the mainstream of political science than have other subfields dealt with in this book. Whilst this survey has been by no means extensive, and has certainly stressed some developments rather than others, it should allow the reader to judge whether this separateness is still a feature of the subfield. Furthermore, it should allow them to assess whether the subfield continues to lag behind other subfields of political science.

At the beginning of this chapter I said that I would return to the issue of the separateness of the subfield from the mainstream of Politics. My own view is that international relations is very much a separate discipline, despite all the overlaps with Politics. Like Politics, it is concerned with issues of power, authority, and morality, and, like Politics, it is studied with a specific set of methodologies. However, the subfield does have a distinct professional structure, that, in the UK at least, has self-consciously established an identity separate to that of mainstream Politics. More saliently, those working in the subfield are as likely to take their cues from debates in economics or sociology as they are from those occurring in Politics. The conferences which they attend, the journals that they read and the people they talk to in their own institution are just as likely to come from the economics, sociology, history or psychology departments as from Politics. Above all, the nature of international relations in the real world does seem to involve rather different issues to those that occupy most political scientists who work on domestic politics. Furthermore, the international environment is crucially different to the domestic environment, since international anarchy does result in a specific structure different from that found within the state.

This does not mean that there are no areas of overlap. The most worrying aspect is that there is little contact between those working in different areas of Politics. In fact, the problems posed by the linkage with economics apply throughout the discipline. Similarly, the problems of method that have bedevilled international relations have also caused similar problems in other areas of Politics. I certainly think that there are massive areas for cooperation between international relations scholars and those in Politics, but, equally, I feel that the professional development of the subfield is leading it away from the mainstream of the discipline. This is simply the result of the way in which the subfield has developed. It has never been exclusively populated by political scientists, and it has never been concerned solely with narrowly defined politics. In short, the concerns of international relations are not merely the extension of those of Politics to the international sphere.

Finally, it is obvious that my opinion of how the subject needs to develop in the next decade reflects my view of what the subject is and should be: nevertheless, the contrast between the areas for development outlined in this and in the other surveys should inform the reader about rather more than my values. If pushed, I would argue that the most pressing need is for the subject to be as open as possible to alternative views, methods and discourses. The dominant approach to understanding international relations does reflect certain values, and it is vital that this dominance does not silence equally valid world-views. After all, the central defining characteristic of the international system is that there is no one morality nor any one universal moral or legal code. The challenge for the subject of international relations is for it to become a truly international and non-hegemonic discipline.

NOTE

I would like to thank Marysia Zalewski and Adrian Leftwich for their helpful comments on earlier drafts of this chapter.

REFERENCES

Alker, H. and Biersteker, T. (1984), 'The dialectics of world order: notes for a future archaeologist of international savoir faire', *International Studies Quarterly,* **28(2)**, pp. 121-42.

Allison, G. (1971), *Essence of Decision* (Boston, Little Brown).

Ashley, R. (1984), 'The poverty of neorealism', *International Organization,* **38(2)**, pp. 225-86.

Bull, H. (1966), 'International theory; the case for a classical approach', *World Politics,* **18(3)**, pp. 361-77.

Bull, H. (1977), *The Anarchical Society: a study of order in world politics* (London, Macmillan).

Butterfield, H. and Wight, M. (ed.) (1966), *Diplomatic Investigations* (London, Allen and Unwin).

Cooper, R. (1968), *The Economics of Interdependence* (New York, McGraw-Hill).

Cooper, R. (1972), 'Trade policy is foreign policy', *Foreign Policy,* **9**, pp. 18-36.

Cox, R. (1983), 'Gramsci, hegemony and international relations: An essay in method', *Millennium,* **12(2)**, pp. 162-75.

Der Derian, J. (1987), *On Diplomacy* (Oxford, Basil Blackwell).

Hoffmann, S. (1977), 'An American social science: international relations', *Daedalus,* **106(3)**, pp. 41-60.

Holsti, K. (1985), *The Dividing Discipline* (London, Allen and Unwin).

Hoole, F. and Zinnes, D. (ed.) (1976), *Quantitative International Politics* (New York, Praeger).

Janis, I. (1972), *Victims of Groupthink* (Boston, Houghton Mifflin).

Janis, I. (1982), *Groupthink* (2nd edn.) (Boston, Houghton Mifflin).

Jervis, R. (1976), *Perception and Misperception in International Politics* (Princeton, Princeton University Press).

Keohane, R. and Nye, J. (eds) (1972), *Transnational Relations and World Politics* (Cambridge, Mass., Harvard University Press).

Keohane, R. and Nye, J. (1977), *Power and Interdependence* (Boston, Little, Brown).

Keohane, R. (1984), *After Hegemony: cooperation and discord in the world political economy* (Princeton, Princeton University Press).

Keohane, R. (ed.) (1986), *Neorealism and its Critics* (New York, Columbia University Press).

Krasner, S. (1978), *Defending the National Interest* (Princeton, Princeton University Press).

Krasner, S. (ed.) (1983), *International Regimes* (Ithaca, Cornell University Press).

Maghroori, R. and Ramberg, B. (eds) (1982), *Globalism Versus Realism: International Relations' Third Debate* (Boulder, Westview).

Mansbach, R., Ferguson, Y. and Lampert, D. (1976), *The Web of World Politics* (Englewood Cliffs, Prentice-Hall).

Mansbach, R. and Vasquez, J. (1981), *In Search of Theory* (New York, Columbia University Press).

Modelski, G. (1962), *A Theory of Foreign Policy* (Princeton, Princeton University Press).

Morse, E. (1976), *Modernization and the Transformation in International Relations* (New York, Free Press).

Northedge, F. (1976a), *The International Political System* (London, Faber and Faber).

Northedge, F. (1976b), 'Transnationalism: the American illusion', *Millennium,* **5(1)**, pp. 21-7.

Rosenau, J. (1966), 'Pre-theories and theories of foreign policy' in R. Barry Farrell (ed.), *Approaches to Comparative and International Politics* (Evanston, Northwestern University Press), pp. 27-92.

Rosenau, J. (ed.) (1967), *Domestic Sources of Foreign Policy* (New York, Free Press).

Rosenau, J. (ed.) (1969), *Linkage Politics* (New York, Free Press).

Rosenau, J. (ed.) (1974), *Comparing Foreign Policies* (Beverly Hills, Sage Publications).

Rosenau, J. (1976a), 'Puzzlement in foreign policy', *The Jerusalem Journal of International Relations*, **1(4)**, pp. 1-10.

Rosenau, J. (1976b), 'Restlessness, change, and foreign policy analysis' in his (edited), *In Search of Global Patterns* (New York, Free Press), pp. 369-76).

Singer, J. (1961), 'The-level-of-analysis problem in international relations' in K. Knorr and S. Verba (eds), *The International System* (Princeton, Princeton University Press) pp. 77-92.

Singer, J. (1969), 'The incompleat theorist: insight without evidence' in K. Knorr and J. Rosenau (eds), *Contending Approaches to International Politics* (Princeton, Princeton University Press) pp. 62-86.

Snyder, R., Bruck, H. and Sapin, B. (1962), 'Decision-making as an approach to the study of international politics', in their (edited) *Foreign Policy Decision Making* (New York, Free Press) pp. 14-185.

Sullivan, M. (1976), *International Relations: Theories and Evidence* (Englewood Cliffs, Prentice-Hall).

Vasquez, J. (1983), *The Power of Power Politics* (London, Frances Pinter).

Walker, R. (1987), 'Realism, change, and international political theory', *International Studies Quarterly*, **31(1)**, pp. 65-86.

Wallerstein, I. (1974), *The Modern World System I: Capitalist Agriculture and the*

Origins of the European World-Economy in the Sixteenth Century (New York, Academic Press).

Wallerstein, I. (1980), *The Modern World System 11: Mercantilism and the Consolidation of the European World-Economy, 1600–1750* (New York, Academic Press).

Waltz, K. (1979), *Theory of International Politics* (Reading, Mass., Addison-Wesley).

Zinnes, D. (1976), *Contemporary Research in International Relations* (New York, Free Press).

10. Marxism and Power

Alex Callinicos

INTRODUCTION AND SCOPE

The intellectual history of Marxism since the late 1960s has followed a rather peculiar course. Enormously invigorated by the social and political struggles of 1968 and after, forms of Marxist inquiry proliferated internationally, penetrating deep into the academic world. The past decade, however, has seen a marked failure of nerve: in some countries – particularly France – there has been a wholesale intellectual retreat from Marxism; in the English-speaking world, where the rise of 'analytical Marxism' has lent great academic prestige to historical materialism, leading practitioners have adopted an increasingly defensive tone, summed up by Jon Elster at the end of his major study of Marx: 'It is not possible, today, morally or intellectually, to be a Marxist in the traditional sense' (1985: 531).

Marxism is thus both widely influential and on the defensive. The reasons for this paradoxical situation are, ultimately, political (see Callinicos, 1982; P. Anderson, 1983; and Harman, 1988). One particular form that the resulting intellectual pressures on Marxism have taken is around a concept central to any claims which Politics might have to be a distinct science, namely that of power. Marxism, it is claimed, cannot account for the phenomenon of power, one of the most pervasive features of human social life. It is this assertion, a contemporary commonplace expressed, as we shall see below, in a variety of intellectual idioms, which I wish to challenge in this chapter. I shall seek to do so by first setting out Marx's central claim – that forms of domination are to be explained in terms of the forces and relations of production – and by then suggesting ways in which that claim can provide the basis of concrete historical accounts of specific power relations. My argument will therefore be that the further development of Marxism in the face of apparently formidable contemporary challenges lies not in the abandonment of its fundamental propositions and concepts but rather in their elaboration and application to, *inter alia*, the analysis of the various forms of domination to which human beings are still subject.

POWER AND DOMINATION

It is necessary, first, however, to distinguish between two senses of the term 'power'. One use of this word is to designate human causal powers – that is, the capacities agents have to alter the course of events. Thus understood, the term 'power' expresses a non-relational concept, at least in the sense that such causal powers are not necessarily exercised over other human beings. The object of human intervention is often either animals belonging to other species or inanimate parts of the physical world.

The concept of power at stake in contemporary debates is, however, a relational one. Here the term 'power' refers to a relationship between individuals or groups such that one party to the relationship is subordinate to the other. In this case, causal powers are necessarily exercised over human beings. Power in this sense is what Marx and Weber both call *Herrschaft* (domination) and I shall, for the purposes of clarity, use the term 'domination' to refer to this second, relational, kind of power. When thinkers as otherwise different as Michael Foucault and Anthony Giddens claim that Marxism lacks a theory of power, it is power in the sense of domination that they have mind (see Callinicos, 1985.)

I disagree with Foucault and Giddens on this matter. The issue can be stated using the distinction I have drawn between causal powers in general and domination. Marxism can be said to identify three kinds of causal power. The first, and least interesting for present purposes, are simply those powers which any healthy, adult human being will have. Second, there is the growing power over nature which human beings derive from their inherent ability to alter and improve their methods of production. I have in mind here what Marx calls the 'productive forces', an expression which he uses to refer to both the physical elements of production (labour-power and the means of production), and the form of social cooperation through which these elements are combined, at a given level of technique, in order to produce use-values. Marx, especially in the *Grundrisse*, identifies the development of the productive forces, involving crucially rising labour productivity, with the expansion of human causal powers. The expression '*Produktivkräfte*' is itself Marx's rendering of Smith's and Ricardo's concept of productive powers.

The third type of causal power identified by historical materialism is a second-order power – a power over powers – which Marx calls the relations of production. These consist (oversimplifying slightly) in the effective control exercised by agents over the forces of production – more specifically, over the physical elements of production, labour-power and the means of production. It is, of course, the differences between sets of production relations which constitute those between modes of production such as slavery, feudalism and capitalism.[1]

We are clearly on the borderline here between causal powers in general and domination. For one thing, under certain conditions – for instance, those where a minority has the appropriate degree of control over the productive forces – production relations involve exploitation, in the form of the extraction of surplus labour by this minority (the ruling class) from the direct producers. Exploitation may not, as John Roemer argues (1982), necessarily involve domination, but, in some cases at least, it does – for example, the slave and feudal modes of production. In these cases, exploitation requires the domination of the direct producers by the exploiters, whether in the form of the absolute control of labour-power implied by chattel-slavery or the coercively sanctioned extraction of rent from peasant producers characteristic of feudalism. This pattern is not, however, universal: Marx argues in *Capital* that capitalist exploitation depends on the separation of the direct producers from the means of production and the resulting economic pressures on proletarians to sell their labour-power to capital. Capitalist domination of labour-power within the process of production presupposes indirect economic mechanisms rather than direct coercive intervention. Moreover, even in the case of feudalism, the exploiters' position cannot be reduced to their domination of the direct producers, but also involves some degree of control over the means of production as well, typically in the form of landed property.

One reason for insisting that the relations of production cannot be reduced to forms of domination is that otherwise the central claim of historical materialism would lose its strength. This is that:

(A)   the forces and relations of production, a complex set of historically developed and changing powers, *explain* relations of domination.

(I shall henceforth call this 'the Marxist claim'.)
   For example, Marx writes:

> It is always the direct relationship of the owners of the conditions of production to the direct producers – a relationship always naturally corresponding to a definite stage in the development of the methods of labour and thereby its social productivity – which reveals the innermost secret, the hidden basis of the entire social structure, and with it the political form of the relation of sovereignty and dependence, in short, the corresponding specific form of the state. (Marx, 1894: 791)

Marx refers here to one form of domination – the political – but there are, of course, many others. Those which have attracted most attention in recent years are those based on gender, race and nationality. I take Marx's claim to be a quite general one, applying to *all* forms of domination. It is this which contemporary philosophers and social theorists find so hard to swallow. This scepticism is inseparable from the privileging of the concept of domination which is such a striking feature of the present intellectual scene. Various factors are involved in this cultural phenomenon, but I shall mention only two here. One is the impact of what are often called the 'new social movements' – feminism, black nationalism, lesbian and gay liberation – each of which addresses a specific form of domination, and all of which have tended in recent years to emphasize the particularity of the oppressions they experience and, consequently, the autonomy of their struggles from the traditional socialist movement for global social transformation. The other is the remarkable return to Nietzsche among large sections of the Western intelligentsia over the past 15 years. In some cases, the return is a direct one: Nietzsche's influence on such key post-structuralist philosophers as Gilles Deleuze, Jacques Derrida and Michel Foucault is evident and acknowledged. In other cases the influence is typically more indirect, typically via the intermediary of Max Weber, whose work takes up Nietzsche's questions in another idiom, which we have come to call sociology. The writing of many of the most interesting English-speaking social theorists – Anthony Giddens and Michael Mann, for example – pursues what is recognizably the Nietzsche–Weber tradition.

The result is something of a problem-shift in social theory. Whereas in the immediate post-war years the sociological orthodoxy – certainly in the English-speaking countries – would be some variant of a functionalist account of domination, where relations of domination are explained in terms of agents' position in the socio-technical division of labour or, more broadly, of the requirements of social reproduction (for example, Talcott Parsons' theory of power), today Nietzscheanism, in one of its variants, is likely to gain the most widespread assent. Such a position typically involves two crucial propositions:

(B)   Relations of domination are necessarily plural, with no one form of domination having causal or explanatory priority over the others.
(C)   Relations of domination are permanent features of all human societies.

The implications of the Marxist claim, stated earlier, are starkly opposed to both these Nietzschean propositions. Proposition (A) is inconsistent with (B) because assigning explanatory primacy to the forces and relations of production implies that the form of domination and struggle directly generated by exploitation – class domination and class struggle – assumes a greater importance than other forms of domination and struggle, particularly from the perspective of possible historical transformations. Given the decisive role which historical materialism assigns to the development and control of the productive forces, the conflicts over that control are likely to be crucial to determining the trajectory of social development. In Marx's own words, the class struggle is the 'immediate driving power of history' (Marx and Engels, 1965: 327).

The Marxist claim is also at odds with the Nietzschean proposition (C), because historical materialism denies that domination is a permanent feature of social life. Marx believed, as the passage cited above makes clear, that relations of domination are a consequence of class exploitation. The overthrow of class society which he believed could be accomplished by the emergence of the proletariat would therefore remove the material basis of all forms of domination.

I take it that these ideas are regarded as eccentric and outmoded these days, even by many people otherwise sympathetic to Marxism. One aspect of what Ellen Wood calls 'the retreat from class' (1986) is that the Nietzschean theory of domination has become part of the common sense of the left intelligentsia. Foucault's importance lies in the eloquence with which he expressed the idea that forms of domination, being both plural and permanent, cannot be removed at all, let alone by a working-class struggle for socialism, but can only be resisted by a necessarily fragmented and decentralized congerie of different movements. (See especially Foucault, 1980.) While comparatively few, perhaps, are prepared to face up to the full force of propositions (B) and (C) which make up the core of the Nietzschean theory of domination, many socialists accept, often enthusiastically, the political conclusions derived from them (see, for example, Laclau and Mouffe, 1985).

Now I wish to defend the Marxist claim, (A), against its Nietzschean critics by considering one particular form of domination, that involved in the military rivalries between nation-states. Before doing so, however, let me first make one particular point of clarification. A feature of theories which become embedded in commonsense beliefs is that their adherents appeal to what they regard as self-evident truths. Thus, contemporary Nietzscheans often invoke the very existence of what I shall henceforth call non-class forms of domination, such as sexual and racial oppression, as if this in itself were a refutation of proposition (A). But this is a bad argument. If it is meant to highlight the failure of historical materialism to consider these forms of domination, then it does not succeed, since classical Marxism has been grappling with such issues as nationality and gender virtually since its constitution, as the writings of Marx on Ireland, and of Engels on the family, show. In any case, the mere fact of non-class forms of domination refutes historical materialism only if we say that such phenomena fall outside the scope of normal theoretical inquiry; for explanatory theory typically proceeds by invoking unobserved, and often unobservable, mechanisms to account for visible phenomena. Marxism, in line with this model, does not deny the existence of, say, sexual oppression, but rather seeks to explain it in terms of something more fundamental – the forces and relations of production. For those (like the post structuralists) who do not reject this kind of intellectual endeavour in principle, the crucial question is how good actual Marxist explanations of non-class forms of domination are.

MILITARY CONFLICTS AND NATION STATES

I shall now try to bring out the strength of such explanations by taking the case of military conflicts between nation-states. This particular form of domination has attracted growing attention from social theorists in recent years, no doubt partly because of its obvious political importance given the outbreak of what is sometimes called the New Cold War in the late 1970s. In any case, it has become a common theme of recent writing that Marxism's privileging of class relations makes it incapable of accounting for an international system of nation-states shaped by military and territorial rivalries. This argument has been perhaps best put by Theda Skocpol (1979), but it is also strongly defended by Giddens (1981) and Mann (1986) among others.

A particular weak point in the Marxist case is generally considered to be the fact that the international state system antedates the predominance of the capitalist mode of production, originating as it did during the emergence of the absolute monarchies of the early modern era. This suggests that military conflicts between states involve a dynamic irreducible to the logic of capital. Such an argument would, however, be gravely undermined if it could be shown that the formation of the state system can itself be accounted for in Marxist terms.

As it happens, an explanation along these lines is to be found in the work of the American Marxist historian Robert Brenner (see Aston and Philpin, 1985). The key to Brenner's argument lies in his analysis of the crisis which afflicted late-medieval Europe. Its roots lay in feudal relations of production, which had two central features:

1. 'the direct producers', the peasants, 'held direct [i.e. non-market] access to their means of subsistence, that is the tools and land needed to maintain themselves';
2. 'in consequence of the direct producers' possession', [the exploiting

class of lords] 'were obliged to reproduce themselves through appro-
priating a part of the product of the direct producers *by means of
extra-economic coercion.*' (Brenner, 1986: 27)

Both lords and peasants therefore had access to the means of reproducing
themselves without entering into market relations: the peasants through
their limited, but real, control over the conditions of production; the lords
through their ability coercively to extract surplus product in the form of
rent from the peasants. Consequently, neither class was subject to the kind
of systematic economic pressure to improve methods of production and
thereby to raise labour productivity which develops when, under capitalism, both direct producers and exploiters come to depend, for their
reproduction, on their ability together to produce goods which can be sold
on the market at competitive prices. Hence, after an initial burst of
innovation, feudal economic growth was primarily extensive, running into
long-term crisis at the end of the thirteenth century as population expansion outgrew the increasingly sluggish development of the productive
forces.

The crucial point for our purposes lies in Brenner's account of the lords'
response to the crisis of feudalism:

> In view of the difficulty, in the presence of pre-capitalist property relations, of
> raising returns from investment in the means of production (via increases in
> productive efficiency), the lords found that if they wished to increase their
> income, they had little choice but to do so by *redistributing* wealth away from
> their peasants or from other members of the exploiting class. This meant they
> had to deploy their resources toward building up their *means of coercion* – by
> investment in military men and equipment. Broadly speaking, they were
> obliged to invest in their politico-military apparatuses. To the extent that they
> had to do this effectively enough to compete with other lords who were doing
> the same thing, they would have to maximise both their military investments
> and the efficiency of these investments. They would have had, in fact,
> continually and systematically, to improve their methods of war. Indeed, we
> can say that the drive to *political accumulation*, to *state-building*, is the *pre-
> capitalist* analogue to the capitalist drive to *accumulate capital*. (Brenner, 1986:
> 31–2)

It is through this process of 'political accumulation' that the state system
of early modern Europe gradually emerged, as stronger and more centralized political units were formed in order the better to wage war with their
rivals. The centrality of war to the formation of the modern state system
has long been a commonplace. The distinctiveness of Brenner's argument
lies in the way in which he grounds this form of almost Darwinian natural
selection in the structural features of the feudal mode of production. It
seems to me that four propositions are crucial to the argument:

(D)   The direct access of both lords and peasants to their means of reproduction implies a long-term tendency to economic stagnation or even, in certain conditions (such as those of fourteenth- and early fifteenth-century France) regression (see Bois, 1976).

(E)   Lords (and peasants) are disposed, other things being equal, to maintain and, where possible, to increase their income.

(F)   The lords' possession of military power provides them with the means to respond to the increasing pressure on their revenues (for example, the falling rate of feudal levy documented by Gus Bois for late-medieval Normandy) by intensifying exploitation or seizing neighbouring land.

(G)   The fragmentation of feudal political power means that there is no imperial state capable of preventing lords from aggrandizing themselves at each other's expense.

I have already discussed propositions (D) and (F), and shall return to (E) below. Proposition (G) refers to a specific feature of medieval Christendom and is, in that sense, at a more concrete level than the preceding four propositions. Various writers have argued that Europe's political fragmentation was essential to the provision of the competitive environment which stimulated the processes of state-building and military innovation characteristic of the late-medieval and modern periods. However, the more abstract analysis of the structural limits of the feudal mode of production provided by Brenner offers the socio-economic context to the centralization of feudal power in the absolute monarchy. To a significant degree, the locus of exploitation was displaced from the decentralized extraction of rent to the imposition of taxes by an increasingly bureaucratized royal state to whose revenues many lords themselves had access via their occupancy of military or civil offices.

Brenner's analysis thus locates the emergence of the modern state system in the crisis of the feudal mode of production. Crucial to an understanding of the subsequent history of that system (and here we part company with Brenner who would not, I think, accept what follows) is the interaction of two competitive logics. The first is that of 'political accumulation', the military struggle between states, involving political centralization and military innovation and regulated by frequent outbreaks of war pursued as a means of dynastic and territorial aggrandizement. The other is that of capital accumulation, the competitive interaction of capitals exploiting wage-labour and producing for the market, and therefore under systematic pressure to reduce costs and thereby prices by productivity increasing investments. As capitalist production relations took root, first in English agriculture and then, from the late eighteenth century, in sectors of industry, so the two competitive logics fused. Military power came increasingly to depend on a capitalist economic base. Already in the eighteenth century the English aristocracy's control of a prodigiously productive agriculture allowed them to spend vast sums, by contemporary standards, on the means of war. Access to war-winning military technology came in the nineteenth century to presuppose the capitalist organization of industry, promoting modernization from above by absolutist regimes such as Prussia and Russia which continued to rest heavily on the old landowning class. By the time Marxists came to analyse the capitalism of their day at the beginning of the twentieth century they – (especially Bukharin, 1920, 1982) – seized on the fusion of the state and private capital, and on the competitive logics of political and capital accumulation as the central feature of what they came to call, following Hobson, 'imperialism'. Imperialism can, indeed, be seen as the final subordination of political to capital accumulation, so that the competitive interaction of capitals took on the form of the military rivalries between states, a change which precipitated what Arno Mayer has called 'the Thirty Years' War of the general crisis of the twentieth century' (Mayer, 1981: 3).

Here then, in absurdly summary form, is an analysis of the international state system which integrates it into the general Marxist theory of the feudal and capitalist modes of production. Let me now consider a couple of objections.

OBJECTIONS

One is, quite simply, the Soviet Union. The process of military competition did not, of course, stop in 1945 at the end of Mayer's Thirty Years' War. It continued in the shape of an arms race formally identical to that before 1914, but this time between the Western capitalist bloc and what we tend to call 'really existing socialism' – the USSR and its allies. But how can historical materialism hope to explain military rivalries between capitalist and supposedly post-capitalist societies, especially when the stronger of the latter behave in exactly the same way as Great Powers have traditionally acted, subjugating smaller states and even going to war with each other?

The USSR is more generally one of the most powerful arguments for the Nietzschean theory of domination (summarized by propositions (B) and (C) above) for it displays just about every form of domination known to class society – denying its citizens democratic rights and oppressing people on the grounds of their gender, race, nationality, religion, and sexual orientation. Nonetheless, it is, apparently, a society where class exploitation, along with the private ownership of the means of production, has been abolished. It seems as if Marxists must either engage in apologetic attempts to deny the realities of Soviet society or give up the claim, (A) above, that forms of domination are to be explained in terms of the forces and relations of production. The Parisian intelligentsia's extraordinarily belated discovery of the Gulag Archipelago in the 1970s helped drive them into the arms of Nietzsche and NATO.

There is, however, another course of action open to Marxists, namely to deny that the USSR is a socialist society. This is attractive for independent reasons. The usual grounds given for the Soviet Union's socialist character – that is, the nationalization of the means of production – involve the error, against which Marx had warned, of confusing a juridical property form (state ownership) with the relations of productions, which are relations of effective *control* over the productive forces. In practice, state ownership in the USSR means the exclusion of the mass of direct producers from control of the means of production, which is concentrated in the hands of a small bureaucratic élite at the top of the party–state apparatus. On this argument, the USSR is a class society. Moreover, the pattern of economic priorities – the subordination of agriculture and consumer industries to heavy industry and the military – replicates the subordination of consumption to production which Marx claimed was a prime effect of capital accumulation. The difference is that Marx argued that the pressure to accumulate capital derives from market competition, while the priority given to the Soviet military–industrial complex springs from the international structure of military rivalries between East and West. Nevertheless, the formal structure is the same (accumulation is enforced by competition) while we have seen that Bukharin argued long ago that the tendency for the state and private capital to fuse is characteristic of modern capitalism. On this account, the USSR is an extreme case of the militarized state capitalisms whose emergence was a fundamental feature of the world system in the first half of this century. (See Cliff, 1988.)

The second major objection to my argument can also be summarized very succinctly: the nation. The state system today differs from its early-modern predecessor in that it is a system of *nation* states. Each state claims to rule, not subjects, but citizens who are united by shared membership of a national community. Forms of national domination are a major source of political conflict in the contemporary world, and it is commonly held to be a fundamental weakness of Marxism that it is apparently unable to account for this phenomenon. Many Marxists do indeed accept this criticism, among them G. A. Cohen, author of the most influential recent defence of orthodox historical materialism (Cohen, 1983).

My own view is that, while nationalism represents a major political challenge to Marxism, it does not constitute an insuperable intellectual problem. The fact that national identifications are the most important form of political allegiance in the modern world is obviously a permanent threat to revolutionary socialist politics, for which the main lines of division are international, class antagonisms between capital and labour. The resulting difficulties posed for socialist strategy were long ago registered by Marxists, as is reflected by the rich and complex debates on the national question in the Second International (see Haupt *et al.*, 1974).

By comparison, explaining the salience of national identifications seems to me much less difficult. Recent reflection and research on the subject, much of it non-Marxist, have highlighted a number of points (see, for example, B. Anderson, 1983; Gellner, 1983). One is the historical novelty of national identities, emerging as they did in a world where allegiances and identifications in most regions were highly localized until well into the nineteenth or even twentieth centuries. A second is the constructed, even fictional, character of national identities, their formation typically involving what the work of some historians has encouraged us to call the 'invention of tradition', the creation of largely mythical histories and cultures to justify actors' mobilization, and often forced incorporation, as part of new political communities defined by an existing, or sought-after state (Hobsbawm and Ranger, 1983).

A theoretical framework for interpreting these phenomena is, in my view, provided by the concept of interpellation introduced by Louis Althusser (1970) and modified by Göran Therborn (1980). The central idea is that ideologies interpellate – that is, address agents under a particular identity. Each such identity has political implications – witness the different modes of address applied to British miners during the Great Strike of 1984–5, as strikers or wreckers, scabs or responsible citizens. The formation of national identities is a case of a particularly successful form of interpellation. The crucial question, however, is to uncover the social forces and political projects which underly the interpellation of particular agents in specific circumstances as members of a given nation.

Rather than seriously to attempt to address this issue here, I shall offer what seems to me an illuminating illustration. Eric Hobsbawm has argued that the invention of tradition was a particularly marked feature of late nineteenth-century Europe, a period of social transformation (proletarianization, industrialization, urbanization) which undermined traditional forms of authority at a time when states felt obliged to extend political rights of citizenship to wider layers of wage-earners (Hobsbawm, 1983,

1987.) A variety of practices developed in these circumstances whose effect (and sometimes whose intention) was to encourage this relatively new, and certainly recently enfranchized, working class as part of what Benedict Anderson (1983) calls the 'imagined community' of nationhood, uniting them with the local dominant class but also dividing them from all the classes of other such communities.

This is a case of what one might call 'interpellation from above', but often, of course, the construction of national identities came from below. The history of most colonial national movements is that of a dissident intelligentsia seeking to weld together a typically heterogeneous population into a coherent nationality capable of serving as a means of both legitimation and mobilization in support of the demand for an independent state. The pattern of urban intellectuals combining politico-cultural struggle with the cultivation of socio-economic grievances is a constant, from nineteenth-century Ireland or Bohemia to twentieth-century Zimbabwe or Iran. Usually, of course, these intellectuals are able to win a popular audience thanks to the anxieties and deprivations bred by capitalist modernization. Often the communities they construct prove, after independence, to be fragile in the extreme.

These remarks are the merest gestures towards a serious account of nationalism (there is, for example, a rich and fascinating body of work developing around the related phenomena of race, nation and tribe in southern Africa: see, *inter alia*, O'Meara, 1983; Ranger, 1985; Marks and Trapido, 1987). All the same, they do at least point in the kind of direction which led to the Marxist claim to explain forms of domination. Of course, my arguments here are doubly illustrative, in the sense that, even if historical materialism could account for national oppression, there are other forms of domination – one of them, namely sexual inequality, of overwhelming importance – for which Marxism must come up with independent explanations.

CONCLUSION: EXPLANATORY CLAIMS OF MARXISM

There is an important sense in which the phenomenon of nationality is of wider significance. Recent work on nationalism has been strikingly anti-essentialist in its insistence on the constructed, contingent nature of national identities. In this respect it is highly congenial to Marxism, which also tends to emphasize the historically specific nature of forms of domination. By contrast, the Nietzschean theory of domination, given its assertion in propositions (B) and (C) above of the irreducible plurality and the permanence of relations of subordination, is liable to eternize and essentialize these relations, treating them as somehow self-explanatory. In this sense, there is a strongly ahistorical undertow to the Nietzschean approach.

Such tendencies are not, however, inescapable. Nietzsche himself inaugurated a particular kind of historical writing, the genealogy of forms of domination, which Foucault sought with such distinction to continue. Nevertheless, there are reasons for thinking that the Nietzschean theory of domination is inherently liable to treat forms of domination as self-explanatory rather than contingent and constructed. One source of this inner fault lies in the Nietzschean proposition (C) that relations of domination are permanent features of all human societies, since one is entitled to ask: why should this be so? Nietzsche's own answer lay in the doctrine of the will to power, an ontological principle according to which reality as a whole is a chaos of competing power centres. But why should one buy this metaphysic? Weber gave the idea a more mundane expression, speaking of 'the fundamental fact of the external struggle of men with one another' (Weber, 1975: 222), at the price of reproducing one of the main axioms of classical bourgeois thought – namely, a conception of human nature as necessarily competitive and aggressive. Foucault's distaste for either essentialism led him into a series of notorious evasions which undermine his conception of power-knowledge. Thus he insisted on the omnipresence of both power and resistance without explaining how resistance can develop within the all-embracing apparatus of power-knowledge, a difficulty which underlies the major theoretical shift represented by the second and third volumes of *The History of Sexuality* (Foucault, 1984a and b)[2].

By comparison, not the least of Marxism's virtues is that it combines a very strong explanatory claim – that the forces and relations of production explain forms of domination (proposition (A)) – with rather weak assumptions about human beings and, indeed, about nature, which Nietzsche and his followers so eagerly assimilate to the social world. A good example is provided by Brenner's analysis of early-modern state-building, one of whose premisses, (E), is the assumption that lords (and peasants) are disposed, other things being equal, to maintain and, where possible, to increase their income. This is a mild and cautious assumption, consistent with a wide range of accounts of human motivation and behaviour. The explanatory weight is taken in Marxism not by general theories about human beings, but by concepts such as those of the forces and relations of production used to specify definite modes of production. This is, I suppose, merely a long-winded way of saying that Marxism is, fundamentally, *historical* materialism.

NOTES

I gave an earlier version of this paper at one in a series of seminars organized by the History Faculty of Cambridge University on Approaches to the Study of Power: I am grateful to all those who participated in the very lively discussion which followed, and to Adrian Leftwich for his comments on the present version.

1. On the basic concepts of historical materialism, see Althusser and Balibar (1968); Hindess and Hirst (1975); Therborn (1976); Cohen (1978); Elster (1985); Callinicos (1987).
2. See my review, Callinicos (1986) and the important critiques of Foucault's thought in Habermas (1985) and Dews (1987).

REFERENCES

Althusser, L. (1970), 'Ideology and the ideological State apparatuses' in *Lenin and Philosophy and Other Essays* (London, New Left Books).

Althusser, L. and Balibar, E. (1968), *Reading Capital* (London, New Left Books).

Anderson, B. (1983), *Imagined Communities* (London, Verso).

Anderson, P. (1983), *In the Tracks of Historical Materialism* (London, Verso).

Aston, T. H. and Philpin, C. H. E. (eds) (1985), *The Brenner Debate* (Cambridge, Cambridge University Press).

Bois, G. (1976), *The Crisis of Feudalism* (Cambridge, Cambridge University Press).

Brenner, R. (1986), 'The social basis of economic development' in J. Roemer (ed.), *Analytical Marxism* (Cambridge, Cambridge University Press).

Bukharin, N. (1920), *The Economics of the Transformation Period* (1971 edn.), (New York, Bergman).

Bukharin, N. (1982), *Selected Writings on the State and the Transition to Socialism* (Nottingham, Spokesman).

Callinicos, A. (1982), *Is There a Future for Marxism?* (London, Macmillan).

Callinicos, A. (1985), 'Anthony Giddens: a contemporary critique', reprinted in Callinicos (ed.) *Marxist Theory*, 1989.

Callinicos, A. (1986), 'Foucault's third theoretical displacement', *Theory, Culture and Society*, **3(3)**.

Callinicos, A. (1987), *Making History* (Cambridge, Polity).

Callinicos, A. (ed.) (1989), *Marxist Theory* (Oxford, Oxford University Press).

Cliff, T. (1988), *State Capitalism in Russia* (London, Bookmarks).

Cohen, G. A. (1978), *Karl Marx's Theory of History* (Oxford, Clarendon Press).

Cohen, G. A. (1983), 'Reconsidering historical materialism', reprinted in Callinicos (ed.), *Marxist Theory*, 1989.

Dews, P. (1987), *Logics of Disintegration* (London, Verso).

Elster, J. (1985), *Making Sense of Marx* (Cambridge, Cambridge University Press).

Foucault, M. (1980), *Power/Knowledge* (Brighton, Harvester).

Foucault, M. (1984a), *L'usage des plaisirs* (Paris, Gallimard).

Foucault, M. (1984b), *Le souci de soi* (Paris, Gallimard).

Gellner, E. (1983), *Nations and Nationalism* (Oxford, Basil Blackwell).

Giddens, A. (1981), *A Contemporary Critique of Historical Materialism* (London, Macmillan).

Gilbert, A. (1983), 'The storming of Heaven' in J. R. Pennock and J. W. Chapman (eds), *Marxism* (New York, New York University Press).

Habermas, J. (1985), *The Philosophical Discourse of Modernity* (Cambridge, Polity).

Harman, C. (1988), *The Fire Last Time* (London, Bookmarks).

Haupt, G. *et al.* (1974), *Les Marxistes et la question nationale 1848–1914* (Paris, Maspero).

Hindess, B. and Hirst, P. (1975), *Pre-Capitalist Modes of Production* (London, Routledge and Kegan Paul).

Hobsbawm, E. J. (1983), 'Mass producing traditions: Europe, 1870–1914' in Hobsbawm and Ranger (eds) *The Invention of Tradition*.

Hobsbawm, E. J. (1987), *The Age of Empire* (London, Weidenfeld and Nicolson).

Hobsbawm, E. J. and Ranger, T. (eds) (1983), *The Invention of Tradition* (Cambridge, Cambridge University Press).

Laclau, E. and Mouffe, C. (1985), *Hegemony and Socialist Strategy* (London, Verso).

Lakatos, I. (1978), *Philosophical Papers* (Cambridge, Cambridge University Press).

Mann, M. (1986), *The Sources of Social Power*, vol. I (Cambridge, Cambridge University Press).

Marks, S. and Trapido, S. (eds) (1987), *The Politics of Race, Class and Nationalism in Twentieth-Century South Africa*, (London, Longman).

Marx, K. (1894), *Capital* III (1971 edn.), (Moscow, Progress).

Marx, K. and Engels, F. (1965), *Selected Correspondence* (Moscow, Progress).

Mayer, A. (1981), *The Persistence of the Old Regime* (New York, Pantheon).

O'Meara, D. (1983), *Volkskapitalisme* (Johannesburg, Ravan).

Ranger, T. (1985), *The Invention of Tribalism in Zimbabwe* (Gweru, Mambo).

Roemer, J. (1982), *A General Theory of Exploitation and Class* (Cambridge, MA., Harvard University Press).

Skocpol, T. (1979), *States and Social Revolutions* (Cambridge, Cambridge University Press).

Therborn, G. (1976), *Science, Class and Society* (London, New Left Books).

Therborn, G. (1980), *The Ideology of Power and the Power of Ideology* (London, Verso).

Weber, M. (1975), *Max Weber* (New York, John Wiley and Sons).

Wood, E. M. (1986), *The Retreat from Class* (London, Verso).

11. Elections and Voting Behaviour

Pippa Norris

INTRODUCTION

The term 'paradigm' is often overused in intellectual histories and in Political Science it has been employed to embrace a variety of concerns, from behaviouralism to traditional political theory (Wolin, 1968; Beardsley, 1977; Almond, 1966). In most cases, political studies have proved so eclectic and diverse that the term 'paradigm' seems inappropriate in its original Kuhnian sense (Kuhn, 1962). Nevertheless in the field of electoral studies it is possible to identify, if not a paradigm, at least a dominant theoretical perspective, incorporating a body of concepts, techniques and methods of inquiry, which came to dominate the study of Anglo-American voting behaviour in the 1960s and early 1970s. In the USA, Angus Campbell, Philip Converse, W. E. Miller and Donald Stokes published *The American Voter* in 1960 which was rapidly accepted as the standard work on the subject, while in Britain David Butler and Donald Stokes established an equally authoritative text with the first publication of *Political Change in Britain* in 1969. It can be claimed that the 'Michigan' model, as it may be termed, shaped the understanding of electoral change for a generation of Political Scientists.

The recent history of electoral studies is, to a large extent, an account of the breakdown of the dominant paradigm. The Michigan model has been challenged by a number of alternative theories. Since the mid-1970s electoral studies have experienced a period of fragmentation of the field into a variety of different approaches. The literature is vast, diverse and complex. The purpose of this chapter is to make some sense of the field by providing a broad thematic overview. The chapter will first outline the development, in the 1960s, of electoral surveys in the USA and UK, before considering more recent revisionist accounts, concluding with some tentative comments about the future of electoral studies.

THE DEVELOPMENT OF ELECTORAL STUDIES IN THE USA

The publication of *The American Voter* in the early 1960s represented the convergence of a number of post-war developments in American Political Science, including changes in methodological approaches, institutional structures and financial resources which brought about what came to be known as the 'behavioural revolution'. There are problems about defining the concept of behaviouralism with any precision given the diversity of those who followed this perspective. In many ways, behaviouralism represented a gradual continuation of the empirical work in pre-war Political Science, rather than a clear-cut revolution. Nevertheless we can identify certain defining features common to this approach (for a fuller discussion see Dahl, 1960; Eulau, 1963, 1969). Essentially, behaviouralism was a research orientation associated with new sources of empirical data and methodological techniques. Within this perspective many wished to draw a sharp demarcating line between behavioural empirical analysis and the more traditional approaches of political theory, political philosophy and descriptive institutional analysis. Behaviouralists felt that Political Science should attempt to follow the Popperian model of scientific progress, with formal hypotheses derived from general theories which could be subject to critical scrutiny against the empirical evidence – in other words, the method of 'bold conjectures and attempted refutations'. The aim was to develop broad generalizations about the nature of voting behaviour in the USA which could be rigorously tested against data from large-scale electoral surveys, irrespective of whether such generalizations were consistent with models of elections in classical democratic theory. The emphasis was on description rather than prescription, the identification of observable uniformities in political behaviour, the validation of findings through replicable research, and the accumulation of knowledge through the development of well tested general theories (Seidelman, 1985; Ricci, 1984).

In the post-war years much of the stimulus for behavioural research came about through the development of survey techniques. These were facilitated by technological changes in mainframe computers which allowed the easy statistical manipulation of large-scale data sets. Serious commercial polling in elections started in the mid-1930s in the USA with the development of applied sampling techniques by the Gallup, Roper and Crossley organizations. Following this, large-scale academic electoral surveys expanded substantially in the post-war years, and much of the impetus towards the behavioural shift came from the explosion of electoral data which was available for secondary analysis.

The most notable institutional development was the creation in 1946 of the Survey Research Center (SRC) at the University of Michigan, joined in 1948 by the Institute for Social Research (ISR), later known as the Center for Political Studies. The work of Angus Campbell and associates at the SRC in Michigan has been responsible for the cumulative series of American National Election surveys which have formed the core of US voting studies since 1948. Over the years these surveys have increased in breadth and sophistication although the core items remain essentially unchanged, representing the largest pool of data available on the American voting population. The expansion of behavioural research was also encouraged by the National Opinion Research Center (NORC) at the University of Chicago, and the Social Science Research Council's (SSRC) Committee on Political Behaviour, chaired by V. O. Key from 1949 to 1953 and by David Truman from 1953 to 1964. In addition, since 1940, the Bureau of Applied Social Research at Columbia pioneered the use of panel and community studies (Rossi, 1959; Natches, 1970). The scale and cost of large-scale surveys means that electoral studies are heavily dependent upon collaborative research, particularly the secondary analysis of data collected through such sources.

In addition to institutional support electoral surveys, one of the most expensive forms of research in Political Science, requires generous financial resources. In the post-war years large philanthropic organizations such as the Ford Foundation, the Carnegie Foundation and the Rockerfeller Foundation gave increasingly strong support to behaviourally-oriented research. The Rockerfeller Foundation helped finance the voting behaviour studies conducted by Lazarfield, Berelson and Gaudet during the 1940 election and the SRC surveys throughout the 1950s.

THE MICHIGAN MODEL IN THE USA

Within this context the foundations were laid for the expansion of electoral studies in American Political Science. Before 1960 there were a number of classic pioneering works, notably *The People's Choice* (Lazarfeld *et al.*, 1944), *Voting* (Berelson *et al.*, 1954) and *Parties, Politics and Pressure Groups* (Key, 1942). But it is fair to say that none had quite the impact on the profession as *The American Voter* (Campbell *et al.*, 1960) which provided the mainstream theory of voting behaviour throughout the 1960s.

The American Voter constitutes an extensive critique of the assumption in traditional liberal theories of representative government that voters rationally choose candidates on the basis of the alternative party platforms. Campbell *et al.* stressed that, according to data in the series of American National Election surveys, the electorate was only marginally informed about, interested in and influenced by political issues. The model specifies three necessary conditions for issue voting: citizens must have an opinion about the issue; they must feel that the issue is important; and they must be able to distinguish between alternative policies offered by the parties. In the mid-1950s, according to *The American Voter*, only about one-fifth to one-third of the American electorate met these criteria on any given issue. Even fewer were found to have a consistent ideological viewpoint structuring their views across a wide range of issues. Converse estimated that only about 3.5 per cent of the population had an ideological perspective while 17 per cent had attitudes with no issue content whatever (Converse, 1964). On many issues, voters were found to have vague or inconsistent views. On a few highly salient issues, voters may have clear preferences about policy outcomes but it is a highly complex process to evaluate which alternative policies will achieve these desired outcomes. It is difficult to evaluate each party's stand on the issues. Party platforms may be vague, either to avoid alienating certain groups or because party leaders are undecided. Policy statements may be highly technical and complex. In the course of campaigns voters will also have to consider many low-saliency issues where the parties do not offer clear-cut alternatives. To evaluate the issues voters therefore needed to invest considerable resources of time and energy in the political process in order to find out what is going on, and Campbell *et al.* found that most people were just not that involved in politics. In line with wider debates in Political Science this seemed to provide further proof of the 'end of ideology'.

But although there is little general interest in politics, many people still feel a duty to participate; hence it follows that voters will seek short-cuts to guide their voting choice. The electorate will therefore tend to vote along the lines of others around them, taking their cues from their family, friends and colleagues, developing in their early years a long-run partisan identification to guide their future voting choice. The essential argument developed in this approach was that most voters remain highly stable over successive elections, with deep and long-term affective loyalties for the Democrats or Republicans.

For Campbell *et al.* the key concept was party identification, which seemed to be highly stable (although not unchangeable). It appeared to develop early in life prior to policy preferences and it appeared to strengthen over time. In this sense party identification was seen as an affective orientation, similar to a religious affiliation, rather than an instrumental evaluation. As people saw themselves as Catholics or Protestants, so they saw themselves as Democrats or Republicans. Partisanship therefore relates to our sense of identity, how we think of ourselves, a feeling of belonging. We would expect some voters to deviate or defect from their habitual party due to short-term factors – for instance, the attraction of specific Presidential candidate, the influence of particular campaign events or other highly salient issues – but most could be expected to return to their normal vote in subsequent elections. Hence we can speak of 'Reaganite Democrats'.

Partisan identification was therefore seen as essentially durable, an 'abiding attachment' or 'standing decision' with an extended time horizon (Converse and Pierce, 1985). Furthermore, once voters have committed themselves to a party, Campbell *et al.* suggested that they will adjust their attitudes, beliefs and values to fit their party identification (Campbell *et al.*, 1960: 120–34). In other words, it is because voters felt that they were Democrats that they saw themselves as supporting government welfare programmes, *détente* and affirmative action rather than vice versa. Therefore, as attitudes are formed simultaneously with alignments, they do not structure the way people vote although they may be closely associated. Instead, according to this theory, the primary factor influencing most voters is their social situation which leads to their habitual party loyalties. Hence long-term changes in the structure and composition of social groups could be expected to have a major impact on partisan alignments. The major social cleavages in American society – the divisions of region, ethnic identity and race, religion, income and gender – are closely associated with party support. As Robert Lane concluded: 'Over the long-run party identification has more influence over a person's vote decision than any other single factor' (Lane 1959: 300). The overall result is to give the Democrats and Republicans stable reservoirs of voting strength which they can call on over successive elections. Party loyalties therefore function to simplify the electoral choice facing voters. Although the argument in *The American Voter* challenged established views about electoral behaviour, the theory had far wider implications leading to certain fundamental and enduring questions in politics concerning the nature of human rationality and citizen participation in liberal democracies.

ELECTORAL STUDIES IN THE UK

The behavioural approach developed more slowly in the UK. The first academic surveys of the national electorate came about 15 years after those in the USA, and indeed the approach never achieved quite the same acceptance within the profession. In Britain, electoral studies prior to the 1960s were dependent upon three main sources of data: aggregate results from constituency returns; a limited range of items from regular Gallup national polls since 1945 and NOP polls since 1957; and surveys restricted to local constituencies (Milne and Mackenzie, 1954, 1958; Birch, 1959; Bealey *et al.*, 1965). The main approach in Britain before national surveys were available is best exemplified by the series of 13 Nuffield studies from *The British General Election of 1945* to *The British General Election of 1987*, authored or co-authored by David Butler since 1951. No other country has such a consistent series of academic studies providing an invaluable historical record of each campaign. The nearest equivalent in the USA was essentially journalistic – Theodore White's blow-by-blow account of *The Making of the President 1960* (1961) and subsequent volumes.

The primary aim of the Nuffield studies has been to account for the major developments within the campaign, including the government's record in office, party fortunes in the run-up to the election, the impact of specific events, the popularity of party leaders, the effectiveness of party organization, strategies and tactics, the coverage by the press and television, and the role of opinion polls, election issues, candidates and constituencies. The accounts include a sophisticated psephological analysis of the constituency results presented in an appendix but, without direct access to original survey data, the predominant approach of other parts of the book has had to remain primarily descriptive or historical rather than behavioural. By focusing on the period of the formal campaign, which can be seen as the tip of the iceberg, these studies cannot take account of long-term trends in electoral behaviour, or broad economic and social changes.

The first national academic survey of voting behaviour originated in the summer of 1963 with David Butler (Nuffield College, Oxford) and Donald Stokes (University of Michigan) just before the return of the first Wilson government. The series of British Election Surveys have subsequently been repeated after every General Election since 1964 under the continued direction of Butler and Stokes until 1970. The series then passed to a team from the University of Essex under the supervision of Ivor Crewe, Bo Sarlvik and James Alt (later joined by David Robertson) who supervised the surveys in February and October 1974 and in 1979. Direction then passed to Tony Heath (Jesus College, Oxford), Roger Jowell, Julia Field and Sharon Witherspoon (Social and Community Planning Research) and John Curtice (University of Liverpool) for the 1983 and 1987 studies. Funding for these surveys came from various sources, notably Nuffield College, the Economic and Social Research Council (previously the Social Science Research Council), and other research grant organizations. Although there is a large degree of continuity in these surveys, in the past they have never enjoyed the sort of institutional base and financial security provided by the SRC/CPS in the USA at Michigan. Nevertheless, the series of eight General Election surveys provide an invaluable cumulative source of data for secondary analysis, the longest academic series of nationally representative sample surveys in Britain. The series includes a panel element, as a proportion of the respondents are usually re-interviewed over successive elections. Recently, this source has been supplemented by the Social Attitudes Study, carried out by Social and Community Planning Research, available annually since 1983.

The approach of Butler and Stokes dominated the study of voting behaviour during the 1960s and early 1970s as they essentially established the field of survey-based electoral research in Britain. The explicit links between the team at Michigan and *Political Change in Britain* were acknowledged in their preface by David Butler and Donald Stokes, with much of the data analysis and writing being carried out at Michigan.

Although there are some important distinctions between the models of voting in the USA and Britain, the methodological, conceptual and theoretical connections proved to be strong. According to Butler and Stokes, during periods of stable partisan alignment, voters in Britain are anchored for long periods of time to the major parties, with an abiding and relatively durable loyalty over successive elections (Butler and Stokes, 1974: 211–28). In exceptional circumstances strong historical forces can sweep away political attachments and create new partisan alignments, hence the decline of the Liberals in the 1920s and the rise of Labour in the 1940s. But such radical changes are rare. Party loyalties proved slightly less stable in Britain than in the USA, as more voters changed their partisan self-image when they changed their vote, but partisanship continued to play an important role in structuring voting choice. The Butler and Stokes study suggests that in the 1960s most electors had little general interest in political issues and politics was remote from most people's lives, although most continued to cast their ballot. As a result, the electorate tended to vote along the lines of others around them, developing a long-run habitual identification to guide their future voting choice. This identification tended to be reinforced over successive elections. The primary factor influencing most voters was their social situation, especially their social class, which led to their habitual party loyalties. Without the range of pluralistic cleavages found in the USA, the role of occupational class was seen as paramount in Britain. As Pulzer noted: 'class is the basis of British party politics; all else is embellishment and detail' (Pulzer, 1967: 98). Both 'objective' and 'subjective' class categories were found by Butler and Stokes to be the strongest predictors of voting choice.

The American Voter and *Political Change in Britain* quickly came to be recognized in the 1960s and early 1970s as the standard works on the subject, the baseline against which other studies had to be judged. The model they embodied seemed to provide a comprehensive and consistent account of electoral behaviour in Britain and the USA, with radical implications for traditional assumptions about human rationality in liberal democratic theory.

Yet by the mid 1970s some were seeking to revise some of the theory's basic assumptions, raising thorny questions about the nature and meaning of partisan identification, the applicability of the concept in European systems, the measurement of issue voting, the role of political ideology, the stability of the system and the continuing influence of partisan alignments, although many wished to modify rather than abandon the basic model. In the 1970s wider changes in the political system, including the rise of divisive new issues, new parties, and a generation of new activists, seemed to challenge many of the basic assumptions about the stable, apathetic and non-ideological electorate. In the USA the theory came to seem increasingly inadequate in the context of violent race riots, mass demonstrations over Vietnam and the resurgence of extremist politics on the far left and right.

PARTISAN DEALIGNMENT IN BRITAIN

Widely observed trends towards weaker party loyalties in the USA and Britain raised questions about the explanatory power of the Michigan model. Since the mid-1970s there has been substantial evidence that Britain has been experiencing the process of 'partisan dealignment', a marked loosening of the electorate's ties with Labour and the Conservatives, as documented in Sarlvik and Crewe's *Decade of Dealignment* (1983). A high proportion of the electorate continue to acknowledge a party identification – 86 per cent in the 1987 General Election. Yet although party loyalties continue to structure the electorate, there has been a decline in the number of strong identifiers; in 1964 some 44 per cent of the electorate were committed partisans, 'very' strong Conservative, Labour or Liberal identifiers. By 1987 the proportion had dropped to 19 per cent. This change has affected both major parties, irrespective of social class, gender and age (Crewe, 1985).

Evidence about the causes of partisan dealignment have been supplemented by further symptomatic evidence provided in a series of studies which have found a substantial fall in official party membership, a decrease in the two-party share of the electorate, increased negative voting, greater switching towards third parties and the growth of electoral volatility between, and within, election campaigns (see Alt, 1984; Sarlvik and Crewe, 1983; Crewe, 1986; Crewe *et al.*, 1977; Rose and McAllister, 1986; Franklin, 1985).

PARTISAN DEALIGNMENT IN THE USA

There is substantial evidence that similar trends in partisan dealignment have been occurring in the USA. From 1964 onwards there was a rise in the proportion of US voters who saw themselves as independents. The proportion rose from 23 per cent in 1952 to 37 per cent in 1980, although many independents are 'leaners' towards one of the main parties (Keith *et al*, 1986). In American elections there has been greater vote-switching than in Britain and massive voting defections from party allegiances in Presidential elections. If there were no defections then the Democrats could be expected to hold the White House, given their consistent lead amongst party identifiers (with the exception of the 1984–86 period). Since the 1960s there have been other indicators of partisan dealignment, including more split-ticket voting, a fall in turnout and a decline in the proportion of strong identifiers. Therefore over the last decades parties-in-the-electorate have weakened.

Other develoments from the early 1970s have lessened the role of parties as organizations, notably the growth of primaries, political action committees (PACs) and candidate-centred campaigns, although the national committees have been reasserting their role in the last few years. The consensus which has emerged is that, in the USA, long-term party loyalties continue to be important in structuring the vote, but they are less important today that they were in the 1950s. If we accept that long-term factors have declined, the question which remains is what short-term factors influence the voter? Prospective policy issues? Evaluations of the government's performance? Campaign-specific factors such as campaign spending, candidate images, media coverage, party strategies? On this matter there is as yet little consensus. We need to consider the alternative accounts, first in the USA then in Britain.

PROSPECTIVE ISSUE VOTING IN THE USA

There were a number of major revisionist works re-examining the role of issues and party identification during the 1970s (Jackson, 1975; Markus, 1979; Franklin, 1984). The primary challenge was *The Changing*

American Voter published in 1976 by Norman H. Nie, Sidney Verba and John Petrocik. Their main argument was that Campbell *et al.* provided an accurate analysis of the electorate in the 1950s during the quiescent Eisenhower years, when there were few salient issues cleavages. As the parties and the electorate were not divided by major issues, habitual party loyalties could be expected to dominate voting choice. And they did. But they argued that *The American Voter* was essentially time-bound.

Nie, Verba and Petrocik suggested that, during the turbulent 1960s, there was an increase in divisive new issues: civil rights and urban riots; demonstrations against Vietnam; the rise of the women's movement; the War on Poverty. Other developments heightened political awareness, from the assassination of President Kennedy to the riots outside the Democratic Convention in Chicago. They argued that during the 1960s more voters developed relatively consistent attitude structures and were able to assess the proximity of their attitudes to those of the candidates, enabling prospective issue voting to play a larger role.

One problem at the heart of this dispute is how issue voting should be measured, avoiding the problems of rationalization and circularity, and some have cast serious doubt on the methods employed by Nie, Verba and Petrocik (Sullivan *et al.*, 1976; Smith, 1980). Without sensitive measures in long-term panel studies it is difficult to estimate the direction of causation with issues: that is, whether voters adopt certain attitudes which are consistent with their established party loyalties, or whether voters habitually vote for a certain party because of their orientation towards salient social, economic or foreign policy questions.

EVALUATIONS OF GOVERNMENT PERFORMANCE IN THE USA

Others agree that the role of affective party loyalties has declined in recent decades but they have reservations about the 'issue voting' model propounded in *The Changing American Voter*. Those who wish to strike a middle route have turned to theories of retrospective voting, one of the largest growth areas in the Political Science literature. Much of the interest has been generated in the field of political economy by those who wish to investigate the relationship between economic conditions and government popularity, using aggregate data or individual level survey data (for reviews, see Frey and Schneider, 1981; Paldam, 1981).

At its most simple, the retrospective model assumes that the primary basis for the voters' choice is their evaluation of the government's past record, although this vague notion is open to a wide range of interpretations. In the literature there is extensive controversy about a series of questions concerning retrospective voting. For example, what is the exact timeframe for voters' evaluations (Lewis-Beck, 1988; Miller and Wattenberg, 1984)? What is the role of affective feelings and cognitive judgements (Conover et al., 1986)? What is the relative influence of economic, social and foreign policy factors on evaluations of the government's performance (Clarke et al., 1986; Gopoian and Yantek, 1988)? What is the impact of personal economic circumstances (simple 'pocketbook voting') versus evaluations of the state of the national economy (Kiewiet, 1983; Kinder and Kiewiet, 1979)? What is the relationship between actual economic conditions (the rate of unemployment, economic growth, inflation or levels of personal income) and voters' perceptions of the government's economic performance (see for example Conover et al., 1986; Eulau and Lewis-Beck, 1988)? What is the relationship between approval of the government's record and government popularity? Is there a well-established cyclical pattern in government popularity which is associated with economic conditions? As one commentator noted, 'Until recently, knowledge about just exactly how economic issues affected voting behaviour was largely confined to the domain of political folk wisdom', yet by the early 1980s 'there has been a veritable explosion of theory and research in this area' (Kiewiet, 1983: 2).

The idea that a government's fate depends upon its performance in the eyes of the electorate, particularly its success in handling 'bread-and-butter' economic conditions, has a long tradition, but it raises complex issues. The classic basis of the general model was developed by Anthony Downs and V. O. Key before being extended more recently by Morris Fiorina (Downs, 1959; Key, 1961; Fiorina, 1981). The value of the retrospective model has been examined in an extensive range of studies in the USA, although there is little consensus about the results as none have employed exactly the same set of assumptions or the same statistical controls (see Kiewiet, 1983; Kiewiet and Rivers, 1984; Eulau and Lewis-Back, 1988).

In the classic account provided by Anthony Downs, rational citizens aim to maximize their utility by selecting parties for government which will be most beneficial to themselves. In making their choice, the most important factor will not be party promises, but the current record of the incumbent since this allows instrumental voters, with a minimum of information costs, to make their decisions on established facts rather than vague conjectures. The theory suggests that voters will evaluate party platforms in the light of what the government achieved during its period in office and what they believe the other parties would have done. Accordingly, citizens judge future policies by past performance.

A more extensive version of this theory has been developed most recently in the USA by Morris Fiorina who suggests that citizens quite rationally discount much information about campaign platforms, given the poor record of politicians in fulfilling their promises and the uncertainty surrounding the most appropriate means to achieve desired policy goals. Although voters are unclear about prospective policies, they have a certain amount of reliable information upon which to base their choice, because citizens know what life has been like under the last government (Fiorina, 1981). Voters will therefore rely more upon past performance than upon plans, proposals and promises about what politicians will do in the future. The electorate can use its vote to express evaluations of the government's past performance, responding to the direct and indirect questions: Are you better off today than you were at the time of the last election? And is the country better off as a result of the actions of the incumbent administration? The retrospective theory assumes that citizens are more concerned with the *outcome* of government actions than the policies used to achieve them.

A further distinction needs to be drawn between *simple* evaluations which are the result of judgements about the respondent's personal situation and *mediated* evaluations which are formed from assessments of the government's general performance (Fiorina, 1981). The theory does not suggest that simple pocketbook voting dominates, that electors are motivated purely by their personal circumstances and narrow self-interest. Rather, it suggests that voters give more weight to their experiences of what the government has done than what the government promises to do.

Work on US Presidential elections has consistently concluded that voter evaluations of national economic conditions have had a greater impact on electoral outcomes than have perceptions of personal economic situations (Kinder and Kiewiet, 1979, 1981; Feldman, 1982; Kinder and Mebane, 1983). Kinder and Kiewiet have called this tendency 'socio-tropic' politics: 'In reaching political preferences, the prototypic socio-tropic voter is influenced most of all by the *nation's* economic condition. Purely socio-tropic citizens vote according to the country's pocketbook, not their own' (1981: 132). The essential point of the retrospective account is that voters are primarily concerned with results rather than the policies which produce them, although we still know relatively little about how voters arrive at their evaluations of the government's performance.

CAMPAIGN-SPECIFIC FACTORS

The widely observed trends in partisan dealignment has caused us to revise our understanding of other aspects of voting behaviour. In the 1950s it was assumed that party loyalties structured the vote in House, Senate and Gubernatorial races as well as in Presidential elections. The concept of 'Presidential coat-tails' was widely used to account for House elections, with models developed to predict Congressional results on the basis of Presidential popularity and national economic conditions in the months prior to the election (Tufte, 1975). One of the major growth areas in US electoral studies has been the field of Congressional elections, as newer studies have emphasized that these contests are essentially candidate-centred campaigns (Jacobson, 1982). Much of the focus of recent work has been to try to explain the influence of other factors within the campaign, notably voting within primaries (Bartels, 1988; Orren and Polsby, 1987), the role of the media in shaping candidate images, campaign financing (Alexander, 1984; Sorauf, 1988), election forecasting (Rosenstone, 1983), the role of PACs (Malbin, 1980), and the contro-versial question of the consequences of party reform (Crotty and Jacob-son, 1980; Sabato, 1988; Polsby, 1983; Polsby and Wildavsky, 1988). There has also been a revival of interest in the fundamental question of whether elections matter, when and where the outcome has had a major impact on public policy (Ginsberg and Stone, 1986). In dealing with these broader questions electoral studies have, in some ways, come full circle, recognizing that the more narrowly behavioural approaches which can be applied to voting behaviour often prove inadequate by themselves when dealing with the more intangible aspects of election campaigning.

ISSUE VOTING IN BRITAIN

Just as there have been revisionist theories in the USA, so the widely noted trends towards partisan and class dealignment have produced a number of responses in British electoral studies. On the one hand, the most radical critique of the Michigan model has been provided by Himmelweit *et al.* in *How Voters Decide*, where the authors suggest that there are problems with the methods and evidence for issue voting used by Butler and Stokes (Himmelweit *et al.*, 1985). Based on a long-term panel survey, extending over 15 years, Himmelweit has argued that, if we take account of how electors respond to changes in issues, it is apparent that most voters display a relatively high degree of consistency in their attitudes. Essentially she suggests that voters can be seen as analogous to consumers in the economic market-place, selecting their voting choice on the basis of rational issue preferences.

Furthermore, far from long-term stability, Himmelweit found that inconsistency over successive elections was the norm. Butler and Stokes saw changes in voting as occasional and unpredictable fluctuations from a firm party loyalty. In their panel study over four successive elections, from 1959 to 1970, Butler and Stokes found that two-thirds of Conservatives remained constant, along with a half of Labour and a quarter of the Liberal voters (Butler and Stokes, 1974). But in their longitudinal panel study covering six general elections from 1959 to 1979, Himmelweit et al. found that consistency proved to be the exception and variability the norm. In this study only 30 per cent of the electorate came to the same decision throughout the period, with the most frequent switch being from a vote to an abstention and vice versa. In each election there was considerable movement to and from the Liberals as a halfway house, but few 'switchers' stayed consistently Liberal. Moreover, when they changed, Himmelweit et al. found that this was not due to apathy. Instead, voters switched because they disliked some aspect of the party they had previously supported, or were positively drawn towards the other side (Himmelweit et al., 1985).

Yet others have suggested that the model provided in the account of Butler and Stokes needs to be refined, rather than abandoned. An extensive debate has been generated about whether the relationship between social class and voting choice has declined over the last decades, and about how social and economic developments have changed the relative size of the working class. The controversy remains unresolved largely due to differences in the measurement and definition of social class. In *British Democracy at the Crossroads* (1985) Dunleavy and Husbands argued that hierarchical occupational classifications are too narrow. Instead, in understanding how social class relates to voting choice, we need to take account of salient consumption as well as production cleavages; that is, we need to consider such factors as whether voters are dependent on public transport, public housing and welfare services, as well as their position in the occupational marketplace.

In *How Britain Votes* (1985) Heath, Jowell and Curtice have argued that we need to redefine traditional occupational classifications based on income levels and lifestyle into categories based on economic interests in the marketplace. They propose a fivefold classification into the salariat, the routine non-manual, the petty bourgeoisie, foreman and technicians and the traditional working class. Using this classification, the authors suggest that there continues to be a strong relationship between social class and voting choice, although there have been changes in the relative size of the working class due to the decline of manual and manufacturing jobs in the economy. Hence they conclude that Britain is still divided politically by class, although the shape of the class structure has altered, leaving Labour with a shrinking electoral base. However, this account has been contested by others who argue that there is clear evidence of class and partisan dealignment in Britain, with controversy surrounding operational definitions of social class, methods of analysis and overall conclusions (Crewe, 1986; Dunleavy, 1987). It seems likely that this debate will continue to be unresolved with class remaining an essentially contested concept.

THE FUTURE OF ELECTORAL STUDIES?

We can conclude that, over the last decades, electoral studies has become more eclectic, lively and diverse, if more fragmented. What can we say of the future? There is good news and there is bad news. A glance through the major British, American and European journals of Politics, shows that the field of electoral studies is clearly alive and well. Internationally, there is a prolific amount of research being carried out on voting behaviour and elections, with approaches ranging from fairly descriptive articles on recent campaigns to highly abstract theoretical models of public choice.

Yet in Britain the field is less secure. The strength of the British humanistic tradition means that the behavioural and quantitative approach has never been as popular as in the USA. Instead, the more philosophical, historical and institutional approaches tend to predominate, even when dealing with those aspects of politics which are most open to quantification. In the 1986–87 *Political Studies Survey of the Profession* out of 1,000 Politics staff in universities and polytechnics under 100 were identified as teaching political behaviour, compared with over 200 in the fields of British Politics, public administration and Political Theory, and over 300 in the field of Comparative Politics and Area Studies (Berrington and Norris, 1987). But this may underestimate the influence of the behavioural persuasion which has become less distinctive. Since the 1950s it has been absorbed at least in part as one of the mainstream approaches within Political Science, coexisting with (although rarely predominating over) alternative traditions within courses on comparative government, British politics and the like.

Certain major threats may be identified. First, survey fieldwork necessary for electoral studies is one of the most expensive forms of research in political science which can be seriously undermined without sufficient resources. While core funding may protect the series of British Election Surveys, in the current climate of academic financial constraints it is difficult to obtain support for more innovative survey-based projects. In recent years, given research prospects, many colleagues in the field have been attracted overseas, notably to the USA.

Second, although electoral studies has always enjoyed a relatively high profile, it remains a minority occupation in British Political Science. Many Politics undergraduates and graduates leaving British colleges lack any except the most rudimentary statistical skills. In many cases, introductory courses in methods and techniques, if available, are strictly optional. Where they are offered they are too rarely integrated with the mainstream Politics course. By contrast, in the USA, over half (54 per cent) of all undergraduate majors in Political Science are required (and a further quarter (27 per cent) are recommended), to take a course in methodology (American Political Science Association, 1987).

The problem is not necessarily one of resources. In Britain large-scale electoral datasets are easily available through the ESRC data archive at Essex. Computers are becoming much more accessible and most departments are acquiring micros capable of running standard statistical packages such as Minitab and SPSS-PC. Yet, in terms of research or teaching, there is little evidence that the profession is responding by changing its dominant methodological approach.

Many are justly critical of the behavioural approach, arguing that much of the available data in politics is too 'soft' to be amenable to rigorous statistical analysis. It can be suggested that many of the central explanatory concerns of Politics cannot be quantified or dealt with through empirical methods. As with any approach, some research is concerned with quantifying the trivial, 'counting votes', but the more imaginative certainly is not. Electoral studies raises fundamental questions which have always been at the heart of politics: do we make rational choices? Or are we creatures of socialized habit? What are the major social cleavages in society – of class, region, gender, religion, language and race – and how do these relate to political divisions? How can we produce a democratic system through the mechanism of parties and elections? Who is active in the body politic? How do we account for political stability and change?

At its heart, through quantitative means, electoral studies try to evaluate these kinds of questions. Without the necessary statistical skills too many Politics graduates lack the essential techniques which provide the basis for an informed evaluation of electoral analysis. In this respect, Political Studies in Britain often seems to be lagging behind other social sciences and other countries. Quantitative skills are of course not the only method of analysis and we need a wide variety of approaches which draw on the rich tradition of British Political Science. But we need to be able to evaluate the use of these techniques, where appropriate. In looking to the future this seems one of the developments which we need to take on board.

REFERENCES

Alexander, H. E. (1984), *Financing Politics* (Washington, DC., OQ Press).

Almond, G. A. (1966), 'Political theory and political science', *American Political Science Review,* **60,** December, pp. 869–79.

Alt, J. E. (1984), 'Dealignment and the dynamics of partisanship in Britain' in R. J. Dalton *et al.* (eds), *Electoral Change in Advanced Industrial Democracies* (Princeton, Princeton University Press).

American Political Science Association (1987), *Survey of Departments, 1986/7* (Washington, DC., American Political Science Association).

Bartels, L. M. (1988), *Presidential Primaries and the Dynamics of Public Choice* (Princeton: Princeton University Press).

Beardsley, P. L. (1977), 'A critique of post-behaviouralism', *Political Theory,* **97(111),** February.

Bealey, F., Blondel, J. and McCann, W. J. (1965), *Constituency Politics* (London, Faber and Faber).

Berelson, B., Lazarfeld, P. F. and McPhee, W. N. (1954), *Voting* (Chicago, Chicago University Press).

Berrington, H. and Norris, P. (1987), *Political Studies in the Eighties* (Newcastle, Political Studies Association of the United Kingdom).

Birch, A. H. (1959), *Small Town Politics,* (Oxford, Oxford University Press).

Butler, D. (1952), *The British General Election of 1951* (London, Macmillan).

Butler, D. (1955), *The British General Election of 1955* (London, Macmillan).

Butler D. and Rose, R. (1960), *The British General Election of 1959* (London, Macmillan).

Butler, D. and King, A. (1965), *The British General Election of 1964* (London, Macmillan).

Butler, D. and Pinto-Duschinsky, M. (1971), *The British General Election of 1970* (London, Macmillan).

Butler, D. and Kavanagh, D. (1974), *The British General Election of February 1974* (London, Macmillan).

Butler, D. and Kavanagh, D. (1975), *The British General Election of October 1974* (London, Macmillan).

Butler, D. and Kavanagh, D. (1980), *The British General Election of 1979* (London, Macmillan).

Butler, D. and Kavanagh, D. (1985), *The British General Election of 1983* (London, Macmillan).

Butler, D. and Kavanagh, D. (1988), *The British General Election of 1987* (London, Macmillan).

Butler, D. and Stokes, D. (1974), *Political Change in Britain,* 2nd edition, (London, Macmillan).

Cain, B., Ferejohn, J. and Fiorina, M. (1987), *The Personal Vote: constituency service and electoral independence* (Cambridge, Mass., Harvard University Press).

Campbell, A., Converse, P., Miller, W. E. and Stokes, D. E. (1960), *The American Voter* (New York, Wiley).

Clarke, H. D., Stewart, M. and Zuk, G. (1986), 'Politics, economics and party popularity in Britain, 1979–83', *Electoral Studies,* **5(2)** pp. 123–41.

Conover, P., Feldman, S. and Knight, K. (1986), 'Judging inflation and unemployment: the origins of retrospective evaluations', *Journal of Politics,* **48(3)** pp. 565–88.

Converse, P. E. (1964), 'The nature of belief systems in mass politics' in D. E. Apter (ed.), *Ideology and Discontent* (New York).

Converse, P. E. and Pierce, R. (1985), 'Measuring partisanship', *Political Methodology*, **11**, pp. 143–66.

Crewe, I. (1986), 'On the death and resurrection of class voting: some comments on "How Britain Votes" ', *Political Studies*, **XXXIV**, pp. 620–38.

Crewe, I. (1985), 'Great Britain' in I. Crewe and D. Denver (eds), *Electoral Change in Western Democracies: patterns and sources of electoral volatility* (London, Croom Helm).

Crewe, I. (1984), 'The electorate: partisan dealignment ten years on' in H. Berrington (ed.), *Change in British Politics* (London, Frank Cass).

Crewe, I. and Denver, D. (1985), *Electoral Change in Western Democracies* (London, Croom Helm).

Crewe, I., Alt, J. and Sarlvik, B. (1977), 'Partisan dealignment in Britain 1964–1974', *British Journal of Political Science*, **7**, pp. 129–190.

Crotty, W. J. and Jacobson, G. (1980), *American Parties in Decline* (Boston, Little, Brown).

Dahl, R. (1960), 'The behavioural approach to political science' in H. Eulau (ed.), *Behaviouralism in Political Science* (New York, Atherton Press).

Downs, A. (1959), *An Economic Theory of Democracy* (New York, Harper and Row).

Dunleavy, P. (1987), 'Class dealignment in Britain revisited', *West European Politics*, **10(3)**, pp. 400–419.

Dunleavy, P. and Husbands, C. (1985), *British Democracy at the Crossroads* (London, George Allen).

Eulau, H. and Lewis-Beck, M. (1988), *Economic Conditions and Electoral Outcomes: the United States and Western Europe* (New York, Agathon).

Eulau, H. (1963), *The Behavioral Persuasion in Politics* (New York, Random House).

Eulau, H. (ed.) (1969), *Behavioralism in Political Science* (New York, Atherton Press).

Feldman, S. (1982), 'Economic self interest and political behaviour', *American Journal of Political Science*, **26**, pp. 446–66.

Fiorina, M. (1981), *Retrospective Voting in American National Elections* (New Haven, Yale University Press).

Franklin, M. (1985), *The Decline of Class Voting in Britain* (Oxford, Clarendon Press).

Franklin, C. H. (1984), 'Issue preferences, socialization and the evaluation of party identification, *American Journal of Political Science*, **28**, pp. 459–75.

Frey, B. S. and Schneider, F. (1981), 'Recent research on empirical politico-economic models' in D. A. Hibbs and H. Fassbender (eds) *Contemporary Political Economy* (Amsterdam, North-Holland).

Ginsberg, B. and Stone, A. (1986), *Do Elections Matter?* (New York, Sharpe).

Gopoian, J. D. and Yantek, T. (1988), 'Cross-pressured economic voting in America: the 1984 election', *Political Behaviour*, **10(1)**, pp. 37–51.

Heath, A., Jowell, R. and Curtice, J. (1985), *How Britain Votes* (Oxford, Pergamon Press).

Heath, A., Jowell, R. and Curtice, J. (1988), 'Partisan dealignment revisited', paper presented at the *Political Studies Association Annual Conference*, Plymouth (April).

Himmelweit, H. *et al.* (1985), *How Voters Decide* (Milton Keynes, Open University Press).

Jackson, J. E. (1975), 'Issues, party choices and presidential voting', *American Journal of Political Science,* **19**, pp. 161–86.

Jacobson, G. (1982), *The Politics of Congressional Elections* (Boston, Little, Brown).

Keith, B. E., Magelby, D. R., Nelson, C. J., Orr, E., Westlye M., and Wolfinger, R. E. (1986), 'The partisan identification of independent "Leaners" ', *British Journal of Political Science,* **16**, pp. 155–86.

Key, V. O., Jr. (1942), *Parties, Politics and Pressure Groups* (New York, Thomas Crowell).

Key, V. O., Jr. (1961), *The Responsible Electorate* (New York, Vintage).

Kiewiet, D. R. (1983), *Macroeconomics and Micropolitics* (Chicago, University of Chicago Press).

Kiewiet, D. R. and Rivers, D. (1984), 'A retrospective on retrospective voting', *Political Behaviour,* **6(4)**, pp. 369–93.

Kinder, D. R. and Kieweit, D. R. (1979), 'Economic discontent and political behaviour: the role of personal grievances and collective economic judgements in congressional voting', *American Journal of Political Science,* **23**, pp. 495–527.

Kinder, D. R. and Kiewiet, D. R. (1981), 'Socio-tropic politics: the American case', *British Journal of Political Science,* **11**, pp. 129–61.

Kinder, D. R. and Mebane, W. (1983), 'Politics and economics in everyday life' in K. Monroe (ed.) *The Political Process and Economic Change* (New York, Agathon Press).

Kuhn, T. (1962), *The Structure of Scientific Revolutions* (Chicago, University of Chicago Press).

Lane, D. (1959), *Political Life* (Glencoe, Ill., The Free Press).

Lazarsfeld, P. F., Berelson, B. and Gaudet, H. (1944), *The People's Choice* (New York, Duell, Sloan and Pierce).

Lewis-Beck, M. S. (1988), 'Economics and the American voter: past, present, future', *Political Behavior,* **10(1)**, pp. 5–21.

Malbin, M. (1980), *Money and Politics in the United States* (New Jersey, Chatham House).

Markus, G. B. (1979), 'The political environment and the dynamics of public attitudes: a panel study', *American Journal of Political Science,* **23**, pp. 338–59.

Miller, A. H. and Wattenberg, M. P. (1984), 'Throwing the rascals out: policy and performance evaluations of presidential candidates, 1952–1980', *American Political Science Review,* **78**, pp. 359–72.

Milne, R. S. and Mackenzie, H. C. (1954), *Straight Fight* (London, Hansard Society).

Milne, R. S. and Mackenzie, H. C. (1958), *Marginal Seat* (London, Hansard Society).

Natches, P. B. (1970), 'Images of voting: the social psychologists', *Public Policy,* **17**, pp. 553–88.

Nie, N. H., Verba, S. and Petrocik, J. R. (1976), *The Changing American Voter* (Cambridge, Mass., Harvard University Press).

Orren, G. and Polsby, N. (eds) (1987), *Media and Momentum: The New Hampshire Primary and Nomination Politics* (New Jersey: Chatham House).

Paldam, M. (1981), 'A preliminary survey of the series and findings on vote and popularity functions', *European Journal of Political Research,* **9**, pp. 181–99.

Polsby, N. W. (1983), *Consequences of Party Reform* (New York, Oxford University Press).

Polsby, N. W. and Wildavsky, A. (1988), *Presidential Elections* (New York, The Free Press).

Pulzer, P. G. J. (1967), *Political Representation and Elections* (London, Allen and Unwin).

Ricci, D. M. (1984), *The Tragedy of Political Science* (New Haven, Yale University Press).

Rose, R. and McAllister, I. (1985), *Voters Begin to Choose* (London, Sage Publications).

Rosenstone, S. J. (1983), *Forecasting Presidential Elections* (New Haven, Yale University Press).

Rossi, P. H. (1959), 'Four landmarks in voting research' in E. Burdick and A. J. Brodbeck (eds), *American Voting Behaviour* (Glencoe, Illinois).

Sabato, L. J. (1988), *The Party Just Begun* (Glenview, Illinois, Scott, Foresman and Co).

Sarlvik, B. and Crewe, I. (1983), *Decade of Dealignment* (Cambridge, Cambridge University Press).

Seidelman, R. (1985), *Disenchanted Realists: political science and the American crisis, 1884–1984* (Albany, NY, State University of New York).

Smith, E. (1980), 'The levels of conceptualization: false measures of ideological sophistication', *American Political Science Review,* **74**, pp. 685–96.

Sorauf, F. J. (1988), *Money in American Elections* (Glenview, Illinois, Scot, Foresman and Co).

Sullivan, J. L., Pierson, J. E. and Marcus, G. E. (1976), 'Ideological constraints in the mass public: a methodological critique and some new findings, *American Journal of Political Science,* **22**, pp. 250–69.

Tufte, E. R. (1975), 'Determinants of the outcomes of midterm Congressional elections', *American Political Science Review,* **69**, pp. 812–26.

White, T. H. (1961), *The Making of the President (1960)* (New York, Harper and Row).

Wolin, S. (1968), 'Paradigms and political theories' in Preston King and B. C. Parekh (eds), *Politics and Experience* (Cambridge, Cambridge University Press).

12.   Rational Choice and Political Analysis

Albert Weale

INTRODUCTION

Rational choice analyses of politics stand in the line of a long tradition. Forerunners of contemporary rational choice approaches to politics include Hobbes, Hume and, on Elster's (1985) interpretation at least, Marx. No doubt other favoured names could also be added. But modern rational choice theory is distinguished from its predecessors by its ability to draw upon the considerable resources of formal social choice and games theory. It is this background of formal theory that provides rational choice analysis both with its power and with its rather forbidding appearance. If you open any textbook on rational choice theory, the likelihood is that you will see an extensive array of formal definitions, equations and mathematical proofs. These are certainly important in yielding insight into the nature of social and political choice. Yet, in many respects, the basic ideas of rational choice theory are simple. The task of this chapter will be to explore these basic ideas, giving sufficient explanation of their application to show how fruitful their use is in understanding politics. My theme will be that rational choice analysis reveals both the richness and the limitations of concepts of instrumental rationality – that is, a notion of rationality that is defined in terms of the adaptation of means to previously specified ends. When applied to political life, such a notion has considerable power to illuminate; but it also has stringent limitations. So, at least, I shall argue.

Rational choice theory regards politics as a particular set of institutions forming a process for amalgamating individual preferences into a collective choice of policy or outcome. Other institutions also perform this function, most notably the market, but the task of the rational choice theorist of politics is to identify and explain what is distinctive about politics in the way that preferences are amalgamated. The term 'preferences' has a broad interpretation. Usually it is taken to refer to the ability of individuals to rank states of affairs in accordance with a scale of value.

The object of the preferences may be candidates in an election, competing policies or alternative states of society. Thus, individuals are expected to know which of the available candidates is their most preferred choice, which their next choice, and so on. In short, individuals are assumed to know enough about their own views and outlook to be able to rank any alternative relative to some other alternative. Individuals are thus assumed always to know how to order alternatives, including the possibility that they may find that they are indifferent between two alternatives.

There is no assumption in rational choice approaches that these preferences are motivated entirely by selfish considerations. True, they may be; but equally they may be motivated by a concern to advance the welfare of others. There is an assumption, however, that whatever preferences persons have they will want to maximize the chance of achieving their most favoured outcome, or at least the outcome that seems most achievable in the circumstances in which they are placed. This maximizing assumption is crucial. It encapsulates the thought that rationality is a question of adapting means to previously specified ends and it often provides a poignant reference point for the outcomes that individuals might have expected to secure in particular types of situation. For example, it is often said that, since people cause pollution, people can stop pollution. Yet, as we shall see, rational choice theory shows why it may be impossible to stop pollution even when this is desired by everyone in society.

Politics would be a trivial activity if all the members of a political community had identical preferences about the course of action the government should follow. There is therefore a need for a process by which diverse preferences are amalgamated so as to provide a collective choice. It is at this point that rational choice theory makes one of its distinctive methodological moves. Instead of asking how, in practice, preferences are amalgamated or how ideally preferences ought to be amalgamated, it asks instead: under what conditions will preferences be amalgamated in a characteristic way? Two characteristics have been of particular interest to rational choice theorists. The first is that of stability. Stability here means that no individual in the system is able to change the outcome from the sum of individual choices, given that none of the other individuals is prepared to change their choices. The second characteristic is that of optimality. Optimality is the principle that everyone is as well-off as they can be, in the sense that no one can be made better off without making someone else worse off. In other words, rational choice theorists typically ask whether collective choice procedures are stable and optimal. The point of the exercise is neither to describe nor to prescribe, but to analyse the conditions under which processes will operate in a specified way.

In order to see the distinctiveness of this approach, it is useful to contrast the rational choice approach with alternative methods of analysis. Consider, for example, the phenomenon of corporatism. This is an arrangement under which government, unions and industry collaborate in the making of economic policy. Political scientists have been interested in determining the conditions under which political systems will evolve corporatist arrangements, and one approach has been to try to determine the answer to this question inductively. Thus, writers in the mould of the 'new institutionalism' (for example, Katzenstein, 1984) have used the method of comparative case studies to identify the circumstances that make for successful corporatism. Another example is provided by studies of consociational democracy, where political scientists (for example, Lijphart, 1968, 1977) have sought to determine the conditions under which elites in practice have negotiated successfully with one another over the government of segmented societies. The ambition of the rational choice approach is to get behind these inductive generalizations to ascertain the logic of the situation according to the nature of the choices that individuals face. In other words, a rational choice theorist would say that an adequate account of phenomena like corporatism or consociational democracy ought to emerge from an examination of the choices facing individuals, and we should not be content with appeals, for example, to political culture or historical contingency.

The power of this method lies in the fact that it is indirect. This means that circumstances of preference amalgamation can be investigated that are possibilities for what is found in the world of experience but of which experience might only give us the merest of glimpses. In order to illustrate these possibilities I shall consider three examples of rational choice analysis:

1. the nature of voting schemes;
2. the existence of patterns of collective choice with sub-optimal, or malign outcomes;
3. rational choice approaches to issues of normative theory.

These examples are chosen not because they provide a comprehensive account of contemporary rational choice theory, but because they provide a representative cross-section of the implications for the study of politics of the analysis of rational choice and also indicate the kinds of new developments which can be expected.

THE NATURE OF VOTING SCHEMES

I have used the notion of amalgamating preferences up to now, but this notion can take several different senses depending on which form of social activity is used to perform the amalgamation. Buying and selling in markets is one way of amalgamating preferences; conducting wars is another; and handing over the decision to a charismatic individual is a third. Politics usually proceeds by the weighing of preferences in some way, however, and the most typical form this takes is voting. Voting I shall simply define as the registering of preferences with a counting device in which the final choice of alternatives is dependent in some way on the result of the counting. Such voting can take place in families, small committees, national elections and international organizations. A very common system of voting is that of majority rule, in which the motion is put to the electors, and the winning alternative is the one that commands a simple majority of those voting. I choose it not only because it is so common and familiar, but also because many people who have been brought up within liberal democracies (whom I suppose to constitute the majority of readers of this volume) will regard it as self-evidently the ideal way to make collective decisions. The extensive analysis that rational choice theory applies to majority rule is therefore doubly instructive: it both illustrates and demythologizes.

Suppose that voters are asked to choose between two alternatives, x and y. These alternatives might concern a variety of issues; for example, whether or not to have a system of capital punishment, or whether or not to allow abortion. Their essential characteristic is that only one of two courses of action can be followed. Then there are good reasons to use the principle of majority rule. Irrespective of the issues involved, majority rule will take into account only the weight of numbers supporting each of the alternatives, thus imparting an egalitarian element to the process of choice. Moreover, if on a subsequent occasion the same alternatives come up for decision and sufficient people have changed their mind for there to be a new majority preference, then the method of majority rule will reflect positively this change of mind. And it has been known for some time (May, 1952) that the method of majority rule is the only decision procedure that operates in this way: that is, it is the only method of social choice that is independent of the issues, independent of who the voters are and positively responsive to changes of mind. Finally, with two alternatives, majority rule will always yield a result. Either one alternative will beat the other, or they will tie for votes. In the latter case the natural inference would appear to be that each alternative is as good as the other in the eyes of the voters.

There is no doubt much attraction in viewing politics essentially as a contest between only two alternatives. Aristotle (1962, v.1) once remarked that the great divisions in politics were between those who favoured the idea of equality and those who opposed it, thus turning politics essentially into a two alternative contest. More recently Schattschneider (1960) argued that division into two camps was essential to the idea of politics. And it is, of course, part of the textbook theory of British politics that it is, and should be, structured so as to produce an alternative in and out of office of two competing parties.

Yet there is no reason, either in logic or in experience, to accept that political choices are essentialy binary in this way. Often there are more than two alternatives from which voters can select. For example, some people in a political community may not be in favour of capital punishment in general, but they may favour it for cases of convicted terrorists. Similarly, some people may not favour abortion generally, but only in cases of rape or incest. So, in these cases, there are not two alternatives, but three. Let us label these alternatives x, y and z. We can now ask whether majority rule will lead to a stable outcome given any possible pattern of preference. Suppose there are three blocks of voters with three distinct patterns of preference. For each bloc we can represent the preference as follows: A: x, y, z, means that bloc A prefers x to y to z. Figure 12.1 gives a possible distribution of preferences for the three blocs.

$$A : x, y, z$$
$$B : y, z, x$$
$$C : z, x, y$$

Figure 12.1   The pattern of cyclical preferences

If the sets of voters designated by the letters A, B, and C are of roughly equal size, so that none is big enough on its own to decide the result, but each by entering a coalition with one other set would be in a majority, then none of the alternatives would be able to secure a majority against both the other two: x would defeat y, y would defeat z and z would defeat x. This situation is known as a majority voting cycle. By majority rule, x beats y, and by the same rule y beats z, but z, which might seem the worst alternative, beats x. This seems irrational, just as it would be irrational for you to prefer wine to beer and beer to cider, but also prefer cider to wine. It also means that, in the majority voting cases, no one outcome emerges as the overall winner: there is a majority vote against any one of them.

One consequence of this is illustrated in Figure 12.2. Suppose that there

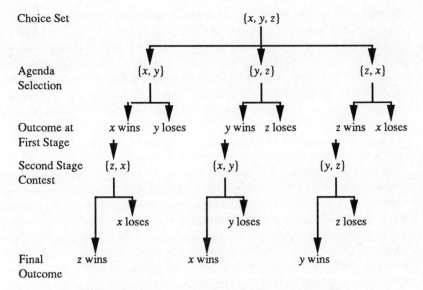

Thus, the final outcome depends upon which pair is
voted on at the first stage of Agenda Selection.

Figure 12.2   The open structure of an agenda under majority rule when
preferences are cyclical

are three alternatives that confront a political community. Careful structuring of the agenda will ensure that if there are cyclical preferences as in
Figure 12.1, then any of the three would be selected by majority rule. It
will depend solely on the order in which alternatives are put to the vote.
Agenda manipulation therefore becomes an important part of the process
by which preferences are amalgamated.

It might be thought that the phenomenon of cycling was an odd
peculiarity of majority rule, but in a justly renowned result Arrow (1963)
showed that this was not so. Arrow showed that a similar problem affects
any collective choice procedure that is not dictatorial ('dictatorial' in the
sense that the collective choice coincides only with the preferences of one
individual). Although Arrow's proof is technically complex (for a clear
version, see McLean, 1987: 172), the insight it embodies is clear: if we
amalgamate individual preferences by means of a series of pairwise
comparisons, then to achieve a coherent outcome we must restrict the
range of preferences we are prepared to respond to. Subsequent work
(summarized in Kelly, 1978) shows how pervasive the Arrow problem is.

Implicitly in the design of any political constitution we always face the trade-off between logicality and fairness (Riker, 1982: 132). The more we seek to design mechanisms of collective choice that always yield consistent and complete outcomes, the more we shall find that we are in effect heeding the preferences of only a minority. If, on the other hand, we wish to reflect the preferences of the majority in a fair-minded way, then we should expect as a matter of logic that our collective choices will be inconsistent.

Since no method of amalgamating preferences, unless it be dictatorial decision-making, is proof against cycling, the other question that analysts have asked is: under what conditions is majority rule prone to cycling? Since majority rule is a widely used and accepted principle of decision-making this question has obvious relevance when we are trying to understand political choices in the real world. This problem is connected with another, namely the question of how many dimensions of conflict are on the agenda. If we distinguish between capital punishment and capital punishment for terrorists, we are implicitly considering two dimensions: one concerned with capital punishment and one concerned with terrorism. The dimension of terrorism enables us to distinguish among those who favour capital punishment in terms of their attitude towards the question of whether terrorism is a special issue. Those who say it is take one attitude; those who say it is not take another. The important thing is that we are now looking at the question from two points of view. We have two dimensions to consider. Now, when we move to two dimensions of political competition, stability of outcome rests upon impossibly stringent conditions. In particular, it has been shown that for stability to exist voters need to be strung out along the dimensions of competition in such a way that the numbers at any point are exactly counterbalanced by the numbers holding the opposite point of view (useful summaries of these results can be found in Austen-Smith, 1983; and Riker, 1982; 181–95).

To see how stringent a condition this is, suppose that members of a political community are divided about two sets of issues – for example, the management of the economy and how liberal the community should be on matters of birth control or abortion. Each candidate for office offers a platform that defines his or her view in relation to these two issues. Then, for there to be a majority winner that is proof against all other candidates, for every economically conservative and socially liberal voter there needs to be an economically liberal and socially conservative voter as a counter-balance. To suppose this to obtain in the real world would be an heroic act of faith. Hence, we may generally expect, in any moderately complex political system, that cycling will be the norm, not the exception.

Cycling allows the possibility of agenda manipulation, and hence of political change. These possibilities are brilliantly illustrated by Riker (1986) in a series of stories intended to show the nature and consequences of agenda manipulation. Riker is able to show that the introduction of new items on to a political agenda is able to disrupt the political basis of a previously dominant political coalition. Since any winning group in politics is sitting on top of a combination of issues that is vulnerable to defeat from some other combination of issues, the task of the opposition is to find that combination. Thus Lincoln was able to use the issue of slavery to break up the Jeffersonian–Democratic coalition that had dominated US politics for most of the previous 60 years. Implicitly the Jeffersonian-Democratic coalition was divided between commercial and agrarian expansionists who characteristically took different attitudes towards slavery. So long as there was no challenge on the issue, the coalition was safe from attack. Once Lincoln was able to deploy the slavery issue, however, the coalition would be split since the commercial expansionists were opposed to slavery. By adding this new item to the political agenda, Lincoln was able to create an electoral cycle that could be exploited by the Republicans.

There is a curious twist of the theoretical dialectic at this point. I noted earlier that rational choice theory might be contrasted with the study of political institutions. Yet, in another way, rational choice theory shows how important it is to study institutions. To understand this point, consider the question of stability. The cycling of outcomes is likely to be a widespread feature of opinion in any complex society. How does it come about therefore that we observe so much stability in society? Certainly Lincoln could break up the opposing coalition with his appeal to the slavery issue, but that coalition had after all dominated US politics for some 60 years prior to that point. The answer must be something along the following lines. Since, *ex hypothesi*, the stability cannot rest in the structure of popular preferences, it must rest in the institutions that are responsible for amalgamating those preferences into a political choice. Theoretically it is possible to show this by appeal to the notion of a 'structure-induced equilibrium'. This concept can be illustrated by the example of the rules of normal committee procedure. Given certain preferences, cycling will arise if voters are allowed to pursue the possibility of further voting on any pair of alternatives. Normal committee rules prevent this. For example, in formal committee procedure, there is only a certain order in which amendments can be put, so that not every alternative is compared with every other. As any eager-minded reformer who has ever come up against the limits of committee procedure can testify, these formal devices can be powerful instruments in the hands of those determined to maintain the status quo. Even if you believe that your proposal

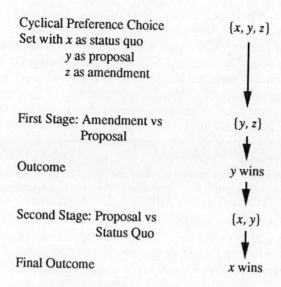

Thus, the status quo is the final outcome, *even if* the amendment, *z*,
is preferred by a majority to the status quo.

*Figure 12.3   Conventional agenda rules as a structure-inducing
              equilibrium*

would defeat the status quo, you may find that voters never have the
opportunity to vote on the question, because your proposal has already
been defeated by an amendment. Rational choice theory shows how
fragile winning coalitions often are, and therefore indicates the need to
study institutions in the light of their capacity to control the expression of
preferences. (See Figure 12.3 for an example.)

Political scientists have long observed that the ability to set the political
agenda, to decide what comes up for decision as well as deploying political
resources when items are up for decision, is an aspect of power that is of
fundamental importance. The problem has always been to show how
agenda manipulation is possible and why it is so pervasive. Rational choice
theory provides an answer to this question. Agenda manipulation exists
when cyclical preferences provide an advantage to persons to manipulate
the outcome to their own advantage. The results of social choice theory
show why this is so. But little is known about the processes by which
political agendas are set and, more importantly, there is little work
comparing the various forums in which agendas can be set. For example,

although the manipulation of committee rules can be regarded as an explicit context within which agenda manipulation can take place, the salience of issues to mass publics, and the chances for politicians to exploit agenda opportunities are poorly understood.

The final aspect of social choice theory that needs to be examined in this respect concerns the implications of the theory for philosophical or normative accounts of democracy. Democracy is sometimes justified in terms of the concept of the 'popular will' and the need to ensure that political decisions reflect its promptings. If, however, the popular will is identified with the preference of the majority, then in most cases it will be a meaningless concept. Over any moderately complex set of alternatives, there is unlikely to be an alternative that would defeat all of the others taken in pairwise comparison. Whatever else it might mean, democracy cannot be taken to require the implementation of the preferences of the majority, since there is unlikely to be a majority preference to be found. Governments who claim mandates for their policies as a result of their being successful in elections are treading on the thinnest of thin ice. Political theorists have hardly risen to the challenge implicit in the central results of social choice theory. An adequate response will almost certainly involve seeing democracy not merely as a mechanism for amalgamating preferences but also as a forum in which the moral and political claims of preferences can be debated so that a consensus is created around a political decision. The point is that we cannot construct a mechanical device that will amalgamate preferences in a satisfactory way if those preferences are allowed to range over all logically possible alternatives. The need is to reduce the diversity of preferences by rational debate, so that the grounds on which persons hold views can be examined. When the process of reflective examination takes place, through reasoned argument, the hope is that this will reduce the diversity of views and lead to a higher level of consensus. We move from instrumental rationality to discursive rationality in the form, for example, discussed by Habermas (1979: 178–205).

STABILITY WITH MALIGN OUTCOMES

The problem of majority rule was presented as a problem of instability. But perhaps there are political circumstances in which it is stability, rather than instability, which is the problem. One such situation that has received extensive consideration is that of the Prisoners' Dilemma. The original version of this game is still the most instructive. Two prisoners are being questioned by the police about a crime they are supposed to have committed. Each is told the following: 'If you confess and your partner

Column
Cooperate Defect

	Cooperate	Defect
Cooperate	3,3	1,4
Defect	4,1	2,2

Row

Where the first cell entry represents the pay-off to Row, and the second to Column. The higher number is always preferred by a player, so that for example Row's preference ordering is:

First preference	: Row defects; Column cooperates	(4,1)
Second preference	: Row cooperates; Column cooperates	(3,3)
Third preference	: Row defects; Column defects	(2,2)
Fourth preference	: Row cooperates; Column defects	(1,4)

Figure 12.4 The Prisoners' Dilemma

does not, then we shall recommend a lenient sentence (one year, say). If you both confess, then both of you will get a harsh sentence (five years). If you do not confess, and your partner does, then you will receive the worst sentence possible (ten years). And, if neither of you confess, we shall get you on a lesser charge which carries a sentence of two years.' Each prisoner can reason as follows: either my partner will or will not confess. If he confesses, then I am better off confessing (five years rather than ten); if he does not confess, then I am still better off confessing (one year rather than two). The upshot is that it seems rational to confess, and yet if both do the rational thing, they both end up worse off than if neither had confessed.

The general form of this game is illustrated in Figure 12.4. In this game there are two players, Row and Column, and each is confronted by two strategies, cooperate or defect. The pay-offs for the four combinations of strategies are given in the matrix, with the figures providing the ordering of the outcomes for each of the players, following the usual convention that Row's pay-offs are entered first and Column's second. The feature of this game that has attracted so much attention is that the rational strategy for each individual player appears to leave both players worse off than they otherwise need be. If both could cooperate, they would find that they could achieve a better outcome than if they each defected. But for each player defection is the dominant strategy (that is, it promises at least as much as the alternative strategy, and under at least one contingency it promises something better).

The Prisoners' Dilemma has been taken to provide a good model for many common political situations. For example, it captures much that is intrinsic to the arms race, where the attempt by each of the two superpowers to steal the advantage on the other results in their both being locked into an expensive and potentially lethal conflict. Similarly, the conflict between capitalist and workers may be thought of along such lines. If capitalists and workers could agree to cooperate then they might both be better off than if they continue to oppose one another. Moreover, the Prisoners' Dilemma game can be generalized from two to many players, and in this N-person form becomes the free-rider problem. In this problem no one individual has the incentive to contribute to a public good (that is a good that will be enjoyed by members of a community whether or not they have paid for it) since there is always the hope that others will contribute sufficient in order for the good to be provided without the individual having to pay. Polluters will continue to pollute hoping that others will be willing to clean up; natural resources will continue to be exploited beyond their long-term limits by those who hope that others will be more restrained in their pursuit of advantage than they are themselves; and the system of commercial morality will be undermined by those willing to trade on the trust of others without being willing to reciprocate on their own part.

The problem here appears to be that individual agents are locked into patterns of decision-making which appear to work to their advantage but in fact work to their disadvantage. And yet this Hobbesian vision of a world in which agents are constantly engaged in a 'war of all against all' does not correspond to what we observe. True there is pollution, overexploitation of natural resources and an erosion of public morality under the pressures of commerce. But, equally, there is sometimes voluntary cooperation to reduce pollution, common agreements not to exploit certain resources and a functioning system of public morality without which commerce could not take place at all. If these situations are truly Prisoners' Dilemmas how do we observe such patterns? One answer that is particularly important is that the rational strategy in a repeated Prisoners' Dilemma is not the same as in a once-and-for-all game. There are clearly identifiable circumstances in which it is rational to cooperate, in the sense that the expected outcome of cooperation is of higher value than the expected outcome of defection. The fundamental insight here is due to Taylor (1976) who shows that a crucial circumstance leading to cooperation is that the players do not discount the future too highly.

To see the logic of this argument, consider the fact that those who cooperate with one another in the Prisoners' Dilemma do better than those who are locked into a pattern of mutual defection, since they are able to reap the advantage of an outcome which both prefer. Of course, if a cooperator plays the game with a persistent defector, then there is no advantage in continuing to cooperate. So what is needed is the opportunity for players to find out whether they are playing against someone who is willing to cooperate or someone who is not. Playing the game a repeated number of times allows this process of mutual discovery to occur, and in particular it allows the playing of the 'tit-for-tat' strategy, by which a player will cooperate as long as the other player continues to do so. 'I will if you will' then becomes a powerful principle making for cooperation. It will work in a repeated number of plays provided that one of the players does not discount the future so heavily in such a way that the immediate gain of defection in the first round does not wipe out the expected benefits of cooperation in future rounds.

In order to illustrate this possibility consider a particular example. Suppose we model the relationship between capitalists and workers in a capitalist society as a Prisoners' Dilemma. Workers want higher wages and capitalists want higher incomes from the profits of the enterprise. If they pursue these goals in competition with one another, one possible set of consequences is strikes, underinvestment and increasing lack of competitiveness in the national economy. If it were possible to institute a system of social partnership under which workers agreed to restrain their wage demands in exchange for the capitalists agreeing to maintain investment, both parties might be better off in the long run than they are under a system of conflict. It can be argued that this is precisely what has happened in western European systems of corporatism, most notably the varieties of corporatism that are found in Austria and Sweden. Under these arrangements, economic management has been conducted precisely to achieve agreement on how wage increases are to be traded off against profits and investment. The key point about these arrangements in the present context is that both Austria and Sweden are countries in which the labour movement has traditionally been reformist and willing to take a long-term perspective (for a parallel but distinct argument, see Przeworski and Wallerstein, 1982).

Understanding the logic of 'tit-for-tat' also helps explain how co-operation can spread in a population. The possibility has been ingeniously illustrated by Axelrod (1984), who organized a tournament of computer programmes to play repeated versions of the Prisoners' Dilemma. 'Tit-for-tat' emerged as the all-round winner among the programmes that were submitted, as it did in a subsequent tournament which Axelrod organized having announced the result of the first. If those who are willing to play 'tit-for-tat' have the opportunity to meet one another sufficiently frequently, then the programme enables them to act on the principle of 'I will if you will' and one can expect a norm of cooperation to become established. Moreover, Sugden (1986: 122–44) has shown that it is not necessary to have interaction just between two persons in order for cooperation to emerge. Provided the members of a group are agreed on a norm of reciprocity ('I will if you will' again), then there can emerge a system of voluntary cooperation to provide public goods. Thus, recent work has shown that one should not be too despairing in the face of the Prisoners' Dilemma – at least in theory. There are strategies of cooperation that do not presuppose excessive or saintly altruism on the part of otherwise rational players. One should of course be less optimistic that the lessons from these results can be translated into practically effective suggestions for reducing the malign effects of Prisoners' Dilemmas as they occur in the real world.

RATIONAL CHOICE AND NORMATIVE THEORY

So far we have been concerned with using the tools of rational choice theory to understand and interpret how politics is conducted and policy choices made. However, one of the key points of interest in rational choice theory is that it provides an analytic framework that can be adapted to the examination of normative questions. The prime example of this approach has been provided by writers in the tradition of modern contract theory. The task of these theorists has been to specify a set of principles to be used for the evaluation of social arrangements. The basic argument has been that we should use principles that would be agreed by rational persons who were ignorant of their own future position in society but who were nonetheless seeking to do as well as they could from social arrangements. In other words, the intellectual strategy has been to hypothesize a choice situation that can in some sense be characterized as yielding 'fair' appraisals, and to imagine the choices that rational individuals would make in such a situation. This approach can be found in the writings of Rawls (1972) and Harsanyi (1976).

These writers have received a great deal of attention in the literature, so I should like to consider another example of the application of rational choice theory that emerges from a quite different tradition of analysis. Roemer (1982) has sought to show how various forms of exploitation might be characterized using the tools of rational choice theory. The basic thought behind his approach is quite simple. It is to say that exploitation exists in an economy if a subset of agents in the economy would, hypothetically, be better off outside the economy than they are within it. For example, suppose we ask the question: in what sense was there exploitation in the feudal economy? Roemer's answer is that there is exploitation if the serfs would have been better off with free labour markets than they were with tied labour obligations. Similarly, there is capitalist exploitation according to Roemer if there is a subset of workers who would be better off outside of the capitalist economy, provided that they can take their per capita share of capital assets in the economy. The strength of Roemer's analysis is that he provides a definite meaning to the various senses in which the notion of exploitation may be used, and he even goes so far as to provide a definition of socialist exploitation, in which differences of skill level become the crucial test.

Despite these strengths, it may be argued that Roemer's use of rational choice theory suffers some of the same defects that have been identified in its use in social contract theory. The main problem is that we are asking what rational actors would do in a hypothetical situation, and then using this hypothetical situation as the benchmark for fairness or lack of exploitation in the real world. But for this to be a useful benchmark, we need to be assured that the hypothetical situation contains reasonable assumptions. In particular, it may be that the characterization of the hypothetical situation already biases the conclusions in one direction rather than another. For example, why should we say that capitalist exploitation exists when workers would be better off outside of the economy with their per capita share of alienable assets? Why not make the relevant benchmark as much as they could get from bargaining, or some specified minimum? Clearly, there is no correct answer to this question. We can understand how rational agents would behave in any of these situations, but we are not sure what is the most reasonable situation in which to place them. Here again, we reach the limits of instrumental rationality.

CONCLUSIONS

As this last example goes to show, rational choice theory is not a means by which fundamental questions about values in politics can be solved. What the rational choice approach has done is provide a series of well-honed intellectual tools with which to formulate and discuss those issues. In some ways the use of rational choice theory in the normative context forces us back to some of the questions that arose in other uses. Rational choice theory provides an elegant account of instrumental rationality when applied to the political world. It sheds new light on a number of familiar features: for example, we can understand why committees have to be chaired well if they are to conduct their business expeditiously or how groups become locked into self-defeating conflict when they take a narrow or short-term view. Perhaps, however, instrumental rationality is not enough. Perhaps we also need some broader notion of rationality in which assumptions and motivations can be debated as well as the means to attain satisfaction. If so, rational choice theory will not be redundant – merely one aspect of the search for reason in human affairs.

REFERENCES

Aristotle (1962), *The Politics*, trans. T. A. Sinclair (Harmondsworth, Penguin).

Arrow, K. J. (1963), *Social Choice and Individual Values* (New Haven, Yale University Press).

Austen-Smith, D. (1983), 'The spatial theory of electoral competition: instability, institutions, and information', *Environment and Planning C: Government and Policy*, **1**.

Axelrod, R. (1984), *The Evolution of Cooperation* (New York, Basic Books).

Elster, J. (1985), *Making Sense of Marx* (Cambridge, Cambridge University Press).

Habermas, J. (1979), *Communication and the Evolution of Society* (London, Heinemann).

Harsanyi, J. C. (1976), *Essays on Ethics, Social Behaviour, and Scientific Explanation* (Dordrecht, D. Reidel).

Katzenstein, P. J. (1984), *Corporatism and Change* (Ithaca and London, Cornell University Press).

Kelly, J. S. (1978), *Arrow Impossibility Theorems* (New York, Academic Press).

Lijphart, A. (1968), *The Politics of Accommodation. Pluralism and Democracy in the Netherlands* (Berkeley and Los Angeles, University of California Press).

Lijphart, A. (1977), *Democracy in Plural Societies* (New Haven and London, Yale University Press).

May, K. O. (1952), 'A set of independent, necessary and sufficient conditions for simple majority decision', *Economica*, **20**.

McLean, I. (1987), *Public Choice* (Oxford, Basil Blackwell).

Przeworski, A. and Wallerstein, M. (1982), 'The structure of class conflict in democratic societies', *American Political Science Review*, **76(2)**.

Rawls, J. (1972), *A Theory of Justice* (Oxford, Clarendon).

Riker, W. H. (1982), *Liberalism against Populism* (San Francisco, W. H. Freeman and Co.).

Riker, W. H. (1986), *The Art of Political Manipulation* (New Haven and London, Yale University Press).

Roemer, J. E. (1982), *A General Theory of Exploitation and Class* (Cambridge, Mass., Harvard University Press).

Schattschneider, E. E. (1960), *The Semi-Sovereign People* (New York, Holt, Rinehart and Winston).

Sen, A. K. (1970), *Collective Choice and Social Welfare* (San Francisco, Holden-Day).

Sugden, R. (1986), *The Economics of Rights, Cooperation and Welfare* (Oxford, Basil Blackwell).

Taylor, M. (1976), *Anarchy and Cooperation* (London, John Wiley).

Index

analytical Marxism 127, 161

behaviouralism 60
 and electoral studies 176–7, 191
 and international relations 144–7

Cold War 129
comparative politics
 approaches 62–9
 and constitutions 61
 and democracy 63, 64 ff.
 and policy outcomes 73–5

democracy
 and affluence 69
 and bills of rights 17
 and convergence models 73
 double-sided nature 16 ff.
 and economic growth 73
 and equality 73
 essence 8
 and human rights 74
 and modernization 69
 and political participation 15
 and social choice 205
 and war 73
democratic autonomy 20 ff.
democratic performance 72
development
 defined 83–4
 dependency and
  underdevelopment 89, 95
 and Marxism 87 ff.
 and modernization theory 88, 93
 and neoclassical political economy
  89
 and social-democratic consenus 89
 and the state 83
developmental state 83, 98
Development Studies 84–6
 and social science 85–7
 theoretical schools 87–90
direct democracy 12

domestic-international politics 148
domination 162

economics of bureaucracy
 problems 117–18
electoral studies
 and British political science 191
 dominant paradigm 176
 future of 190–91
 and statistical skills 191
 in UK 180–82
exploitation 163

feminism
 and femininity 27–31
 and International Relations 154–5
 and patriarchy 31–3
 and politics 24–8
 and poststructuralism 39 ff.
 problems of 41
 and psychoanalysis 29–30
 radical 27–9, 30
 and science 34–6
 and social science 34–5
 and the state 31 ff.
 and teaching Politics 37–8
 and women's movement 24–5
feminist thought
 history 25–7
feudalism
 relations of production 166, 168
forces and relations of production
  162, 166, 173

historical materialism 161, 165, 169,
  173

Institute for Social Research 178
International Relations
 and behaviouralism 144–6
 and critical theory 155
 the discipline 143, 157
 ethnocentrism 151
 and feminism 154–5

and the future 154–8
and international economics 155–6
middle-range theory 145–5
and political economy 150
and Politics 143, 157
Realism 143, 147
role of state 148, 153
and values 151–2
interpellation 171–2
issue voting
Britain 188
USA 185

liberal socialism 20 ff.

Marxism 161 ff., 173
analytical 127, 161
and Development Studies 87–8
and nationalism 170–72
and Public Administration 111–12
and the state 168
modes of production 163

National Opinion Research Center
178
New Left 10 ff.
New Right 9 ff.
Nietzsche
and power 164
Nufield Studies 181

partisan dealignment
Britain 182
USA 184
partisan identification 180, 182
party identification 179
philosophy
applied 131
and politics 131–3
politics and political philosophy
127
'political accumulation' 167, 168
political philosophy
anti-foundationalism 131, 139
and conversationalism 136 ff.
foundationalism 131, 134
future prospects 139–40
and the good life 133
revival 129–31
Politics (the discipline)
and Development Studies 82 ff.,
90 ff.

the discipline 2 ff., 24–5, 34–5
and feminism 25 ff.
and interdisciplinary studies 91
relationship to practical politics
4–5
politics (the activity)
central problem 4
definitions 82–4
and development 82 ff.
primacy of 5–6
positivism 128
power
conceptions 162–3
preference cycling 200–202
Prisoners' Dilemma 205–209
Public Administration
approaches 110–19
critical approach 112–13
and economics of bureaucracy
116–17
and neo-Marxist state theory
112–13
new directions 119–23
organizational sociology approach
111
policy approach 110–11
and political science 109
and public choice 115–16
and public management 113–14
and privatization and deregulation
122–23
study and teaching 107
theories 108–9
and X-efficiency 115

radical feminism 27–9, 30
rational choice
and corporatism 198
and game theory 196
and institutions 203
and optimality 197
and stability 197
and voting 199–205
rational choice theory
defined 196–8
and exploitation 209

Social Attitudes Study 182
Social and Community Planning
Research 182

Social Science Research Council
    (USA) 178
State
    and civil society 11 ff., 49
    definitions 44 ff.
    and development 97
    and feminism 31 ff.
    and other institutional orders 54–6
    and social formations 46
    theories of 43 ff., 56–9, 168–9
state building 48

state-centred theories 50–51
state theory
    and public administration 111 ff.
Survey Research Center 178

voting
    and rational choice 199–205
    retrospective 185
    and social class 182–3, 189
    stable 179

welfare state 8